Subscores

This authoritative guide directs consumers and users of test scores on when and how to provide subscores and how to make informed decisions based on them. The book is designed to be accessible to practitioners and score users with varying levels of technical expertise, from executives of testing organizations and students who take tests to graduate students in educational measurement, psychometricians, and test developers. The theoretical background required to evaluate subscores and improve them is provided alongside examples of tests with subscores to illustrate their use and misuse.

The first chapter covers the history of tests, subtests, scores, and subscores. Later chapters go into subscore reporting, evaluating and improving the quality of subscores, and alternatives to subscores when they are not appropriate. This thorough introduction to the existing research and best practices will be useful to graduate students, researchers, and practitioners.

SHELBY HABERMAN is a statistician with substantial experience in educational testing. He currently works as an independent consultant. Previously he taught at the University of Chicago, Hebrew University, and Northwestern University and was later employed by the Educational Testing Service (ETS). He is a fellow of the Institute of Mathematical Statistics, the American Statistical Association, and the American Academy for the Advancement of Science and was the 2019 recipient of the National Council on Measurement in Education Award for Career Contributions to Educational Measurement. Haberman is the author of *The Analysis of Frequency Data*, *Analysis of Qualitative Data*, and *Advanced Statistics*.

SANDIP SINHARAY is a distinguished presidential appointee in the Research & Development division at the ETS in Princeton, New Jersey. He is the current editor of *Psychometrika* and a past editor of the *Journal of Educational Measurement* (2020–2022) and the *Journal of Educational and Behavioral Statistics* (2010–2014). He has received seven awards from the National Council on Measurement in Education. These awards include the Outstanding Service Award (2023), Bradley Hanson Award for Contributions to Educational Measurement (2018 and 2020), Annual Award for Outstanding Technical or Scientific Contribution to the Field of Educational Measurement (2015 and 2009), Jason Millman Promising Measurement Scholar Award (2006), and Alicia Cascallar Award for an Outstanding Paper by an Early Career Scholar (2005). He received the ETS Scientist award in 2008 and the ETS Presidential award twice. Sinharay has coedited two published volumes, including the *Handbook of Statistics*, Volume 26 on psychometrics (which he coedited with Prof. C. R. Rao), and authored or coauthored more than 100 articles in peer-reviewed journals and edited books.

RICHARD A. FEINBERG is a principal psychometrician at the National Board of Medical Examiners and also teaches a course on research methods at the Philadelphia College of Osteopathic Medicine. Feinberg has received several awards and recognitions, including the National Council on Measurement in Education Jason Millman Promising Measurement Scholar Award (2018), the American Educational Research Association Division I Established Researcher Award (2017), and the Outstanding Research Publication Award (2022), and is a six-time winner of the Educational Measurement: Issues and Practice Cover Graphic/Data Visualization Competition. He has coedited one published volume and authored numerous articles across a broad range of statistical applications in the educational and psychological literature.

HOWARD WAINER is an independent statistician and author with experience in educational testing and data visualization. He has taught at the University of Chicago, Princeton University, and the Wharton School of the University of Pennsylvania. He was employed by the ETS from 1980 until 2001 and was the Distinguished Research Scientist at the National Board of Medical Examiners from 2001 until 2016. Wainer is a fellow of the American Statistical Association and American Educational Research Association, and the author or editor of 25 previous books.

Subscores
A Practical Guide to Their Production and Consumption

SHELBY HABERMAN
Independent consultant

SANDIP SINHARAY
Educational Testing Service

RICHARD A. FEINBERG
National Board of Medical Examiners

HOWARD WAINER
Independent consultant

CAMBRIDGE
UNIVERSITY PRESS

Shaftesbury Road, Cambridge CB2 8EA, United Kingdom

One Liberty Plaza, 20th Floor, New York, NY 10006, USA

477 Williamstown Road, Port Melbourne, VIC 3207, Australia

314–321, 3rd Floor, Plot 3, Splendor Forum, Jasola District Centre, New Delhi – 110025, India

103 Penang Road, #05–06/07, Visioncrest Commercial, Singapore 238467

Cambridge University Press is part of Cambridge University Press & Assessment, a department of the University of Cambridge.

We share the University's mission to contribute to society through the pursuit of education, learning and research at the highest international levels of excellence.

www.cambridge.org
Information on this title: www.cambridge.org/9781009413688

DOI: 10.1017/9781009413701

Work excluding Chapter 5 © Dr. Howard Wainer, Dr. Shelby Haberman, and National Board of Medical Examiners 2024

Chapter 5 © Educational Testing Service 2024

This publication is in copyright. Subject to statutory exception and to the provisions of relevant collective licensing agreements, no reproduction of any part may take place without the written permission of Cambridge University Press & Assessment.

First published 2024

A catalogue record for this publication is available from the British Library

A Cataloging-in-Publication data record for this book is available from the Library of Congress

ISBN 978-1-009-41368-8 Hardback
ISBN 978-1-009-41366-4 Paperback

Additional resources for this publication at www.cambridge.org/9781009413688

Cambridge University Press & Assessment has no responsibility for the persistence or accuracy of URLs for external or third-party internet websites referred to in this publication and does not guarantee that any content on such websites is, or will remain, accurate or appropriate.

To Paul W. Holland, who has, for decades, provided wise counsel and guidance to us and others who toil in the same fields

To my late wife Penny and to my children Shoshanah, Chasiah, Sarah, Milcah, Boaz, and Devorah (SH)

To my parents, Puspamita and Radhanath Sinharay, who taught me that anything is possible except reporting subscores for unidimensional tests; to my siblings Joydeep and Manidipa for their continuous support and encouragement; and to my wife, Lopamudra, whose multidimensional skills have helped me become who I am (SS)

To my family, Betsy, Nathan, and Daniella Feinberg, for being genuinely excited whenever I have something to share (RF)

To Linda; to Laurent, Lyn, Koa, and Sophie; and to Sam – all of whom continue to bring joy and enlightenment (HW)

Contents

Preface		*page* ix
Acknowledgments		xv

1 Introduction   1
Background and historical context on what subscores are, using the US census and testing programs in the military as clarifying examples.

2 How Are Subscores Reported?   18
Different modalities for communicating subscore information, across varied testing purposes and audiences, are illustrated through excerpts from real score reports. Connections to general score reporting best practices and development are discussed.

3 When and How Should Subscores Be Reported?   45
A comprehensive review of the statistical requirements, methods to quantify value, and how to determine if subscores are worth reporting.

4 A Survey to Explore the Conditions under Which Subscores Have Added Value   88
Actual data from 36 operational testing programs are used to assess the extent to which reported subscores have added value.

5 What to Do When Subscores Do Not Have Added Value: Augmentation, No Subscore Reporting, and Some Other Options   110
Several approaches are recommended for what can be done when subscore information is needed yet the original subscores lack sufficient quality to be reported.

6   Coda: Lessons Learned, Conclusions, and Recommendations   136
Guidance for how subscores should be reported is discussed
as well as what might be done when subscores ought not
be reported. Advice is also given to help practitioners
respond to pressure from various stakeholders when subscores
would be misleading to report.

Appendix   150

Glossary   154
References   158
Name Index   169
Subject Index   172

Preface

Subscores have long been popular for intelligence tests. Psychologists have used results from different types of comparisons of the subscores on the Weschler Adult Intelligence Scale–Revised, Stanford–Binet Intelligence Scale, and so on to interpret performance on those tests. These analyses are often referred to as *profile* or *scatter* analyses. Subscores on educational assessments were prevalent but received scant attention during the twentieth century.

However, the first decade of the twenty-first century saw a change. There was a huge surge of interest in diagnostic scores for educational assessments, possibly due to the No Child Left Behind Act of 2001, which demanded, among other things, that students receive diagnostic reports to allow teachers to address their specific academic needs. Testing organizations responded by accelerating their recently begun or already ongoing efforts of reporting subscores and other types of diagnostic scores. Measurement researchers responded to the demand by suggesting various ways of computing diagnostic scores.

Despite good intentions, these efforts on subscore reporting had their limitations. Many of the reported subscores were based on only a handful of items, thus possessing dubious psychometric properties. Unfortunately, there was not much guidance for practitioners on when and how to report subscores. We began to feel the need to address one or more of these issues during the period from the late 1990s to 2010.

How We Became Involved with Subscores

The seed for the book was sown in the late 1990s when Kathy Sheehan reached out to her colleague Howard Wainer at the Educational Testing Service (ETS) with a knotty problem associated with a teachers' licensing examination. The score users wanted subscores; however, Kathy was hesitant to comply because many of the potentially reportable subscores were based on only a few items. She felt that it would be unethical to supply scores that had unacceptably low reliability. Howard subsequently ran into his colleague Nick Longford at lunch, who suggested using the other items on the test to help stabilize the subscores and thought that this was a made-to-order application for an empirical Bayes approach. Nick sketched the idea on a napkin. Howard did the necessary algebra and handed it over to the remarkable Xiaohui Wang, who had just joined ETS as a data analyst. Xiaohui used the afternoon to write the code and run the program on Kathy's data to compute what are now called augmented subscores. Their reliabilities were stunningly high. It is now known that augmented subscores computed from any largely one-dimensional test will have high reliability regardless of the number of items formally constituting those subscores. But in the 1990s, the result looked too good to be true. This led Howard and Xiaohui to check the algebra and code several times. They later published three landmark papers on augmented subscores between 1998 and 2001. David Thissen insisted on referring to the augmented subscores as Wainer subscores in 2001, following Stigler's law of eponymy that nothing is ever named after the right person (which Stigler attributed to Robert Merton).

Despite this breakthrough, there remained the need for a widely accepted method for the parsimonious characterization of the psychometric quality of subscores. Enter Shelby Haberman, who joined the staff at ETS in 2002 shortly after Howard left ETS for the National Board of Medical Examiners (NBME).

Shelby, who joined the faculty of the University of Chicago in 1970 along with Howard Wainer (though they hardly knew each other in Chicago), became involved with subscores shortly after he arrived at ETS. He learned of ETS's interest in supplying diagnostic scores despite the possibility of their feeble psychometric properties. There were several ongoing projects, both from internal researchers and from external vendors, focused on producing subscores for ETS tests despite the very real questions about the prospective utility of these subscores. In response, Shelby tried to provide criteria for the utility of subscores and for methods to improve them. He published a paper in 2008 that suggested a simple yet elegant approach that summarizes a comprehensive evaluation of the psychometric quality of a subscore in a single number. That paper is widely regarded as a breakthrough in research on subscores and, as of January 2023, had been cited 265 times. Sandip Sinharay joined ETS in 2001, partially because his doctoral supervisor (Hal Stern – currently at the University of California–Irvine) knew of a job vacancy at ETS from his friend Howard Wainer. Sandip joined Shelby's research team for the study of subscores in the mid-2000s. Sandip's initial goal was disseminating to ETS colleagues and outsiders the ideas behind Shelby's brilliant subscore-related papers that were highly technical and thus ill-suited for the faint of heart. Shelby and Sandip went on a vigorous spree of examining various aspects of subscore reporting in a series of papers, often involving ETS colleagues like Gautam Puhan and Kevin Larkin. Their research is documented in more than 20 technical reports, journal articles, and chapters in edited volumes. This earned them the euphonious appellation of the subscore police from their esteemed colleague Paul Holland and also the 2009 annual award for technical or scientific contribution to the field of educational measurement from the National Council on Measurement in Education.

In the meantime, Howard Wainer – who left ETS to join NBME in 2001 and was busy working on testlets, measurement problems in medical licensing tests, and several books on various topics – read Shelby's 2008 paper and figured that the next logical step would be the equating of subscores, which would make an excellent dissertation topic. Howard mentioned this topic to his NBME colleague Mike Jodoin, who contacted Richard A. Feinberg, then both a staff member at NBME and a graduate student at the University of Delaware. Rich was in the process of considering different plausible dissertation ideas. In 2010, Richard met with Howard to further discuss the idea, which instigated a productive research agenda between the two of them. Rich began communicating with Sandip and Shelby, who told him that ETS colleagues were already investigating equating of subscores (two papers on the topic were published in 2011). This led Howard and Rich to think carefully about other important practical questions that could add value to the rapidly growing subscore literature. Richard's dissertation evolved and led to several papers on previously unexplored and practical issues related to subscores.

The Origin of This Book

In July 2021, after completing work on his 25 book and passing beyond the biblically prescribed life span of 3 score and 10 years, Howard realized that he probably did not have many books left in him. He was looking for the right topic for a book that would have a lasting impact on operational testing and would allow him to "go out with a bang." He alit on subscores as the topic that he was looking for. He contacted Sandip, Richard, and Shelby, all of whom thought that a book on subscores was a great idea. The book project would also provide an opportunity for the four authors, who had narrowly missed collaborating in the past (e.g., when Howard left ETS immediately after Sandip joined ETS and a year before Shelby joined ETS), to team up on a topic of common interest. The four of us then contacted Lauren Cowles of Cambridge University Press, who shared our enthusiasm, and the ball started rolling. The book was to be a coherent compendium of all of our past research as well as other new, relevant research. Thus, the version of the book that you now hold in your hand includes new material that we developed to bridge gaps in the literature that were exposed once we had collected prior work into a coherent whole. The section on canonical scores in Chapter 3 is one prime example of this, as are many of the figures in Chapters 4 and 5. Finally, the summary recommendations for practice appearing throughout the book are new.

The Need for This Book and the Purpose That We Intend It to Serve

If there's a book that you really want to read, but it hasn't been written yet, then you must write it.

Toni Morrison (1981)

Given the popularity of subscores and the high variability of their utility that is encountered in practice, the authors felt the need for a single, coherent, and authoritative source that provides a succinct and easily accessible summary of best practices supported by existing research. Because such a source did not exist, we felt compelled to follow Professor Morrison's advice and write it. We believe that this book will provide direction to both producers and consumers of psychological and educational test scores about when and how subscores should be provided, how to interpret reported subscores appropriately, and how to make informed decisions based on the subscores. The book will provide graduate students and researchers with a thorough introduction to existing research on subscores and guide them to future research topics related to subscores. We hope that it will contribute to improved understanding and more sensible and ethical use of subscores among psychometricians, test developers, institutional and individual users of assessment results, and management of testing organizations that currently report subscores or are considering their use. Thirteen years after Rich and Howard started their quest to find unsolved problems on subscores, many of the same problems still exist, which suggests a larger conversation is needed between psychometricians, test developers, governance stakeholders, and score recipients regarding how to estimate a subscore's value, its limitations, appropriate modalities of reporting, and so on. We hope that this book can contribute to that conversation.

A Brief Outline of This Book

We begin with an introductory chapter that provides a brief account of the long history of tests, subtests, scores, and subscores. Chapter 2 focuses on the reporting of subscores and provides examples of the various ways in which subscores are reported for several large-scale operational tests. Chapter 3 focuses on the importance of evaluating the quality of subscores and suggests various ways of assessing the psychometric quality of subscores. Chapter 4 includes the results from a survey regarding the quality of subscores using data from 34 operational tests. Chapter 5 provides some alternatives when subscores are demanded but do not satisfy contemporary standards of psychometric quality and consequently ought not, in good conscience, be provided. Chapter 6 includes concluding remarks and our recommendations for practice.

Acknowledgments

We would like to take this opportunity to acknowledge the help of, and express gratitude to, the individuals and organizations who contributed in various ways to the publication of the book.

First, organizational thanks are due to the ETS that employed three of the authors when they first became involved with subscores. The authors are especially grateful to Amit Sevak, Walt McDonald, and Kurt Landgraf, present and former presidents of ETS – their wise leadership was instrumental in providing continued support for basic research. Henry Braun, Drew Gitomer, Ida Lawrence, Kadriye Ercikan, and John Mazzeo, the former and current vice presidents of research at ETS, ensured the smooth running of ETS allocation projects that provided support for the research. Their enthusiasm and wise counsel were appreciated then and now. Paul Holland, Daniel McCaffrey, and Matthew Johnson have all provided valuable support, encouragement, and advice.

Second, the authors are grateful to the NBME and its then president, Donald Melnick, and current president, Peter Katsufrakis, who supported the work of Howard and Richard over many years. The enthusiasm of the NBME senior vice presidents Michael Jodoin and Ye Tong for the work in this book is much appreciated.

Third, we are indebted to Katherine Castellano for creating the cover graphic and to the following colleagues for their assistance, encouragement, review, and valuable suggestions: Neil Dorans, Kevin Larkin, Charles Lewis, Yi-Hsuan Lee, Nick Longford, John Mazzeo, Gautam Puhan, Yasuyo Sawaki, Kathy Sheehan, Xiaohui Wang, Jonathan Weeks, and Lili Yao (all currently or formerly at ETS); Mike Jodoin (formerly at ETS and now NBME); Amanda Clauser, Brian Clauser, Jerusha Henderek, Daniel Jurich, Francis O'Donnell, and Kimberley Swygert (current NBME employees); April Zenisky (at the University of Massachusetts, Amherst); Ronald Hambleton (formerly at the

University of Massachusetts, Amherst); and David Thissen (at the University of North Carolina).

Fourth, the authors would like to express gratitude to Cambridge University Press (the outlet Isaac Newton chose to publish his *Principia*) and the mathematics editor Lauren Cowles and her assistant Arman Chowdhury for ready acceptance of the book proposal, encouragement, and help in making this book the best it could be.

Fifth, any long-term project accumulates debts to many others whose help was important. Most important are Clare Dennison and Amala Gobiraman, whose work ethic and keen sense of organization kept everything in order.

We would like to end by thanking Shenghai Dai (Washington State University), Xiaolin Wang (Pearson VUE), and Dubravka Svetina (Indiana University–Bloomington) for preparing the *R* package *subscore* and Alexander Robitzsch for preparing the *R* package *sirt* that can be used to implement the aforementioned approach of Haberman that is the cornerstone of this book. The packages have facilitated the application of the authors' research to a variety of problems and immensely helped us while writing the book.

1
Introduction

Standardized tests, whether to evaluate student performance in coursework or to choose among applicants for college admission or to license candidates for various professions, are often marathons. Tests designed to evaluate knowledge of coursework typically use the canonical hour; admissions tests are usually two to three hours; and licensing exams can take days. Why are they as long as they are? To answer this question, we must consider the purposes of the test. Most serious tests have serious purposes – admission to a college or not, getting a job or not, being allowed to practice your profession or not. The extent to which a test score can serve these purposes is its validity, which is usually defined as "the degree to which evidence and theory support the intended interpretations of those test scores."[1] But the validity of a test's scores is bounded by the test's reliability.[2] Reliability is merely a standardized measure of the score's stability, ranging from a low of 0 (essentially a random number) to a high of 1 (the score does not fluctuate at all). A test score that has low reliability must perforce have an even lower validity, and its usefulness diminishes apace.

Thus, the first answer to the question "Why are tests so long?" that jumps immediately to mind is derived from the inexorable relationship between a test's length and its reliability. However, even though a test score always gets more reliable as the test generating it gets longer, *ceteris paribus*, the law of diminishing returns sets in very quickly. In Figure 1.1, we show the reliability of a typical professionally prepared test as a function of its length. The figure shows that the marginal gain of moving from a 30-item test to a 60- or even 90-item one is not worth the trouble unless such small additional

---

[1] Linda Steinberg, October 26, 2020, personal communication.
[2] More accurately, the validity is bounded by the *square of its reliability*. So, for example, if a test's reliability is 0.90, its validity can be no higher than 0.81.

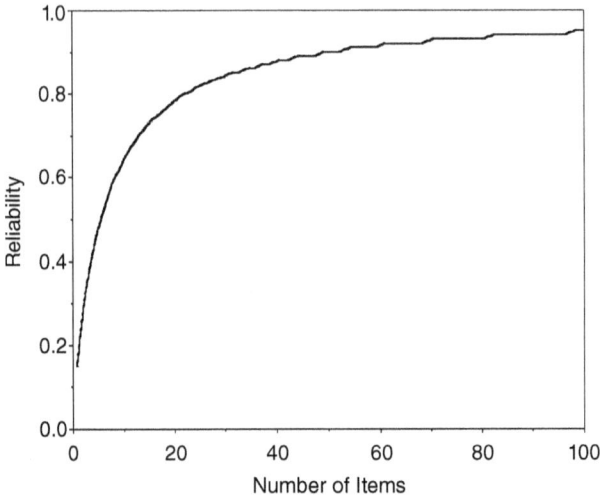

Figure 1.1 Spearman–Brown function showing the reliability of a test as a function of its length, if a one-item test has a reliability of 0.15.

increments in reliability are of practical importance. We must also note that reliability does drop precipitously as test length shrinks from 30 toward zero. But the puzzle still remains: Why are typical tests so long if, after a test's length surpasses 30, it is about as reliable as we are likely to need. So, if such extra precision is rarely necessary, why are tests as long as they are?

1.1 A Clarifying Example: The US Census

Our intuitions can be clarified with an example, the decennial US census. According to the 2020 decennial census, the United States had 331,449,281 residents; however, the Bureau of the Census estimates that this number has a nontrivial error of uncertain size. The estimate is that 782,000 more people resided in the United States than were reported, but it is also estimated that about one third of the time the estimate would be that the decennial census overcounted the population by at least 30,000 or undercounted the population by no less than 1,620,000 people. The budget of the 2020 census was $14.2 billion, or approximately $42.84 per person counted. Is it worth this amount of money to just get this single number? Before answering this question, consider the function shown in Figure 1.2, which provides the results of all decennial censuses for the past 150 years. The curve shown is a fitted quadratic function

1.1 A Clarifying Example: The US Census

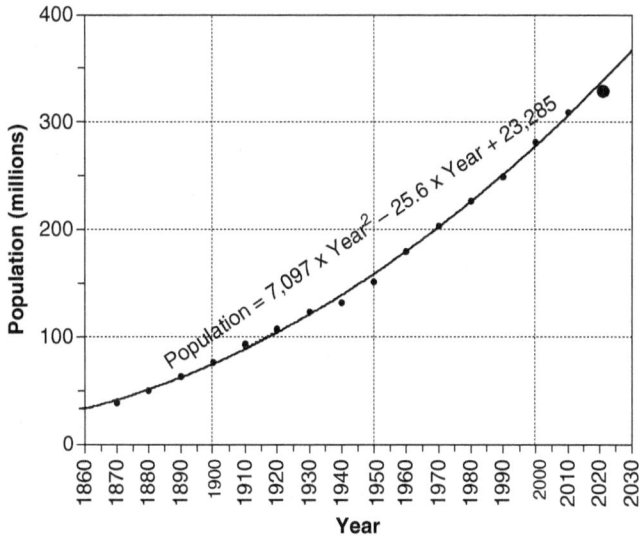

Figure 1.2 US population from 1870 to 2020.

to the data from 1870 through 2010. The large dot associated with 2020 is the actual population estimate from the 2020 census; the value of the curve, which passes slightly above it, is the estimate obtained from this fitted function – 331,943,913. The difference between the two is 494,632 people, or 0.1%, an error certainly comparable to the estimated error from the decennial census. Obtaining this estimate cost only about an hour of a statistician's time – totaling perhaps a couple of hundred dollars.

Fitting a connecting function, like the quadratic shown in Figure 1.2, can have many uses. By far, the most important purpose is to provide, at a glance, an accurate representation of more than a century's growth of a nation's population – Henry D. Hubbard (in the preface to Brinton, 1939) memorably characterized this use when he pointed out the following: "There is a magic in graphs. The profile of a curve reveals in a flash a whole situation – the life history of an epidemic, a panic, or an era of prosperity. The curve informs the mind, awakens the imagination, convinces."

Although the fitted curve provides only an approximation of the population between censuses, we can, by adopting very credible regularity assumptions, confidently use the curve to interpolate between censuses and obtain accurate estimates for any time in the 150-year range of the data.

A third use, and the one that we have illustrated here, is extrapolation 10 years beyond the 2010 census. Extrapolation, like interpolation, relies on regularity assumptions, but those assumptions become more heroic the further the estimate is from the data. As we have seen, predicting the 2020 US population from prior census results ending in 2010 yielded an estimate that is likely accurate enough for most applications. Were we to use the same function to predict further into the future, we would be less sure, and our uncertainty would, naturally, expand with the size of the extrapolation. Of course, there are more data-rich methods that could improve the accuracy of such extrapolations by making their inevitable underlying assumptions more credible.[3]

And so, returning to the original question, is it worth $14.2 billion to just estimate this single number when it could have been determined as accurately in just a few minutes and be paid for out of petty cash? It doesn't take a congressional study group or the Office of Management and the Budget to tell us that the answer is no. If all the census gave us was that single number, it would be a colossal waste of census workers' time and taxpayers' money. However, the Constitution and acts of Congress require that the census enumerate the resident population and report on population sizes for very small geographical regions, including for 2020 about 11,000,000 census blocks and 73,000 census tracts. These population values for small areas are needed for apportionment of the House of Representatives and for apportionment of state legislatures and other governmental units. They, together with survey data from the American Community Survey, are also valuable for allocation of social services, among other uses. The census provides such small area estimates admirably well, but to be able to do so requires massive data collection and so incurs a huge expense. Yet the importance of providing accurate answers to many crucially important small area questions makes its impressive cost unavoidable.

There are the two key lessons we should take from this census example:

1. Obtaining an accurate estimate of the grand total is easy and cheap.
2. Obtaining accurate small area estimates is hard and expensive, and hence should not be attempted unless such small area estimates are important enough to justify the vast increases in the resources of time and treasure that are required.

---

[3] For example, the change in the population of the United States at any given time after a full census is the sum of four factors: (1) the number of births since the census, (2) the number of deaths since then, (3) the number of immigrants since then, and (4) the number of emigrants. When all of these are added together, we find that the net increase in the US population since 2010 is one person every 13 seconds, and so to get an accurate estimate of the total population at any moment, one merely needs to ascertain how much time has elapsed since the last estimate, in seconds; divide by 13 and add in that increment. Note that a single clerk with access to a pocket calculator in a minute or two could use this method to estimate the change from the previous census (to an accuracy of $\pm 0.1\%$).

1.2 Back to Tests

Now let us return to tests. Instead of characterizing cost in terms of dollars (a worthwhile metric, for sure, but grist for another mill), let us instead use examinee time. Is it worth using an hour (or two or even more) of examinee time to estimate just a single number – a single score? Is the small marginal increase in accuracy obtained from a 60- or 90-item test over, say, a 30-item test worth doubling or tripling examinee time?

A glance at the gradual slope of the Spearman–Brown curve shown in Figure 1.1 as it nears its asymptote tells us that we aren't getting much of a return on our investment. And multiplying the extra hour spent by each examinee by the millions of examinees that often take such tests makes this conclusion stronger still. What would be the circumstances in which a test score with a reliability of 0.89 will not suffice, but one of 0.91 would? Off hand, it is hard to think of any.

But, returning to the lessons taught us by census, perhaps there are other uses for the information gathered by the test that require additional length – the equivalent of the small area estimates of census. In testing, such estimates are usually called subscores – small area estimates on aspects of the subject matter of the test. On a high school math test, these might be subscores on algebra, arithmetic, geometry, and trigonometry. For a licensing exam in veterinary medicine, there might be subscores on the pulmonary system, the skeletal system, the renal system, and so on. There is even the possibility of cross-classified subscores; perhaps one on dogs; another on cats; and others on cows, horses, and pigs. Such cross-classified subscores are akin to the census having estimates by ethnic group and also by geographic location.

Thus, the production of meaningful subscores needed for important purposes would be a justification for tests that contain more items than would be required merely for an accurate enough estimate of total score. What is a meaningful subscore? *It is one that is reliable enough for its prospective use and one that contains information that is not adequately focused (or is overly diluted) in the total test score.*

There are at least three prospective uses of such subscores:

(i) To provide institutions with information used for major decisions such as admission, licensure, and immigration qualification
(ii) To aid examinees in assessing their strengths and weaknesses, often with an eye toward remediating the latter
(iii) To aid individuals and institutions (e.g., teachers and schools) in assessing the effectiveness of their instruction, again with an eye toward remediating weaknesses

In the first case, subscores need to be highly reliable, given the life-changing decisions dependent upon them. The demands on reliability *increase* when subscores must exceed a fixed value and when multiple subscores are involved.

In the second case, helping examinees, the subscores need to be reliable enough so that attempts to remediate weaknesses do not become just the futile pursuit of noise. And, obviously, the subscores must contain information that is focused on performance on the specific topic of interest and is not diluted over the broad range of topics contained in the total test score. We might call these two characteristics of a worthwhile subscore *reliability* and *specificity*. But for a subscore to have a specific focus apart from the total score, its information must be somewhat orthogonal to the total score; hence we shall designate this characteristic of a useful subscore *orthogonality*. Shortly, we will provide an introductory discussion of each of these two important characteristics and then tell the full story in Chapter 3. But first, let us drop back in time and see where the concept and use of subscores came from.

1.3 A Brief Account of the Long History of Tests and Subtests, Scores and Subscores

The use of mental tests appears to be almost as ancient as Western civilization. The Hebrew Bible (in Judges 12:4–6) provides an early reference to testing in Western culture.[4] It describes a short verbal test that the Gileadites used to uncover the fleeing Ephraimites hiding in their midst. The test was one item long. Candidates had to pronounce the word שיבולת (transliterated as *shibboleth*). Ephraimites apparently pronounced the initial *sh* as *s*. The consequences of this test were quite severe (the banks of the Jordan were strewn with the bodies of the 42,000 who failed). Obviously, any test that consists of but a single item can have no subscores. But there were much earlier tests that were longer and had subscores.

In his 1970 *History*, Philip DuBois reported that tests had been around for millennia, and whenever they consisted of more than a single item, the appeal of computing subscores has been irresistible.

There was some rudimentary proficiency testing that took place in China around 2200 BCE, which predated the biblical testing program by almost a thousand years! The emperor of China is said to have examined his officials

---

[4] Judges 12:6. "Then said they unto him, Say now Shibboleth: and he said Sibboleth: for he could not frame to pronounce it right. Then they took him and slew him at the passages of Jordan: and there fell at that time of the Ephraimites forty and two thousand."

every third year. This set a precedent for periodic exams in China that was to persist for a very long time. In 1115 BCE, at the beginning of the Chan dynasty, formal testing procedures were instituted for candidates for office. Job sample subtests were used, with proficiency required in (1) archery, (2) arithmetic, (3) horsemanship, (4) music, (5) writing, and (6) skill in the rites and ceremonies of public and social life. The Chinese discovered the fundamental truth that underlies the validity of testing – that a relatively small sample of an individual's performance, measured under carefully controlled conditions, can yield an accurate picture of that individual's ability to perform under much broader conditions for a longer period of time. The procedures developed by the Chinese are reasonably similar to the canons of good testing practice used today. For example, they required objectivity – candidates' names were concealed to ensure anonymity; they sometimes went so far as to have the answers redrafted by another individual to hide the handwriting. Tests were often read by two independent examiners, with a third brought in to adjudicate differences. Test conditions were as uniform as could be managed – proctors watched over the exams given in special examination halls that were large permanent structures consisting of hundreds of small cells. The testing process was so rigorous that sometimes candidates died during the course of the exams.

This testing program was augmented and modified through the years and has been praised by many Western scholars. Voltaire and Quesnay advocated its use in France, where it was adopted in 1791, only to be (temporarily) abolished by Napoleon. It was cited by British reformers as their model for the system set up in 1833 to select trainees for the Indian civil service – the precursor to the British civil service. The success of the British system influenced Senator Charles Sumner of Massachusetts and Representative Thomas Jenckes of Rhode Island in the development of the examination system they introduced into Congress in 1868. This eventually led to George Hunt Pendleton proposing the eponymously entitled US Civil Service Act in January 1883.

The US military has arguably one of the most widely used and consequential testing programs in the United States, in terms of both number of examinees and length of time it has been in use. It also has been carefully thought through and researched over the better part of a century. Few testing programs can match the careful seriousness of its construction and use. We feel this makes it a worthy and informative illustration of the use of tests and subscores in support of evidence-based personnel decision-making. In the following narrative, we first trace the history of military testing in the United States, then move to a discussion of decisions based on total test scores and the use of subscores, and then conclude with an evaluation of the success of this approach as a guide to others who would like to use both test scores and subscores to generate evidence supporting claims about individuals and groups.

1.4 The Origins of Mental Testing in the US Military

During World War I, Robert M. Yerkes, president of the American Psychological Association, took the lead in involving psychologists in the war effort. One major contribution was the implementation of a program for the psychological examination of recruits. Yerkes formed a committee for this purpose that met in May 1917 at the Vineland Training School in New Jersey. His committee debated the relative merits of very brief individual tests versus longer group tests. For reasons of objectivity, uniformity, and reliability, they decided to develop a group test of intelligence.

The criteria they adopted (described in detail on page 62 of Philip DuBois' 1970 book on the history of testing) for the development of the new group test were:

1) Adaptability for group use
2) Correlation with measures of intelligence known to be valid
3) Measurement of a wide range of ability
4) Objectivity of scoring, preferably by stencils
5) Rapidity of scoring
6) Possibility of many alternate forms so as to discourage coaching
7) Unfavorableness to malingering
8) Unfavorableness to cheating
9) Independence of school training
10) Minimum of writing in making responses
11) Material intrinsically interesting
12) Economy of time

In just 7 working days, they constructed 10 subtests with enough items for 10 different forms. They then prepared one form for printing and experimental administration. The pilot testing was done on fewer than 500 subjects. These subjects were broadly sampled and came from such diverse sources as a school for those with intellectual disabilities, a psychopathic hospital, a reformatory, some aviation recruits, some men in an officers' training camp, 60 high school students, and 114 marines at a navy yard. They also administered either the Stanford–Binet intelligence test or an abbreviated form of it. They found that the scores of their test correlated 0.9 with those of the Stanford–Binet and 0.8 with the abbreviated Binet.

The items and instructions were then edited, time limits were revised, and scoring formulas were developed to maximize the correlation of the total score with the Binet. Items within each subtest were ordered by difficulty, and four alternate forms were prepared for mass administration.

By August, statistical workers under E. L. Thorndike's direction had analyzed the results of the revised test after it had been administered to 3,129 soldiers and 372 inmates of institutions for mental defectives. The results prompted Thorndike to call this the "best group test ever devised." It yielded good distributions of scores, and it correlated about 0.7 with schooling and 0.5 with ratings by superior officers. This test was dubbed *Examination a*.

In December of the same year, *Examination a* was revised once again. It became the famous *Army Alpha*. This version had only eight subtests; two of the original ones were dropped because of low correlation with other measures and because they were of inappropriate difficulty. The resulting test (whose components are shown below) bears a remarkable similarity to the structure of the modern Armed Services Vocational Aptitude Battery (ASVAB).

Test	Number of Items
1. Oral Direction	12
2. Arithmetical Reasoning	20
3. Practical Judgement	16
4. Synonym-Antonym	40
5. Disarranged Sentences	24
6. Number Series Completion	20
7. Analogies	40
8. Information	40

This testing program, which remained under Yerkes' supervision, tested almost 2 million men. Two thirds of them received the *Army Alpha*, and the remainder were tested with an alternative form, *Army Beta, a* nonverbal form devised for illiterate and non-English-speaking recruits. Together they represented the first large-scale use of intelligence testing.

The success of the *Army Alpha* led to the development of a variety of special tests. In 1919, Henry Link discovered that a card-sorting test aided in the successful selection of shell inspectors and that a tapping test was valid for gaugers. He pointed out that a job analysis coupled with an experimental administration of tests thought to require the same abilities as the job and a validity study that correlated test performance with later job success yielded instruments that could distinguish between job applicants who were good risks and those who were not. L. L. Thurstone developed a "rhythm test" that accurately predicted future telegraphers' speed.

Testing programs within the military became much more extensive during World War II. In 1939, the Personnel Testing Service was established in the Office of the Adjutant General of the Army. This gave rise to the *Army General Classification Test* (AGCT) that was an updated version of the *Army Alpha*. The chairman of the committee that oversaw the development of the AGCT was Walter V. Bingham, who served on the 1917 committee that developed Alpha. This test eventually developed into a four-part exam consisting of tests of (1) reading and vocabulary, (2) arithmetic computation, (3) arithmetic reasoning, and (4) spatial relations. Supplemental tests for mechanical and clerical aptitude, code learning ability, and oral trade were also developed. By the end of the war, more than 9 million men had taken the AGCT in one form or another. The navy and the army air forces participated in the same program but with some different tests that they required for their own purposes.

In 1950, the *Armed Forces Classification Test* was instituted to be used as a screening instrument for all services. It was designed to ensure appropriate allocation of talent to all branches. This was the precursor of the *Armed Forces Qualification Test* (AFQT) that led in turn to the *Armed Services Vocational Aptitude Battery* (ASVAB).

1.4.1 The ASVAB and Scores Derived from It

The ASVAB consists of nine subtests, each of which is scored separately. Each of those scores range from 1 to 100 and is scaled so that the mean is 50. The nine subtests are:

1. Arithmetic Reasoning
2. Mathematics Knowledge
3. Word Knowledge
4. Paragraph Comprehension
5. General Science
6. Electronics Information
7. Auto & Shop Information
8. Mechanical Comprehension
9. Assembling Objects

The scores on the first four of these subtests (Arithmetic Reasoning, Mathematics Knowledge, Word Knowledge, and Paragraph Comprehension) are combined into a composite score and dubbed into the Armed Forces Qualification Test (AFQT) score that specifically determines whether a candidate is eligible for enlistment in the military. Each branch has a different minimum AFQT score requirement.

The five subtests that make up the balance of the ASVAB are not used for enlistment decisions but rather for placement in jobs within the military. Selected groups of the scores from these 9 subtests are used for 10 different composite scores. For example, five of these composite scores are:

Clerical Score: Has same four subtests as the AFQT

Combat Score: Uses Word Knowledge and Paragraph Comprehension but then also includes the scores from Auto & Shop Information and Mechanical Comprehension

Operators and Food Score: Has, oddly, exactly the same components as the Combat Score

General Technical: Is the same as Clerical Score except that it excludes Mathematical Knowledge

Field Artillery: Uses Arithmetic Reasoning and Mathematics Knowledge and adds in Mechanical Comprehension

It is striking to note that the various subscores are not used individually but instead are combined into various scores based on longer tests that are used for impactful decisions by the military. So how is it anticipated that the actual individual subscores are to be used? The military answers this question in their advice to potential enlistees:

Understanding how your ASVAB scores are calculated will help you be strategic when studying, <u>so you can focus on specific areas you want to do well in</u>. (emphasis ours)

1.4.2 How Well Does the ASVAB Work?

The ASVAB, like any well-constructed mental test of sizable length, provides a reliable ordering of its examinees, so interpreting the differences between candidates well separated by score is not likely to be interpreting noise. A dramatic illustration of its efficacy was described by John Flanagan in his 1948 monograph. He told of how military leaders were not fully convinced of the efficacy of using test scores to select candidates for aviation training. Accurate selection was of crucial importance because the training was expensive and failure in training could have catastrophic consequence. Flanagan convinced military leaders to test all of the candidates but then to ignore the results and select trainees on whatever basis they had been using previously. Then after training was complete, some candidates made it through, and some didn't. He showed that their test scores were a very accurate predictor of success in aviation training. After this demonstration, all subsequent candidate decisions were made on the basis of their test scores. Of course, once the population of trainees was highly selected, the strength of the relation between test score and training outcome was, predictably, diminished. Harold Gulliksen often referred to Flanagan's work as "the only true validity study that has ever been done."[5] Apparently military leaders eventually came to see the value of such a testing program, and they initiated work that 20 years later resulted in the inauguration of the ASVAB and the general practice of basing the lion's share of military personnel decisions on it.

One of the reasons that the ASVAB works well is because it is composed of test items spanning a range of topics that panels of experts agree tap into abilities that are important for success in military performance. Crucial to this is the reliability of the total test (AFQT) scores that range between 0.94 and 0.97 depending on the grouping of examinees being considered. Such reliability is generally agreed to match or exceed the standard for useful scores.

But what about the ASVAB's subscores and the various composites that are made from them? The reliability of ASVAB subscores varies depending on the subtest, the subpopulation of examinees, and the mode of administration, but it is generally in the 0.8 range.[6] Why are ASVAB subscores so much lower than the aggregate score (the AFQT)?

1.5 Subscore Reliability

Subscores' reliability is governed by the same inexorable rules of reliability as overall scores – as a test's length decreases, so too does its reliability. Thus, if we need reliable subscores, we must have enough items for that purpose. A glance at the low end of the curve in Figure 1.1 shows clearly that the marginal value of each additional item to a score's reliability is much greater when there are few items than when there are many (the right side of the curve in Figure 1.1). But this means that to have reliable subscores, the overall length of a test would have to be greater than would be necessary for merely a single reliable total score.

---

[5] Harold Gulliksen, October 1966, classroom lecture, Princeton University.
[6] See www.officialasvab.com/researchers/test-score-precision/ for technical details of ASVAB reliability.

For the second use, helping institutions, the test's length might not have to increase, for the reliability would be calculated over the number of individuals from that institution who took the items of interest. If that number was large enough, the estimate could achieve high reliability.

And so it would seem that one key justification for what appears at first to be the excessive lengths of most common tests is to provide feedback to examinees in subscores calculated from subsets of the tests. Certainly, that is what was conveyed by the military's guidance to examinees, "*so you can focus on specific areas you want to do well in*." In general, how successful are test developers in providing such subscores in various testing programs? Not particularly (see Chapters 4 and 5), for such scores are typically based on few items and hence are not very reliable.

1.6 Subscore Specificity

Earlier we proposed that a "subscore is meaningful when it is reliable enough for its prospective use and contains information that is not adequately focused (or is overly diluted) in the total test score" (Haberman, 2008a). Having just discussed reliability, let us turn our attention to specificity.

If a subscore is merely reproducing the same information that is in the total score, we gain nothing from its use – indeed we are fooling ourselves into thinking that we have new, potentially valuable, information when we do not.[7] Continuing with our examination of the ASVAB as an example of a professionally polished test with subscores that potentially impact the lives and careers of its examinees, let us ask the extent to which its various composite scores provide information that is at least somewhat orthogonal to the information obtained from the total score.

The short answer is that they do not. In a sequence of reports in the early 1990s, Malcolm Ree, who for a decade was chairman of the ASVAB Technical Committee, repeatedly showed that the ASVAB and all its composite scores were essentially unidimensional, so any index formed by combining the ASVAB subtests yielded the same result (within the bounds of stochastic variation).

So, while the ASVAB does an admiral job of rank ordering examines and so improves the efficacy of selection for military training, the use of the myriad of indices based on their scores on various subtests is a chimera.

---

[7] More technically, if the covariance matrix of all the subscores is essentially of rank one, all of the subscores are saying the same thing as the total score, albeit less reliably.

1.7 Is the ASVAB Like the Census?

The ASVAB is a serious test taken annually by more than a million people. When it was a linearly structured, paper-and-pencil test, it took more than three hours to complete. In the 1980s, the military undertook an ambitious project to transform the ASVAB to computerized administration and then to make it adaptive (W. A. Sands and his colleagues at the Navy Personnel Research and Development Center provide a full description in their 1997 technical report). This transformation allowed the test to be administered in only a little more than half the time with the same overall accuracy. The annual budget for the ASVAB is somewhere north of $20 million. The ASVAB is not the same size project as the census, but it is a serious test with serious goals. And although its developers desired efficacious subscores, it has been only partially successful in supplying them – they are reliable enough for many purposes but are not independent enough of one another to give guidance that is not more reliably given by the total score (AFQT).

Next, we shall compare the success of other testing programs with parallel goals.

1.8 Other Testing Programs That Want to Use Subscores

Over the past 20 years, due primarily to the passage of No Child Left Behind (and its sequel Every Student Succeeds), there has been a marked acceleration in K-12 testing in the United States. The act requires assessment in grades 3 through 8 with separate scores in mathematics, reading or language arts, and science. In a very real sense, the score on each of these topics is a subscore. They are calculated on various subpopulations of examinees, designated by race, geographic location, and so on, but are not reported back as individual scores to examinees and their families. Because what are calculated are mean scores over the subpopulations of interest, we probably need not be concerned about the reliability of the reported mean scores, at least for large subpopulations; however, concerns remain about the orthogonality of these subscores (see Chapter 4 for details). The stated goal of these subscores is to guide remediation of schools and districts. The aim is for each school to make at least adequate yearly progress (AYP) as defined by the act. Such goals are very serious indeed. Schools have at their disposal several, possibly draconian, actions to remediate less than AYP. These include "restructuring the school by: (1) reopening as a public charter school or (2) replacing all or most of the staff (which may include the principal) relevant to the AYP failure."

There is no doubt that the goal is to have subscores that are accurate enough to make judgements about both the overall level of students' performance in each of several subject matter areas and are also stable enough to estimate changes in them from one year to the next. This simply cannot be done effectively without reliable and orthogonal scores. The annual budget for this work is $250 million to cover roughly 50 million students, or $5 per student.

Compare this with the $40 per person cost of census or even the $20 per examinee cost of the ASVAB. We see that despite the seriousness of the consequences of poorly estimated subscores, the government has not seen fit to provide resources on the same level for them as they have for the census or for military testing.

1.9 Summing Up

I What's Needed
1) Tests have been around for a long time (at least 4,000 years) and have been used to generate scores to provide evidentiary support for claims that users would like to make (e.g., this person should be admitted, be hired, be allowed to practice their profession).
2) But to provide valid support, a score must possess a number of critical characteristics. Two of these are:
   (i) Be relevant for its potential use
   (ii) Be reliable, remembering always that score reliability is immutably connected to the length of the test that generated it
3) For as long as there have been tests and test scores, there have been subtests and subscores.
4) For a subscore to be reliable enough to be useful, the test containing the subtest that generates that subscore must be longer, often much longer, and the more subscores, the greater the length of the test that contains it.
5) The extent to which a subscore yields unique information is directly related to the extent to which that subscore is orthogonal to the total test score.

II What We've Got
6) The inevitable conclusion is that constructing and administering a test whose score is valid and reliable is a straightforward task and has been accomplished successfully for millennia; but constructing such a test containing a number of subtests with scores that are also valid and reliable is much more difficult and expensive (expensive in both money and examinee time), and successful attempts are very rare indeed.

7) A model for success is the US decennial census, with small area estimates that are an analog to subscores. But obtaining such detailed information increases the cost of the census dramatically (to $42 per person counted).
8) A model for marginal success is the US military's ASVAB program that, after almost a century of experience, evolved a combination of careful test construction and the optimization of item presentation that is possible with adaptive technology. It has thus been able to yield a set of eight subtests with associated subscores that are all reliable enough for most prospective uses. Unfortunately, it is not clear that any of the various composite scores calculated from these subscores (used for placement) yield any information that is distinct from any other composite, or indeed distinct from that obtained from the total score (which is, of course, considerably more reliable). At about $20 per person, the per examinee cost of the ASVAB is less than half that of census.
9) Another testing program we described briefly, which is typical of other, smaller, programs that also require subscores for various kinds of decisions, was one instigated by the 2001 No Child Left Behind Act (and its 2015 sequel Every Child Succeeds Act). There are potentially profound consequences for schools whose students' subscores are unacceptably low (e.g., close the school or replace the principal and the faculty). Because of their known unreliability, these subscores are, sensibly, not reported to students or parents. But they are likely highly dependent on one another, so considering shortcomings on multiple subscores as replicated independent evidence is likely a mistake. The per student cost of these programs at $5 per person is about one fourth the ASVAB cost and one eighth that of census.

III What's Next

In the coming chapters, we will expand and deepen this introductory discussion of subscores.

This will include, in Chapter 2, a description of how subscores are reported (and in Chapter 6 how we believe they should be reported).

There is next (in Chapter 3) a careful description of how to tell if a subscore is worth reporting, including statistical measures of the potential value of a subscore.

Then (in Chapter 4) we take the next step and discuss some viable subscores by giving examples of tests whose developers have actually succeeded in providing subscores that add value and the lessons that we can infer from these special tests. We then (in Chapter 5) provide some advice on what might be done when the subscores obtained ought not be reported. Finally, we move on to some potential avenues that research has shown can yield valid subscores.

So far, though, nothing that we have learned allows one to construct a test with more information for less money/effort. Paraphrasing architect Philip Johnson, all good tests share one characteristic – they cost a lot of money or use a lot of examinee time, or usually, both.

Thus, so far at least, there is still no free lunch.

2

How Are Subscores Reported?

> There is no such thing as information overload. There is only bad design.
>
> *Edward Tufte*

Daisy, a 10-year-old fifth grader at Lakeville Elementary school, is a bright, enthusiastic, hard-working student. Her parents have set an extremely high standard for her education and thus, although Daisy consistently performed well above average among her classmates, her family was concerned that she was not reaching her full potential. Without any prompts from the school, pediatrician, or other care providers, Daisy's parents brought her to a psychologist to be assessed for a learning disability, specifically asking to check if she was behind in her reading and vocabulary. As requested, the psychologist administered a battery of relevant assessments and provided the parents with a report summarizing the results. Contrary to her parents' concern, Daisy scored very well in reading and vocabulary. However, the subscores on one of the assessments happened to be normed within-person, designed to identify an individual's relative strengths and weaknesses by contrasting their subscore performance against their overall assessment performance. In school Daisy always performed above average in math, but on this particular assessment, due to her extremely high reading proficiency, it now appeared as if Daisy had a weakness in math.

Her parents were ecstatic; this was exactly what they had hoped for, as they interpreted Daisy's relative weakness as evidence that she had a learning disability and needed additional support. Daisy's parents built a case around this single math subscore to try to pressure the school into qualifying her for an individualized education plan, which would grant curriculum and testing accommodations. Given Daisy's stellar academic performance, the school resisted, as they would rather reserve these essential resources and services for struggling students who were truly in need. However, Daisy's parents were very demanding – threatening litigation – and the school district was mindful of the broader consequences within the community if the issue was not quickly resolved. Now with mounting pressure from the district, the school reluctantly granted Daisy's parents the requested accommodations, thus formalizing a learning disability in her academic record. With her newly diagnosed learning disability, Daisy was protected under the Individuals with Disabilities Education Act (IDEA), and her school, as well as future schools that she would attend, was required by federal law to provide a variety of entitlements and interventions.

Daisy's is a fictionalized account of a true story and reflects a situation that has been worsening over time as more and more parents and students interested in an academic advantage seek diagnoses to qualify for educational and testing accommodations (Lovett & Harrison, 2021). This story highlights the intricacy of subscore reporting by illustrating how subscores can be misinterpreted and misused, leading to serious practical consequences. Reporting a subscore is no different from reporting a total score, and thus the same principles for best practices in score reporting are applicable. In their comprehensive review of student score reports, Goodman and Hambleton (2004) noted several reoccurring challenges around how results are presented, such as too much statistical jargon, lack of descriptive information, and dense tables and graphs. Reporting subscores adds a layer of complexity to these existing concerns because they often contain poor psychometric properties.

In Chapter 1 we described what a subscore is, why there is a desire to report them, and a sense of the effort involved when they need to be accurate. But exactly how subscores are reported varies based on several important considerations, including the psychometric quality of the data underlying the subscores, the inferences that need empirical support, the type of assessment, and the nature of the users who will be receiving and acting upon the subscore information.

We will cover how to determine when subscores are reportable from a statistical perspective in Chapter 3. Additionally, the conditions that impact the psychometric value of a subscore and what to do when they are not worth reporting will be covered in Chapters 4 and 5. Thus, for this chapter, we will assume that the reported subscores have at least some value. Depending on that value, as well as other considerations discussed later in this chapter, there are many ways to present the same subscore results.

2.1 Subscore Value

For a hypothetical student and test composed of five content areas, Figure 2.1 illustrates how the same subscore information can be presented in a few different ways: (a) raw scores, (b) percent correct and percentile scores, (c) profile bands, or (d) categorical performance indicators.

Figure 2.1a is the most detailed at the subtest level and provides raw information that may be the simplest for a score user to interpret, making transparent how many items are in each content area and the number of correct responses. In Figure 2.1b, percent correct scores instead of raw scores are reported, which obscures the number of items and makes it difficult for the score user to know how many items were responded to incorrectly. However, this can be advantageous in facilitating comparisons among categories if there are substantive

(a)

Content Area	Number Correct
Category 1	31 out of 44
Category 2	15 out of 43
Category 3	14 out of 26
Category 4	28 out of 39
Category 5	28 out of 43

(b)

Content Area	Percent Correct Score	Percentile Score
Category 1	70	89
Category 2	35	48
Category 3	54	61
Category 4	72	92
Category 5	65	74

(c)

Scale Score Profile

| | 100 | 200 | 300 | 400 | 500 | 600 | 700 | 800 |

Category 1
Category 2
Category 3
Category 4
Category 5

Your Performance

(d)

Content Area	Low Performance	Average	High Performance
Category 1			X
Category 2	X		
Category 3		X	
Category 4			X
Category 5		X	

Figure 2.1 A few illustrations of the variety of ways to report subscores. (a) Raw scores; (b) percent correct and percentile scores; (c) profile band; (d) categorical performance.

discrepancies in the number of items, sometimes referred to as weighting, between content areas. For instance, a raw score of 9 points should be interpreted differently if it was out of 10 total points compared to 30 total points. Additionally, the normative information in Figure 2.1b adds context for how users can understand their performance as a percentile relative to some meaningful comparison group. For instance, 89% of the students in the school district scored lower than the student in Category 1.

Instead of numeric scores, Figure 2.1c provides profile bands – sometimes referred to as performance bands, confidence bands, or score intervals – with the placement of the students' numeric scale scores marked in the center. Traditionally, the width of the interval is an illustration of measurement error, with narrower intervals representing greater accuracy and wider intervals having lesser accuracy. Presenting subscore information in this format can provide a more direct sense of imprecision to help mitigate overinterpretation of minor score differences between categories – usually accompanied by text explaining that overlapping bands should be interpreted as similar performance.

Lastly, Figure 2.1d altogether removes the burden of asking users to interpret measurement errors and instead reports discretized categories that incorporate the measurement error to identify whether an examinee's performance differed from a relevant reference point. Although useful to facilitate interpretations, it should be noted that the categorizations also contain error, can sometimes be less reliable than the scores from which they are constructed (Ramsay, 1973), and can even be used fraudulently to skew the results (Wainer, Gessaroli, & Verdi, 2006). Further, the consequences of either random or systemic error that puts an examinee's true score in the wrong category might be more of a risk compared to a more subtle difference of a few points. Thus, caution is needed when defining thresholds for determining how continuous scores are converted into discretized categories, which is no different from specifying pass/fail on a classification test (Angoff, 1971) or implementing indicators of subscore performance (Feinberg & von Davier, 2020) as low, average, or high as illustrated in Figure 2.1d.

Figure 2.1a–d also reflect a continuum of decreasing granularity of the subscore information. There are, of course, other modalities of presenting subscore results not displayed here, some of which will be illustrated later in this chapter when describing sample reports from operational testing programs. Generally, more specificity can be supported for subscores of higher precision and accuracy, which in turn helps to mitigate misinterpretation. However, there could be other scoring implications that make reporting the more intuitive raw or percent correct scores less appropriate than a scale score that has gone through further processing. For instance, a student may have a lower raw score in Category A compared to Category B, but if the items in Category A were more difficult, then a lower raw or percent correct score may not necessarily reflect a lower underlying proficiency. In such cases, an adjustment is needed to correct for difficulty, which could be done between categories on the test as well as across different forms of the test (alternatively, report users should be explicitly cautioned about differences in difficulty). Another example is when the reported score has been scaled relative to a particular group of interest, often referred to as a norming group, which could be any subgroup relevant to the score users such as a school, state, national population, first-year college students, successful job applicants, or individuals diagnosed with posttraumatic stress disorder (PTSD) (Mertler, 2018). A normed scale score provides context and supports inferences against the relevant comparison group. Thus, a seeming loss of granularity can be offset by providing more subscore utility.

2.2 Types of Assessment

Beyond psychometric properties and needs for other statistical and scaling adjustments, considerations for how to display subscore information also depend on the type of assessment and corresponding inferences the test publisher claims users can make with the subscores. For our purposes, we will refer to two broad categories of assessments, formative and summative

Formative assessments are often low-stakes and used within educational programs to identify what students misunderstand in an effort to improve instruction and learning (Perie, Marion, & Gong, 2009). At an individual test-taker level, formative assessment is designed to provide feedback to the user, typically on their relative strengths and weaknesses against a relevant criterion. In terms of purpose, formative assessment total scores and subscores serve to inform remediation for learning and preparation for future assessments. The criterion for this feedback could be the user (e.g., interpret performance relative to oneself), a norm group (e.g., interpret performance relative to other students in a similar training program, year of matriculation, proficiency level), or a standard (e.g., interpret performance relative to grade level expectations set by the state). On an aggregate level, the criterion could be how the students at one school performed relative to other cohorts within or across institutions, though the focus would principally be on school-level remediation, such as improving curriculum. There are different types of formative assessments, such as a practice test, a self-assessment, or a progress test that an individual may repeat periodically to track their improvement over time. These types include formative assessments that users may intentionally not prepare for or complete at the start of their learning journey if they are interested in their baseline knowledge or performance. As the primary focus of formative assessment is on supporting improvement, careful consideration should be given to whether and how results are shared with other decision-makers to reduce concerns of having academic consequences for poor performance.

Summative assessments are high-stakes and often shared with decision-makers because they are designed for evaluation (Perie, Marion, & Gong, 2009). Examples of summative assessments include admission tests used in a selection process, achievement tests to assess learning of a particular construct, licensure and certification tests designed to classify test takers as either passing or failing, or national assessments linked to defined accountability standards. Though the main results of a summative assessment are intended to be communicated to stakeholders beyond the examinee to support consequential decisions, subscores are commonly included to support remediation and help users better understand their performance. Thus, though subscores naturally align within a formative assessment context, they can be a major component of how results are reported on summative assessments. For assessing broader group-level trends, such as on the National Assessment of Educational Progress (NAEP), subscores are aggregated over different subsets of students to support various targeted inferences such as by type of school, ethnicity, gender, geographical location, race, and disability status (NAEP, 2023).

However, because summative assessments are designed for evaluation, building quality subscores to support formative uses is often deprioritized in the tradeoff to maximize the primary inference. When this does occur, test publishers may attempt to find a compromise in reporting coarser subscore information (e.g., performance intervals or categories rather than numeric scores) to reduce misinterpretation. Thus, many of the concerns of reporting subscores with poor psychometric value stem from summative assessment programs that are in a difficult situation of trying to both satisfy the primary inference for the overall test score and support score users who desire diagnostic feedback.

2.3 Types of Users

When we think of a standardized assessment, we often first envision high school students sitting for the SAT after months of preparation and managing the stress that often accompanies knowing their performance qualifies them to get into their desired college. These users, though hopefully knowledgeable about the quantitative content on the test, would likely (1) not have any expertise in interpreting complex subscores and (2) be highly motivated to receive detailed diagnostic feedback to understand their performance. In this instance, students eagerly awaiting their SAT results are no different from premed students after completing the Medical College Admissions Test (MCAT) or aspiring accountants completing the Certified Public Accounting (CPA) examination. To assist with score interpretation, test publishers commonly include explanatory language on the score report as well as other supplementary materials (e.g., a video walkthrough of interpreting a score report on their website). Additionally, these users may share their score reports with teachers, faculty, advisors, or learning specialists to help them interpret and make their results actionable. Test publishers would also want to design and refine the report by engaging a representative sample of stakeholders with surveys, cognitive interviews, and focus groups so as to ensure that users can correctly interpret the results.

In an aggregate case, when subscores may be compiled across students within a program or institution, the user may be a teacher, a program director, or another institutional administrator looking for feedback to make curricula enhancements. This could also include governing boards or agencies if results are compiled across schools and districts to inform higher-level decisions about policies, funding, or educational reform. These types of users, faculty, administrators, and government representatives routinely interpret score reports and thus may require less detailed score interpretation materials or protection from misinterpretation.

Similarly, psychologists who frequently administer assessments often score them manually and summarize the results, consulting a manual only for general guidance on the scores when needed. In some cases, the test publisher may provide only a scoring rubric, as the psychologist would be compiling a comprehensive summary, usually across multiple assessments, for a client that also includes background information, behavior observations, and their clinical interpretation.

Thus, in addition to the varying psychometric quality of subscores, many types of assessments report subscores for different purposes and communicate them to different types of users, all of which are factored into how a testing publisher determines what to report. The next section will review a few sample score reports to illustrate how this appears in practice.

2.4 Score Report Examples

2.4.1 Praxis®

The Praxis is a certification test used by many states as one of several requirements to become a certified teacher in the United States (PRAXIS, 2023). Figure 2.2 presents an excerpt from a sample score report from Sinharay et al.

2.4 Score Report Examples

Test / Test Category*	Your Raw Points Earned	Average Performance Range**
ELEMENTARY EDUCATION: CURRICULUM, INSTRUCTION, AND ASSESSMENT (5017)		
I. READING AND LANGUAGE ARTS	33 out of 37	23–29
II. MATHEMATICS	26 out of 31	19–25
III. SCIENCE	15 out of 20	11–15
IV. SOCIAL STUDIES	14 out of 17	9–13
V. ART, MUSIC, AND PHYSICAL EDUCATION	13 out of 15	6–12

* Category-level information indicates the number of test questions answered correctly for relatively small subsets of the questions. Because they are based on small numbers of questions, category scores are less reliable than the official scaled scores, which are based on the full sets of questions. Furthermore, the questions in a category may vary in difficulty from one test to another. Therefore, the category scores of individuals who have taken different forms of the test are not necessarily comparable. For these reasons, category scores should not be considered a precise reflection of a candidate's level of knowledge in that category, and ETS recommends that category information not be used to inform any decisions affecting candidates without careful consideration of such inherent lack of precision.

** The range of scores earned by the middle 50% of a group of test takers who took this form of the test at the most recent national administration or other comparable time period. N/C means that this range was not computed because fewer than 30 test takers took this form of the test or because there were fewer than eight questions in the category or, for a constructed-response module, fewer than eight points to be awarded by the raters. N/A indicates that this test section was not taken and, therefore, the information is not applicable.

Figure 2.2 Excerpt from a Praxis score report. Copyright © 2023 by Educational Testing Service (ETS). Reproduced with permission. All rights reserved.

(2019) showing how the Praxis subscore information is reported along with the corresponding explanatory text. Subscore information is conveyed at a very granular level, similar to Figure 2.1a, along with normative information on how the middle 50% of a recent group of test takers from a national administration performed on this form of the test. Based on these results, the recipient can see that they performed above average in all categories. Going further, the recipient might infer that mathematics and science are areas to focus on for additional preparation, given that they missed five points in each category. However, the explanatory text in the footnote discourages making any serious inferences due to the quality of the subscores: "For these reasons, category score should not be considered a precise reflection of a candidate's level of knowledge in that category, and ETS recommends that category information not be used to inform any decisions affecting candidates without careful consideration of such inherent lack of precision." Interestingly, the footnote also references symbols of N/C for not computed and N/A for not applicable, but neither are observed in the report. Most likely this is standard language on a template used for multiple forms of the Praxis, though it could still be confusing to score users who wonder if something is missing or even why the reference is included at all.

2.4.2 SAT

The SAT is a summative assessment designed to inform college admission decisions and reports subscores on the math and evidence-based reading and writing sections. Similar to how Praxis scores by themselves do not qualify someone to be a teacher, there is no minimum acceptable SAT score, as

Figure 2.3 Excerpt from an SAT score report. © Copyright 2021 College Board. "SAT Suite Results: 2020 (State Reports)." All rights reserved. Reprinted with permission.

different colleges and universities apply different thresholds and use the SAT as a component within a comprehensive admissions process. Figure 2.3 presents an excerpt from a sample SAT score report that includes an individual's total score, performance on different sections, and then subscores at the bottom (SAT, 2023). Subscores on the SAT report are presented as scale scores but with little additional score information. Instead, language on the report directs students online, where they can find a more interactive experience that allows them to explore their skills and connect to appropriate remediation resources if desired. Thus, based on only this report, a recipient can compare their performance between categories, but they would lack context relative to a meaningful group or the significance of the observed scaled score differences (e.g., whether a two-point difference is worthy of attention).

2.4.3 ACT

Like the SAT, the ACT is also a summative assessment that is primarily designed to inform college admission decisions, but it defines the construct slightly differently and reports subscores from the English, math, reading, science, and writing sections of the test. Figure 2.4 presents an excerpt from a sample ACT score report (ACT, 2023). Subscore information includes the number correct out of the total number of items in a particular content area, the corresponding percentage correct, and then a visual indicator representing whether the student's performance was in the readiness range – which is also communicated with a checkmark. As indicated in the explanatory text at the bottom of the report, the readiness range "shows where a student who has met the ACT College Readiness Benchmark on this subject test would typically perform." The explanatory text also notes that meeting the readiness range indicates that "you have at least a 50% chance of obtaining a B or higher or about a 75% chance of obtaining a C or higher in specific first-year college courses in the corresponding subject area." A recipient of this report can see that all their science and all but one of their math subscores were below the readiness range and thus are in need of remediation if they view these grade probabilities as a meaningful goal. This interpretation also aligns with their US and state rankings that illustrate mostly below-average performance in math and science.

2.4.4 American Board of Internal Medicine Maintenance of Certification (ABIM MOC)

The American Board of Internal Medicine Maintenance of Certification Examination (ABIM MOC) is a classification test for practicing physicians to

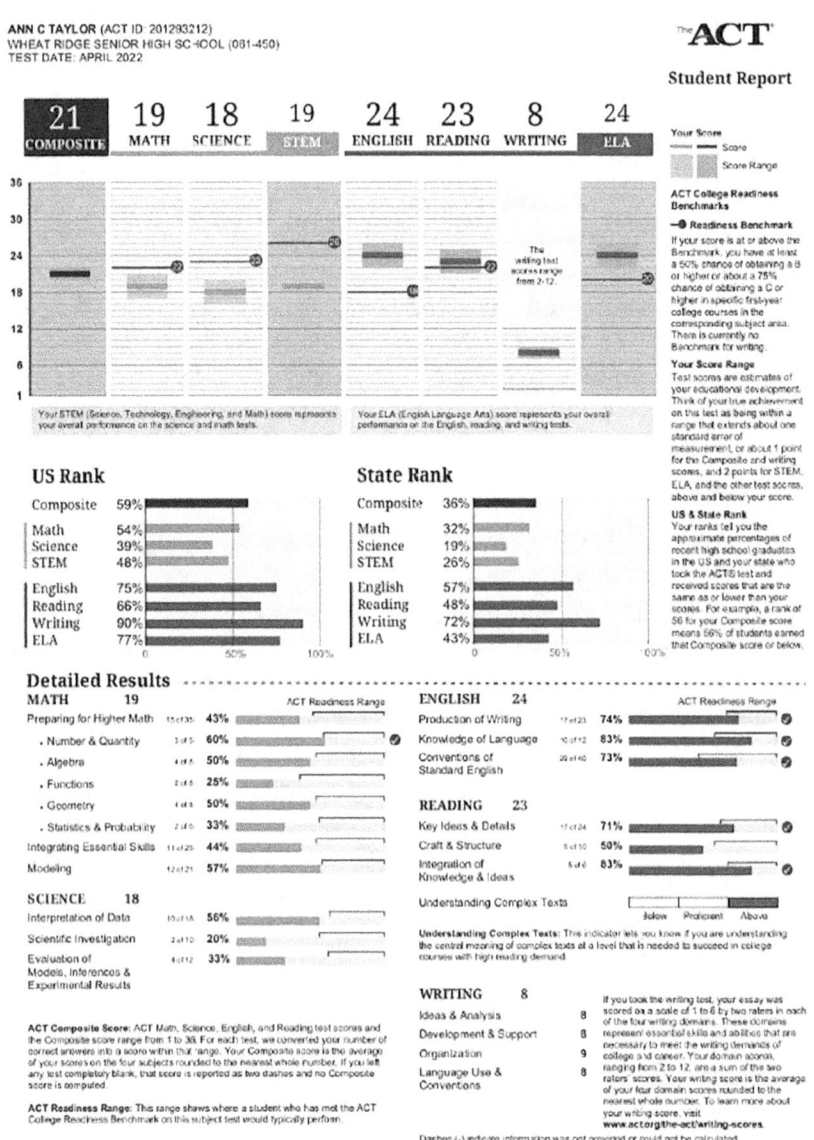

Figure 2.4 Excerpt from an ACT score report. Copyright © 2021 by ACT. Reproduced with permission. All rights reserved.

maintain their specialty credentials by completing and passing the test every 10 years. Figure 2.5 presents an excerpt from the second page of a sample ABIM MOC score report (ABIM MOC, 2023). Subscores for each medical

INTERPRETATION OF OVERALL PERFORMANCE

The American Board of Internal Medicine Internal Medicine Maintenance of Certification Examination is a standardized test that ensures all examinees experience the same level of difficulty to successfully complete the exam. Overall performance is reported on a standardized scale ranging from 200 to 800 points. Your performance on the entire exam determines the exam pass-fail decision. To pass the exam, your standardized score must equal or exceed the **standardized passing score** of 366. The graph on page one shows your performance relative to both the standardized passing score and to a **reference group** of diplomates who took this exam in recent years. The links to the right provide more information related to understanding your overall performance.

More Information

- Passing Scores
- Reference Group Information
- Standardized Score Scale
- Standard Error of Measurement
- Test Standardization

CONTENT AREA SUBSCORES AND FEEDBACK

The table below is an overview of your relative strengths and weaknesses in the medical content areas. Your standardized score in each medical content area is reported in standard deviation units above and below the reference group average (vertical dotted line). Due to the limited number of questions in each content area, content area subscores are less precise than the overall score. Narrower boxes indicate a greater level of precision in calculating your score. Because the overall score and the content area subscores are on different scales, they cannot be directly compared. The links to the right provide more information related to understanding your performance in medical content areas. Also provided on the following page is a detailed listing of exam content, showing the blueprint content description and cognitive task, that you missed in each area.

More Information

- Content Area Subscores
- Exam Blueprint

YOUR PERFORMANCE IN MEDICAL CONTENT AREAS

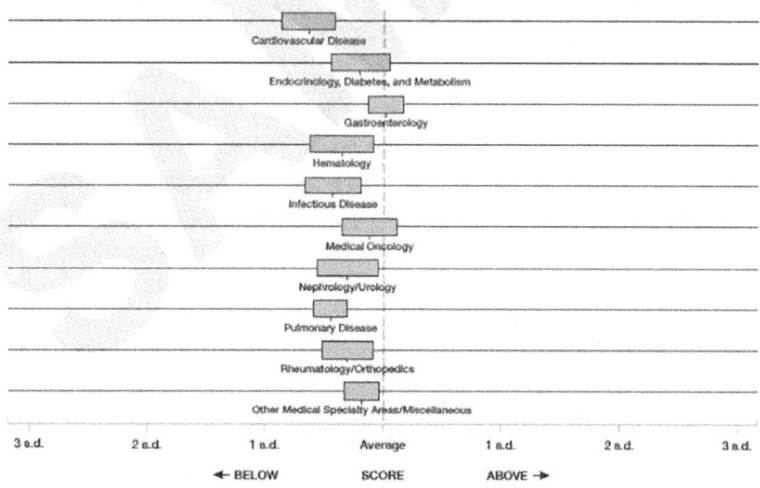

Figure 2.5 Excerpt from the second page of the ABIM MOC score report. Reproduced with permission. All rights reserved.

content area are reported as profile bands standardized to a recent group of diplomates, with a vertical line indicating average performance. As noted in the interpretive text above the graph and similar to Figure 2.1c, the width of the bands is a reflection of score precision. Subsequent pages of the report, not shown here, provide item-level information for missed content as a brief phrase descriptive of the concept targeted by the item. The recipient of this report would see that they performed slightly below average across most subscores. Given the overlap across profile bands, there are no specific areas for remediation; rather, the recipient would benefit from additional preparation on every aspect of the content domain.

2.4.5 Armed Services Vocational Aptitude Battery (ASVAB)

As we discussed in Chapter 1, the Armed Services Vocational Aptitude Battery (ASVAB) is a summative assessment designed to inform military entrance eligibility and help determine what branch of service would be a good fit for an applicant. Figure 2.6 displays an excerpt from a sample score report that individuals receive after completing the ASVAB (ASVAB, 2023). Subscore information displayed under the ASVAB tests section is a hybrid of Figure 2.1b and c, showing percentile ranks for different norming groups and a visual presentation of the subscores in a profile (score bands) format to assist with interpreting relative differences. Unlike the excerpt from the ABIM MOC report, the subscore profiles in this sample have far less overlap, likely reflecting greater reliability (e.g., narrower bands) and validity (variability in performance), although it is possible that the bands were constructed differently, based on a lower standard error criterion or using a different standard deviation, which could be used to distort the results and create the perception of greater reliability and validity. The recipient of this report can see that they performed considerably better in Word Knowledge than in Electronics Information. When considering the purpose of the ASVAB and that the subscores are used to determine entrance eligibility, this level of detail is important in placement decisions for various career positions and branches of service.

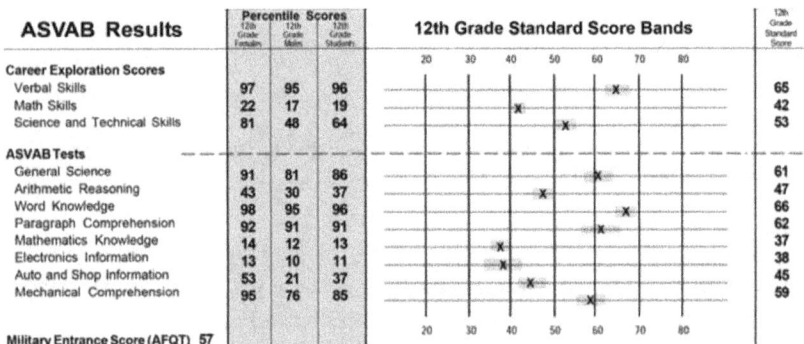

Figure 2.6 Excerpt from an ASVAB score report.

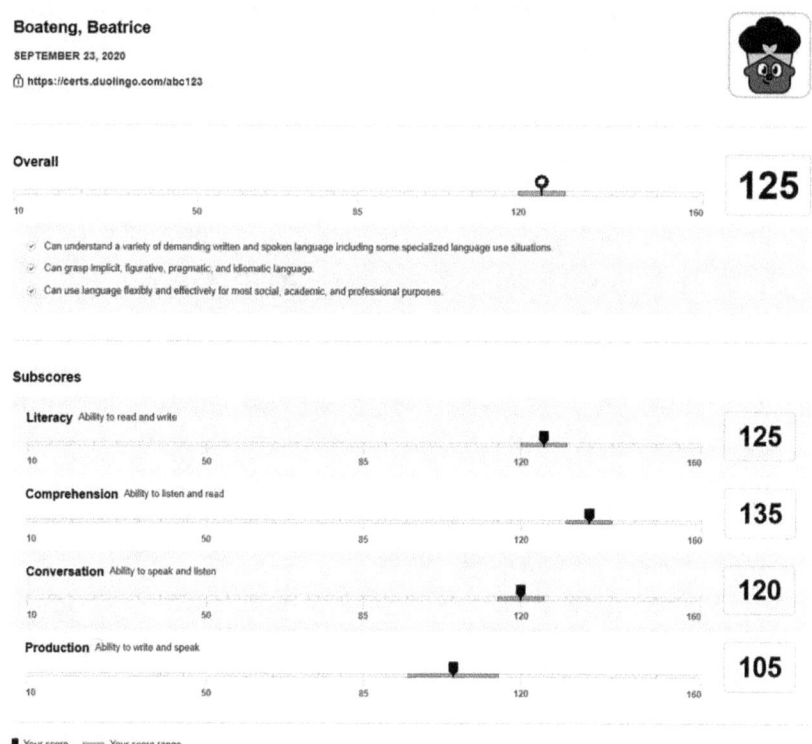

Figure 2.7 Excerpt from the sample Duolingo English Test Certificate. Reproduced with permission. All rights reserved.

2.4.6 Duolingo English Test

The Duolingo English Test is a summative assessment designed to inform undergraduate and graduate admission decisions related to general English language proficiency. Figure 2.7 presents an excerpt from a sample certificate (score report) test takers would receive after completing the test (Duolingo, 2023). Similar to how subscores are reported on the ASVAB report, students receive both their numeric score and a score range on a comparable scale across all subscores. In this example, due to the nonoverlapping score ranges (profiles), the student can see that they performed relatively better in Comprehension and relatively worse in Production. The wider score range for Production likely suggests less precision, and possibly fewer items, compared to the other content areas. Also similar to the ASVAB, the lack of explanatory text on this certificate makes it difficult to know exactly how the score ranges were computed and whether the separation between ranges reflects greater reliability and validity. However, though not mentioned directly on the certificate, the Duolingo website does include a research report (LaFlair, 2020) that describes the psychometric properties of the subscores and evidence for how they can be used. A comprehensive review of recommended approaches for assessing subscore value will be covered in Chapter 3.

2.4.7 South Carolina College- and Career-Ready Assessments (SC READY)

The South Carolina College- and Career-Ready Assessments (SC READY) are formative assessments designed to measure the extent to which students are on track for the next grade and ultimately college and career readiness based

How do my child's mathematics scores compare with his/her scores from previous years?

Your Child's Mathematics Score History						
	Grade 3	Grade 4	Grade 5	Grade 6	Grade 7	Grade 8
Scale Score	570	565		548		
Performance Level	Exceeds	Exceeds		Meets		

How does my child's mathematics score compare with other students?

Percentile Ranks

The table to the left shows your child's percentile ranks. A percentile rank compares your child's score to other students in a group. Percentile ranks range from 1 to 99, with 99 being the highest. The rank is the percentage of students in the comparison group who scored the same as or below your child's score. The South Carolina percentile rank compares your child's score to the scores of students in South Carolina that have taken the test this year. The "Other States with Comparable Standards" percentile rank compares your student's performance to the performance of other students in other states with comparable content standards, during a typical test administration.

Your Child's Mathematics Percentile Rank Comparisons	
South Carolina	55
Other States with Comparable Standards	45

How did my child perform on the mathematics academic standards?

Reporting Category	Your Child's Performance		
	Low	Middle	High
The Number System		✓	
Ratios and Proportional Relationships	✓		
Expressions, Equations, and Inequalities		✓	
Geometry and Measurement			✓
Data Analysis and Statistics			✓

Interpretation of SC READY 2021-22

The SCDE advises caution when interpreting assessment results this year due to the ongoing pandemic. Consider how conditions for learning, disrupted by the pandemic, may have impacted student performance. As a reminder, a single score does not provide a complete or precise measure of student achievement. When interpreting results, please take into consideration other measures of achievement.

Figure 2.8 Excerpt from the fourth page of the sample SC Ready Individual Student Report. Reproduced with permission. All rights reserved.

on state-defined standards set by the South Carolina Department of Education (SC READY, 2023). Students complete versions of this assessment throughout their elementary and secondary education in English language arts (ELA), mathematics, science, and social studies. Figure 2.8 presents an excerpt from a sample sixth-grade student score report that displays categorical subscores relative to meeting academic standards in mathematics. This report would be provided to students and their parents as well as the school to inform curriculum improvements and identify areas where students may need additional support. Additionally, score information is aggregated across schools and districts for the South Carolina state-level summary of results. In the excerpt, the student would see that their overall mathematics performance met sixth-grade expectations, but it also reflects a decrease from their performance in third and fourth grades. Exploring the categorical subscores suggests that their performance relative to the state's academic standards was low in Ratios and Proportional Relationships, which may explain the decrease in overall mathematics performance and represent a key area for remediation.

2.4.8 Comprehensive Clinical Science Examination (CCSE)

The Comprehensive Clinical Science Examination® (CCSE) is designed to assess learning progress and readiness for medical students to take the United States Medical Licensing Examination® (USMLE) Step 2 Clinical Knowledge Examination (CCSE, 2023). Figure 2.9 presents an excerpt from the third page of a sample CCSE score report in which subscores are presented in a categorical format as either lower, same, or higher relative to a comparison group of medical students enrolled at accredited schools testing for the first time. Additionally, the report provides the student's equated percent correct score for each content area and the average for the comparison group. Interpretive text on the prior page explains that the equated percent correct scores "may be slightly lower or higher than the actual percentage of questions you answered correctly on this specific exam form because they are statistically adjusted to account for slight variations in exam form difficulty."

The score report also includes the percent of questions per content area, which reveals substantial differences in weighting between categories. This may be useful to score users in helping interpret the results – lower performance in a category with fewer items may be worth less remedial effort than average performance in a category with many items. Additionally, it can be deduced by the weights that items are coded multiple times across the system, discipline, and physician task (not shown) dimensions. This is likely the result of creating realistic test questions but could also have implications where the overlap causes the subscores to become more redundant (Feinberg & Wainer, 2014).

SUBJECT EXAMINATION PROGRAM
COMPREHENSIVE CLINICAL SCIENCE EXAMINATION (CCSE)
EXAMINEE PERFORMANCE REPORT

ID: 000000000
Name: Student A
000000 - Generic Medical School

Total CCSE Score: 230
Test Date: Month Day, Year

	Your EPC Score	Comparison Group Average EPC Score	Score Comparison: Lower Same Higher	% of Questions
Performance by System				
Legal/Ethical, Professionalism, System-based Practice, Pt Safety	87	81		10 - 14%
Cardiovascular System	73	72		8 - 10%
Immune System & Blood & Lymphoreticular Systems	63	78		7 - 11%
Gastrointestinal System	63	75		7 - 9%
Respiratory System	60	72		7 - 9%
Musculoskeletal Sys/Skin & Subcutaneous Tissue	70	71		6 - 10%
Behavioral Health	55	80		6 - 8%
Nervous System & Special Senses	63	74		6 - 8%
Endocrine System	65	78		4 - 6%
Female Reproductive & Breast	66	75		4 - 6%
Multisystem Processes & Disorders	57	74		4 - 6%
Pregnancy, Childbirth & the Puerperium	83	75		4 - 6%
Renal & Urinary System & Male Reproductive	74	77		4 - 6%
Performance by Discipline				
Medicine	66	75		50 - 60%
Surgery	68	74		25 - 30%
Pediatrics	73	76		20 - 25%
Obstetrics & Gynecology	80	77		10 - 20%
Psychiatry	64	81		10 - 15%

Figure 2.9 Excerpt from the third page of the CCSE Examinee Performance Report. Copyright © 2022 by the National Board of Medical Examiners (NBME). Reproduced with permission. All rights reserved.

2.4.9 United States Medical Licensing Examination (USMLE) Annual School Report

The United States Medical Licensing Examination (USMLE) is a three-step exam sequence to obtain medical licensure in the United States. In addition to individual score reports to medical students, annual reports are provided to schools meeting certain criteria (e.g., at least 20 students) to facilitate comparisons within and between institutions (USMLE, 2023). Figure 2.10

2.4 Score Report Examples

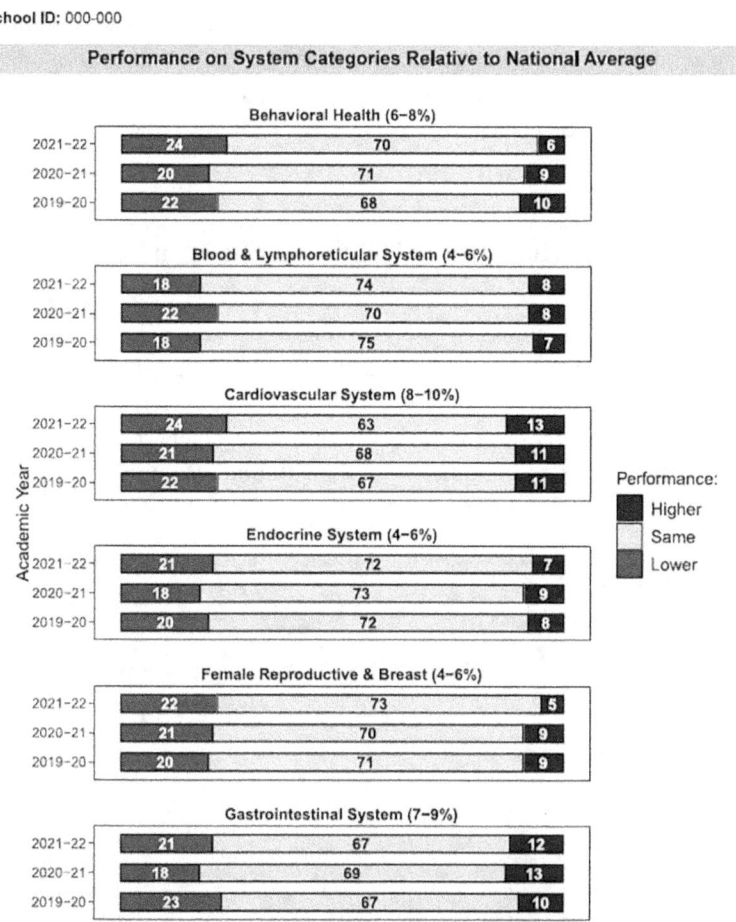

Figure 2.10 Excerpt from the seventh page of the USMLE Step 2 CK School Report. Copyright © 2022 by the Federation of State Medical Boards (FSMB) and National Board of Medical Examiners (NBME). Reproduced with permission. All rights reserved.

presents an excerpt of the subscore performance summary from a sample annual school report on the Step 2 Clinical Knowledge (CK) examination. For each content area, the percent of students from the particular school that performed higher than, similar to, or lower than a national comparison group are displayed as well as what those percentages were for the previous two years. This reporting style supports two inferences – by comparing against the national average, users can interpret the between-school normative context, and with the prior years' information, users can also interpret the within-school historical context. The similarity in results across categories is likely a sign that the subscores are highly correlated. Additionally, category weights are clearly displayed to convey the relative importance and precision of the underlying scores.

2.4.10 Critical Thinking Assessment

Figure 2.11 presents an institution score report excerpt from a postsecondary education critical thinking assessment designed to assess a common set of skills and competencies deemed relevant to learning outcomes for college graduates. In this case, the lighter wider profile band is expressed as a box plot of average scores for all institutions in the comparison group, with the box representing the middle 50% of institution average scores and the

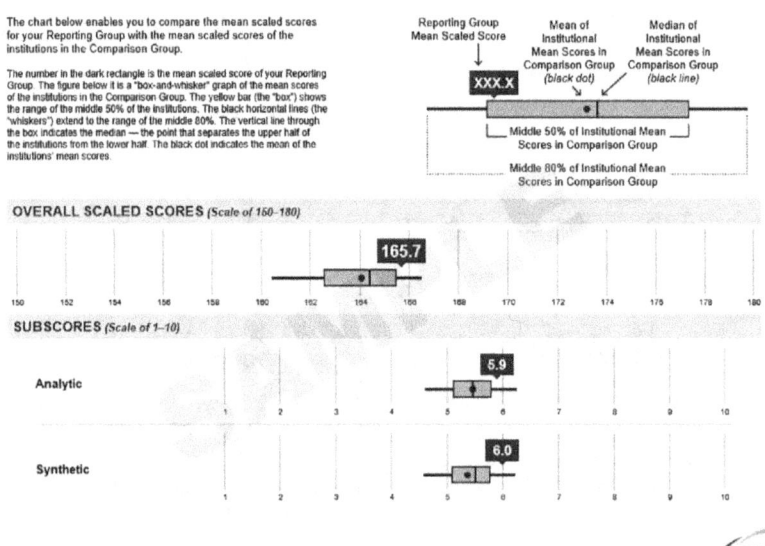

Figure 2.11 Excerpt from an institutional report for an assessment measuring critical thinking. Copyright © 2023 by Educational Testing Service (ETS), www.ets.org. Reproduced with permission. All rights reserved.

middle 80% within the whisker boundaries. The solid circle and vertical line inside the box indicate the grand mean and median, respectively. The darker narrower band represents the average student performance from this particular institution. Using this information, the recipient can infer that the participating students from their institution performed above average in both the analytic and synthetic subscores. Not shown here, other elements in the full report provide contextual information on what overall score ranges fit with developing, proficient, or advanced proficiency levels. However, subscore ranges are not mapped to these descriptions, so it would be difficult for the recipient to know the extent to which any of the subscores met expectations.

2.4.11 Law Enforcement, Corrections, and Public Safety Personality Assessment Inventory® (PAI)

The Personality Assessment Inventory (PAI),[1] first published in 1990, is a 344-item self-report measure of personality and psychopathology that includes 22 scales, 10 of which contain subscores (Morey, 2004). The PAI Law Enforcement, Corrections, and Public Safety Selection Report was specially designed by licensed psychologists to assess emotional stability during the selection process and is based on a normed sample of 18,000 public safety job applicants (PAI, 2023). Figure 2.12 presents an excerpt of an applicant's subscore profile relative to job applicants (*PS*), the general community (*PAI*), and a matching ethnic-gender group, which in this case was Caucasian males. Performance for each subscore is represented by a T score, which is scaled to have a mean of 50 and standard deviation of 10, normed within the respective comparison group. Raw scores are also provided, but the wide variability likely indicates substantial differences in the number of items, making them difficult to interpret. The profile reveals that the sample job applicant is similar across most subscales for all comparison groups but did demonstrate elevated levels of grandiosity and, relative to other job applicants and the specific ethnic-gender comparison groups, slightly higher levels of health concerns and phobias than would be considered typical for the general community. The evaluating psychologist could use this information to follow up on whether advancing the candidate presents a risk or if additional measures are needed to further explore potential concerns.

---

[1] The PAI is a copyrighted instrument and may not be used or reproduced in whole or in part, in any form or language, or by any means without written permission of PAR (www.parinc.com).

How Are Subscores Reported?

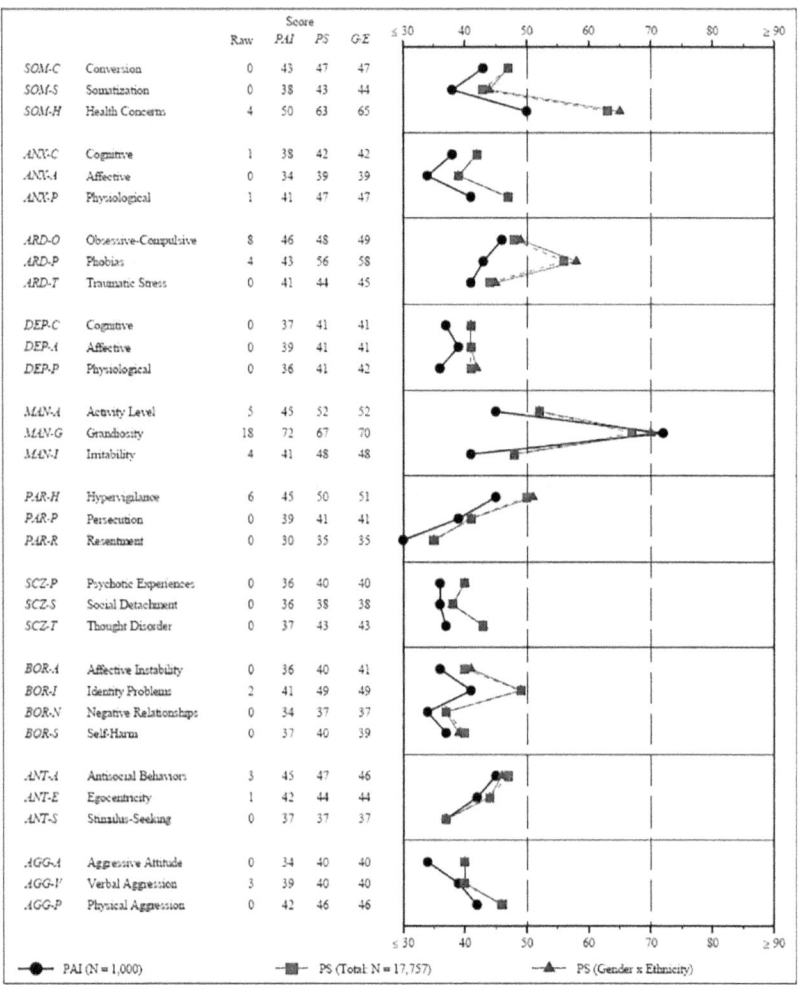

Note. This profile is based on calculations from all applicants in the screening process, regardless of the final selection decision. Ethnic group used for gender- by ethnic-specific profile is Caucasian Male. Refer to the Professional Issues chapter of the manual for the gender by ethnic group sample sizes.

Figure 2.12 Excerpt from the PAI Law Enforcement, Corrections, and Public Safety Selection Report. Adapted and reproduced by special permission of the Publisher, Psychological Assessment Resources, Inc. (PAR), 16204 North Florida Avenue, Lutz, Florida 33549 from the Personality Assessment Inventory by Leslie C. Morey, PhD, Copyright 1991. Further reproduction is prohibited without permission of PAR.

2.4.12 Assessment Tools for Teaching and Learning (asTTle)

New Zealand's Assessment Tools for Teaching and Learning (asTTle) is a formative assessment system administered by the country's Ministry of Education and provides diagnostic performance information to support student learning outcomes and improve instruction (Brown, O'Leary, & Hattie, 2019). The assessment system is not intended to be used for evaluation or punitive purposes – only for informing improvement. Figure 2.13 presents an excerpt from an asTTle console report that is an interactive online score dashboard. Teachers use the subscore information, which in this format is presented as gauge plots and boxplots to explore performance for a cluster of students or drill into performance for a particular student. In the figure, for instance, the user could infer that the students from New Zealand schools are demonstrating lower knowledge and understanding compared to other students at the same year level, but they do have a positive attitude. The gauges without any information could indicate that those characteristics were not assessed or perhaps reflect extreme poor performance, which is impossible to know without additional explanatory text.

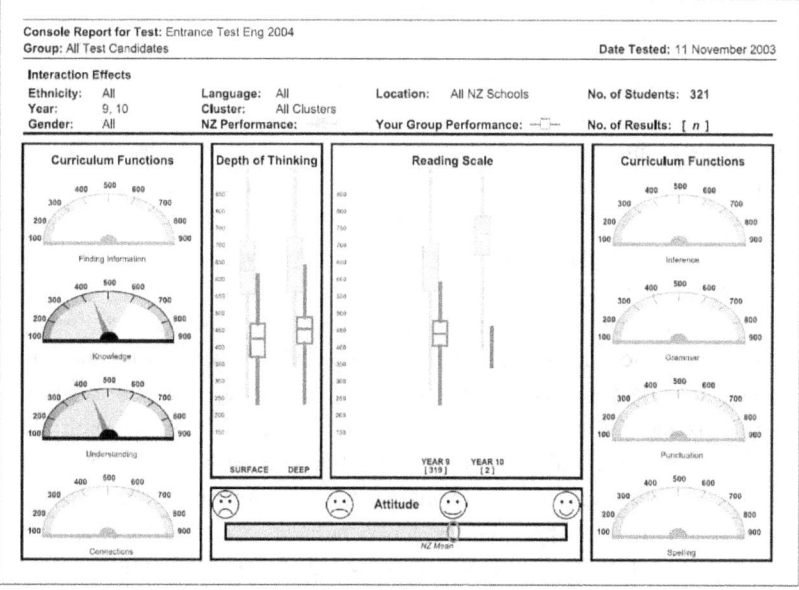

Figure 2.13 Excerpt of an asTTle console report.
From Brown, O'Leary, and Hattie (2019). Reproduced with permission. All rights reserved.

2.5 Generalizing Score Reporting Best Practices to Subscore Reporting Best Practices

The decision on what to report is a function of the intended inferences, using data displays that support those inferences at an appropriate level of granularity (*psychometric quality*) and presented in a way that users can correctly interpret those inferences (*type of users*). If they follow current best practices in the assessment industry, then the test publisher knows the intended inferences and who the users of the results are, as those details would have been clearly defined in the initial test design. A test's design, sometimes referred to as test specifications, articulates all critical aspects of the assessment life cycle to align the purpose of the test and eligibility requirements with the desired inferences carried through to score reporting (Lane et al., 2015).

However, how does the test publisher know users are making the correct inferences from the score report? How does the test publisher know if users desire additional unsupported inferences or are not finding utility in certain reported results? If so, why is there a disconnect? Are there differences in any of these questions between types of users, by either construct-relevant proficiencies or perhaps construct-irrelevant factors like gender, race, native language, or disabilities? Additionally, the information to be presented and the needs of score users may change over time as other relevant factors evolve such as shifts in practice and curriculum, technology enhancements, the composition of the examinee population, and competition from rival testing organizations. This can be particularly troublesome for subscores as users increasingly demand more detailed feedback for diagnostic purposes that were never part of the original test design, which ultimately leads to a desire to receive subscores that lack sufficient psychometric properties.

These concerns can be addressed by a systematic approach to score report development. Several researchers have proposed similar iterative and multistep frameworks for score report design that include gathering information on user needs and user characteristics pertinent to reporting, creating preliminary mockups, engaging with stakeholders to collect feedback (e.g., focus groups), refining a prototype, and then finalizing the score report template for operational deployment (Zapata-Rivera, VanWinkle, & Zwick, 2012; Zenisky & Hambleton, 2012; Hambleton & Zenisky, 2013; Zenisky & Hambleton, 2015; Slater, Livingston, & Silver, 2019). Utilizing a comprehensive framework in score report design not only helps a test publisher understand user needs and optimize alignment with a test's purpose but can also reveal concerns that may be overlooked from a measurement perspective.

Previous research has suggested general principles for displaying data in either a table (Feinberg & Wainer, 2011) or a graph (Tufte, 2001; Friendly & Wainer, 2021), though research specifically on displaying information on score reports suggests there is no such thing as a "best visualization," as it depends on many factors, including the purpose of the display, prior knowledge, information needs, and characteristics of the user (Hegarty, 2019). There are, of course, many ways to poorly display data, which include showing too little or too much information, emphasizing the trivial, skewing the axes on a graph, and presenting needless decimals (Wainer, 1984). Another important consideration is including links to relevant documentation concerning the reliability and validity of the subscores. Some test publishers include this information in a technical report or manual on their website and certainly when required, such as for state and federal assessments like the New York State Testing Program (NYSTP, 2023). Some of the sample score reports mentioned in this chapter included generic links to the publisher's website, but none provided a clear path to this technical information, and many private test publishers do not make this information publicly available.

A systematic approach to score report development can explore how the target recipients perceive the results, exploring questions such as how much detail is too little or too much, interactions with working memory and capacity for attention, and how best to organize information to facilitate comprehension. Additionally, there is an emotional component to interpreting a score report. For instance, a failing grade on a high-stakes test often can have several implications beyond needing to retest – embarrassment among the test taker's friends and family, financial implications of a delay or stop in a career path, and managing the psychological disconnect if the results are vastly different from what was expected. It may not be the job of the test publisher to provide a solution for these concerns, but being aware of the holistic interpretation can help test publishers be more sensitive in communicating disappointing information and present themselves as an advocate.

A serious example of empathy in communicating results described by Wainer (2015) involves the genetic reports a patient would receive when waiting to find out if they carry one of several mutated genes that substantially increase their risk of developing breast cancer. Figure 2.14 presents a current version of the report that provides ample detail and description but obfuscates the key finding – that no mutation was detected. Figure 2.15 presents a suggested redesign, where the important finding is now much more obvious. However, if a mutation had been detected, then the recipient may prefer the current version (Figure 2.14) with plenty of explanatory text and a more sensitive presentation. It may be challenging from an operational perspective, but with different combinations of results and types of recipients, more than one score reporting template may improve how results are being received.

CONFIDENTIAL

Integrated BRACAnalysis®
BRCA1 and BRCA2 Analysis Result

PHYSICIAN	SPECIMEN	PATIENT	
John Smith, MD Comprehensive Medical Center 1100 Grand Ave Away, GA 12345	Specimen: Blood Draw date: Aug 01, 2010 Accession date: Aug 02, 2010 Report Date: Jun 22, 2011	Name: Date of Birth: Patient ID: Gender: Accession #: Requisition #:	Doe, Jane April 1, 1492 000000 Female 00000000-BLD 000000

Test Results and Interpretation

NO MUTATION DETECTED

Test Performed:	Result:	Interpretation:
BRCA1 sequencing	No Mutation Detected	No Mutation Detected
comprehensive rearrangement	No Mutation Detected	No Mutation Detected
BRCA2 sequencing	No Mutation Detected	No Mutation Detected
comprehensive rearrangement	No Mutation Detected	No Mutation Detected

It is our understanding that this patient was identified for testing due to a personal or family history suggestive of hereditary breast and ovarian cancer. Analysis consists of sequencing of all translated exons and immediately adjacent intronic regions of the BRCA1 and BRCA2 genes and a comprehensive rearrangement test of both BRCA1 and BRCA2 by quantitative PCR analysis (BRACAnalysis Rearrangement Test, BART). The classification and interpretation of all variants identified in this assay reflects the current state of scientific understanding at the time this report was issued. In some instances, the classification and interpretation of such variants may change as new scientific information becomes available.

No deleterious mutation was found in BRCA1 or BRCA2 in this individual by sequencing and quantitative PCR analysis. This test is designed to identify mutations in 22 exons and approximately 750 adjacent intronic base pairs of BRCA1 as well as 26 exons and approximately 950 adjacent intronic base pairs of BRCA2 (a total of over 17,600 base pairs analyzed). This test is also designed to detect duplications and deletions involving the promoter region and coding exons of BRCA1 and BRCA2. There are other, rare genetic abnormalities in BRCA1 and BRCA2 that this test will not detect. This result, however, rules out the majority of abnormalities believed to be responsible for hereditary susceptibility to breast and ovarian cancer (Ford D et al., Am J Human Genetics 62:676-689, 1998). If this individual has never had breast or ovarian cancer, it is recommended that testing an affected relative be considered to help clarify the clinical significance of this individual's negative test result.

Please contact Myriad Professional Support at 1-800-469-7423 to discuss any questions regarding this result.

Director Name Here   Director Name Here
Qualifications Here   Qualifications Here

These test results should only be used in conjunction with the patient's clinical history and any previous analysis of appropriate family members. It is strongly recommended that these test results be communicated to the patient in a setting that includes appropriate counseling. The accompanying Technical Specifications summary describes the analysis, method, performance characteristics, nomenclature, and interpretive criteria of this test. This test may be considered investigational by some states. This test and its performance characteristics were determined by Myriad Genetic Laboratories. It has not been reviewed by the U.S. Food and Drug Administration. The FDA has determined that such clearance or approval is not necessary.

Figure 2.14 Notice of negative finding of gene mutation from Myriad Laboratories. *Source:* Wainer (2015).

CONFIDENTIAL

Integrated BRACAnalysis®
BRCA1 and BRCA2 Analysis Result

PHYSICIAN	SPECIMEN	PATIENT
John Smith, MD Comprehensive Medical Center 1100 Grand Ave Away, GA 12345	Specimen: Blood Draw date: Aug 01, 2010 Accession date: Aug 02, 2010 Report Date: Jun 22, 2011	Name: Doe, Jane Date of Birth: April 1, 1492 Patient ID: 000000 Gender: Female Accession #: 00000000-BLD Requisition #: 000000

Test Results and Interpretation

NO MUTATION DETECTED

Test Performed:	Result:	Interpretation:
BRCA1 sequencing comprehensive rearrangement	No Mutation Detected No Mutation Detected	No Mutation Detected No Mutation Detected
BRCA2 sequencing comprehensive rearrangement	No Mutation Detected No Mutation Detected	No Mutation Detected No Mutation Detected

Figure 2.15 Suggested revision of notice of negative finding of gene mutation that emphasizes the principal message.
Source: Wainer (2015).

2.6 Concluding Remarks

The decision of how subscores should be reported is complex and depends on many factors. Most important are the prospective uses of the subscores, their psychometric properties, the type of test and associated purpose, and the stakeholders to whom the results would be reported. For summative assessments, reporting subscores is particularly challenging, as they tend to lack sufficient psychometric properties (Sinharay, 2010) – more on that in the next chapters. However, this is not a surprising finding, given that constructing a test primarily designed to support inferences from a single total score, which is typically the case in summative assessments, leads to including items that correlate highly with the overall score because they are deemed essential to maximize reliability. The items that have lower correlations with the overall score, because they measure a slightly different construct and have the potential to contribute more toward subscore value, are likely to be systematically excluded. Thus, efforts to improve subscore distinctiveness (validity) would in turn diminish test reliability and the utility of the total score and, hence, detract from the primary purpose of the assessment. As stated by Brennan (2012), "If test scores fit a unidimensional model, a psychometrically compelling argument cannot be mounted for reporting any subscores since, by definition, there is only one proficiency or latent trait." Thus, tests that are designed for summative assessment will almost always struggle to have meaningful subscores to report, as that would inevitably confound the primary purpose.

Further, when subscores in a raw score format do have value, they should be reported numerically only after being converted to an established scale. Observed differences between raw subscores either within the same score report or compared longitudinally against a prior attempt, may be confounded due to differences in how the underlying subtests were constructed. Test publishers may be tempted to make the subscore scales comparable to the total score scale (e.g., same mean and standard deviation) or equal to a fraction of the total score scale such that the sum of all subscores equals the total. These choices often contribute to misinterpretation, given that subscores typically have lower reliability than the total score. Therefore promoting comparisons using the same scale can be problematic as subscores are expected to contain more error than the total score and their summation would include compounding error. In addition, reported subscores should be equated or at least linked so that the definition of strong performance in one content area does not change between forms of a test within a single administration or over time. In typical cases, equating is feasible for the total score but not for subscores due to the small number of items. Some work on equating subscores has been done by Puhan and Liang (2011).

Given these challenges, other than not reporting subscores at all, the potential to mislead users can be mitigated with less granular reporting styles and appropriate interpretive language, which can be determined only by engaging with a representative group of users and assessing the extent to which they correctly interpret the score information. Consider how Daisy's story would have been different had the presentation of her results been organized in a more coherent report at a valid and defensible level of detail. Perhaps her parents would have continued pursuing their desired outcome, but at least they wouldn't have perceived evidence from an official score report that could be weaponized to pressure the school.

However, before score users can be engaged to consider and help evaluate report design, the test publisher needs to first understand the psychometric properties of the subscores. Knowledge of the subscore statistical characteristics can inform realistic conversations about their limitations and appropriate next steps on what is defensible to report, if anything, or what could be done to improve their value, if anything. How exactly can a test publisher evaluate subscore quality? How much is good enough? That is the focus of our next chapter.

3
When and How Should Subscores Be Reported?

3.1 Introduction and Chapter Outline

Although demand for subscores exists, we must consider what are professionally responsible ways to report subscores are. Subscores are useful only if they provide information that score users can act upon. For this purpose, the accuracy of the information must be evaluated and reported to score users. As suggested by Standards 1.14, 2.3, and 5.0 of the American Educational Research Association et al. (2014), Haladyna and Kramer (2004), and Haberman (2008a), subscore evaluation involves three related issues: subscore reliability and validity, the strength of the relationships of the subscore to the total score and to other subscores, and the score reporting itself. In the remainder of the introduction to this chapter, we summarize the chapter contents.

3.1.1 Reliability

Because evaluation of subscores relies strongly on the reliability of both subscores and total scores, we begin in Section 3.2 by considering score reliability. We regard the score, whether a subscore or a total score, as an imperfect attempt to measure an underlying but unobserved true score. This approach has a very long history within psychology, as evident in Spearman (1904) and Kelley (1923). Corresponding to the subscore is the true subscore, while the true total score corresponds to the total score. In principle, multiple attempts with parallel forms may be used to measure this true score that is the average score that would be obtained were a parallel form employed rather than the form administered; however, these multiple attempts rarely exist. The reliability coefficient is the correlation of the test score and one parallel-form test score. Thus, the reliability coefficient of a test score measures the strength of the relationship between two parallel test scores. As in Section 3.3, the reliability coefficient provides a measure of the relative accuracy of the observed score in predicting the true score.

In Sections 3.2 to 3.7, we proceed as if we know reliability coefficients; however, as is evident in Sections 3.8 and 3.9, practical estimation of reliability coefficients is difficult. A fundamental principle in this chapter is that a testing organization should not report a score without estimating its reliability coefficient and verifying that the coefficient appears to be sufficiently large. As we note in Section 3.3, the exact standards for a satisfactory reliability coefficient vary depending on the use of the score.

3.1.2 Options for Prediction of True Subscores

Even if a subscore has a satisfactory reliability coefficient, a testing organization should still not report the subscore by itself if it predicts the true subscore less well than does the total score; however, the testing organization may have good justification to report an augmented subscore in which both the subscore and total score predict the true subscore. These decisions on score reporting rely on the reliability coefficients of the subscore and total score and on the correlation of the subscore and total score.

In our evaluations of predictions of true subscore, we will judge predictions in terms of mean square error (MSE), the average squared difference between the predicted true score and the actual true score. As a baseline to compare predictors of the true subscore, we will also consider the mean squared error from prediction of the true subscore by the mean subscore. For the various predictions of the true subscore, we make comparisons in terms of the proportional reduction in mean square error (PRMSE) from use of the prediction rather than from use of the mean subscore. We describe the prediction options in Sections 3.3 to 3.5.

In Section 3.3, we predict the true subscore from the subscore by use of Kelley's formula. With this predictor, the proportional reduction in mean squared error $PRMSE_{sub}$ is the reliability coefficient of the subscore. We apply this interpretation to develop criteria for adequate reliability coefficients for subscores. Because subscores are generally less reliable than total scores and they are highly correlated with total scores, it is possible, as seen in Section 3.4, that prediction of a true subscore by the total score is more accurate than is prediction of that true subscore by the subscore. We define the value-added ratio (VAR) to be the ratio of the proportional reduction in mean square error $PRMSE_{sub}$ from prediction by the subscore to the proportional reduction in mean square error $PRMSE_{tot}$ from prediction by the total score. We contend that the subscore should not be used by itself if the VAR is less than 1 or if the reliability of the subscore is inadequate. Nonetheless, as we show in Section 3.5, we can provide an augmented subscore that applies both the subscore and the total score to predict the true subscore. In virtually all practical cases, the proportional reduction in mean square error $PRMSE_{aug}$ from prediction of the true subscore by the augmented subscore is larger than both $PRMSE_{sub}$ and $PRMSE_{tot}$.

3.1.3 Comparing True Subscores and True Total Scores

Sections 3.2 to 3.5 examine prediction of individual true subscores. In practice, multiple subscores often exist for a single test, and, as in the story of Daisy in Chapter 2, score users and testing organizations may want to compare scores rather than just predict individual subscores. In Section 3.6, we compare the true subscore to the true total score. For example, instead of considering the proficiency of a test taker in speaking, we consider the extent to which the test taker is more or less proficient in speaking than expected, given the true total score. Such a comparison might indicate whether the examinee should devote added attention to improving speaking proficiency. We examine this comparison by prediction of residual true subscores. Such a residual is the prediction error from linear prediction of the true subscore by the true total score. In principle, this residual indicates information about a true subscore that is not provided by the true total score. For example, a negative residual true speaking subscore suggests less proficiency in speaking than is indicated by overall language fluency. Whether this information is useful for instructional purposes involves the study of incremental validity, a topic explored in Section 3.11. Nonetheless, the question of incremental validity necessarily relies on the proportional reduction of mean square error from the best linear predictor of the residual true subscore by the subscore and total score. This predictor is a multiple of the residual subscore, which is the prediction error from the best linear prediction of the subscore by the total score. We then find the proportional reduction of mean square error $PRMSE_{res}$ by comparing the mean square error from prediction of the residual true subscore to the mean square error from the trivial prediction of the residual true subscore by its mean of 0. Use of the predicted residual true subscore is helpful only if $PRMSE_{res}$ is sufficiently large, as judged by standards considered in Section 3.3.

In Section 3.7, we explore a profile of several subscores that sum to the total score. We consider two related issues. We use principal components analysis to examine the extent to which the profile of true subscores corresponding to the profile of subscores can be well approximated by a small fraction of the principal components of the correlation matrix of the true subscores. If such an approximation is available, then the true subscores in the profile are largely redundant, so the subscores are not measuring well-distinguished skills. We use canonical analysis to address the use of composite scores derived from the profile of subscores to predict the profile of true subscores. The resulting Wainer-augmented scores generalize the augmented scores of Section 3.5. The proportional reduction in mean square error $PRMSE_{waug}$ from use of a Wainer-augmented subscore is always at least $PRMSE_{aug}$.

3.1.4 Estimation of Reliability

Through Section 3.7, we have assumed that we know reliability coefficients, but in reality, we must estimate them from data. This task has been a serious problem since Spearman (1904). in Section 3.8, we obtain estimates of reliability coefficients by true-score theory. We consider Cronbach's alpha (Cronbach, 1951), stratified alpha (Cronbach et al., 1965), repeated tests (Spearman, 1904), and half tests (Spearman, 1910; Brown, 1910).

Analysis in Sections 3.2 to 3.7 relies on Cronbach's alpha and on stratified alpha. This approach is limited to test scores obtained by adding up item scores from a single test form. In practice, testing organizations report scaled scores rather than the sums of item scores. For example, in the case of cut scores, a test taker passes or fails a test if the test score exceeds a specified value. In addition, in adaptive tests, different test takers receive different items, and the choice of the next-presented item depends on responses of the test taker to previously presented items. In Section 3.9, we address these issues with item-response theory. We provide estimates of true scores and proportional reductions in mean square error for these problems, and, when possible, we compare results to those based on Cronbach's alpha and stratified alpha.

3.1.5 How Long Is Long Enough?

In Section 3.10, we apply Sections 3.8 and 3.9 to the effect of changing test length on the analysis in this chapter. Increasing test length normally increases reliability coefficients for both subscores and total scores. Except in the rare case in which true subscores and true total scores have correlation 1, the VAR criterion exceeds 1 if the number of items in the subscore is sufficiently large. Thus, increasing test length can permit subscores to be worth reporting. Nonetheless, the number of items required for subscore reporting to become appropriate may become too large for the resulting test to be practical.

3.1.6 Incremental Validity: Does the Subscore Really Help?

In Section 3.11, we look at incremental validity in evaluation of subscores. This section complements Section 3.6. The problem is now evaluation of how much the subscore contributes to prediction of an external validity criterion. For example, does the speaking subscore provide a prediction concerning the quality of work by a teaching assistant beyond the prediction provided by the total score of the language test? Incremental validity is bounded above by the reliability coefficient of the residual subscore developed in Section 3.6. If this reliability coefficient is small, then the incremental validity measure also must be small. On the other hand, a larger reliability coefficient of the residual subscore does not ensure that incremental validity results are satisfactory.

3.1.7 Aggregate-Level Subscores

In Section 3.12, we evaluate average subscores at an aggregate level. These average subscores apply to groups of test takers rather than individuals. Groups may be classes of students, students in specific universities, or adults in specific countries. Evaluation techniques are quite similar to those in Sections 3.2 to 3.8; however, the true subscore of a group is now the average true score of group members, and not all members of the group are actually observed. It is possible that a subscore is not helpful for individuals in the group but is helpful in group evaluation. On the other hand, the subscore may be useful for comparison of individuals but not for comparison of groups.

3.1.8 Conclusions and Recommendations

In Section 3.13, we provide conclusions and recommendations based on results of this chapter. Recommendations depend on the use of the test scores, the presumed knowledge of score users, and legal constraints. Nonetheless, it is essential that testing organizations provide estimates of reliability coefficients of test scores and correlations of test scores as well as information concerning the basis of these estimates.

3.1.9 Data

To illustrate the methods developed in this chapter, we use data from an administration of a language test to 9,617 test takers.[1] (The actual name of the test cannot be employed due to restrictions imposed by the provider of the file.) As shown in Table 3.1, the test provides a total score and four subscores: listening, reading, speaking, and writing.

---

[1] The data are freely available under an Apache 2.0 license in file *FORM1ANOX.TXT* in the repository https://github.com/EducationalTestingService/MIRT/tree/master/Examples. The 34 listening items are in columns 22 to 55, the 42 reading items are in columns 57 to 98, the 6 speaking items are in columns 100 to 105, and the 2 writing items are in columns 107 to 110.

Table 3.1 *Structure of the language test*[2]

Subscore	Number of items	Score categories
Listening	34	0/1
Reading	39	0/1
	3	0/1/2
Speaking	6	0–4
Writing	2	0, 2–10
Total	**84**	

In addition, other examples from published literature illustrate methods and results in this chapter. A more extensive review of results from the literature appears in Chapter 4.

3.2 Reliability

The reliability coefficient is a fundamental measure in the evaluation of any test score. This measure is applied in this chapter to both a subscore s and a total score x. The subscore and total score depend on two populations, a population of test takers and a hypothetical infinite population of parallel forms. First, a test is randomly selected from the population of tests, and then we obtain the subscore and total score by testing a randomly selected member of the population of test takers. For the same selected test taker, we would observe the parallel-form subscore s' and parallel-form total score x' if we selected another test at random from the population of tests and administered that test rather than the one administered. The mean subscore $E(s)$ is the same as the mean parallel-form subscore $E(s')$, the mean total score $E(x)$ of the test taken is the same as the mean parallel-form total score $E(x')$, the variance $\sigma^2(s)$ of the subscore is the same as the variance $\sigma^2(s')$ of the parallel-form subscore, and the variance $\sigma^2(x)$ of the total score is the same as the variance $\sigma^2(x')$ of the parallel-form total score. We assume that the subscore and the total score both have positive variances. The exchangeability assumption then implies that the correlation $\rho(s,x)$ of the subscore and total score is the same as the correlation of the parallel-form subscore

---

[2] The listening score is the sum of 34 item scores with possible values 0 (incorrect or missing) and 1 (correct). The reading score is the sum of 42 item scores, of which 39 have possible values 0 (incorrect or missing) and 1 (correct), and 3 have possible values 0 (completely incorrect or missing), 1 (partially correct), and 2 (correct). The speaking score is the sum of 6 item scores with possible integer values 0 to 4, with 4 being the best score. The writing score is the sum of 2 item scores with possible integer values 0 and from 2 to 10, with 10 being the best score. The total score is the sum of the listening, reading, speaking, and writing subscores.

and total score. The reliability coefficient ρ_s^2 of the subscore s is the correlation $\rho(s,s')$ of the subscore s and s', while the reliability coefficient ρ_x^2 of the total score x is the correlation $\rho(x,x')$ of the total scores x and x'. Thus, reliability coefficients address the reproducibility of test scores. A higher reliability coefficient indicates a more stable test score.

For each population member, the true subscore s_t is the mean of all parallel-form subscores associated with that population member, while the true total score x_t is the conditional mean of all associated parallel-form total scores x'. The parallel-form subscore has the same true score as the subscore, and the parallel-form total score has the same true score as the total score. The subscore and true subscore have the same mean, and the total score and true total score have the same mean. The measurement error s_e of the subscore is $s - s_t$, while the measurement error x_e of the total score is $x - x_t$. For the parallel-form test, the measurement error s_e' for the subscore is $s' - s_t$, and the measurement error x_e' for the total score is $x' - x_t$. All measurement errors have mean 0. The variance of measurement for both the subscores and parallel-form subscores is the variance $\sigma^2(s_e)$, while the variance of measurement of both the total score and parallel-form total scores is $\sigma^2(x_e)$. Whenever a measurement error of the test and a measurement error of the parallel-form test have positive variances, then they are assumed to be uncorrelated. The variance of the subscore is the sum of the variance of the true subscore and the variance of measurement of the subscore, and the variance of the total score is the sum of the variance of the true total score and the variance of measurement of the total score. If the reliability coefficient of the subscore is positive, then the coefficient is the square $\rho^2(s_t,s)$ of the correlation $\rho(s_t,s)$ of the true subscore and the subscore. If the reliability coefficient of the total score is positive, then the coefficient is the square $\rho^2(x_t,x)$ of the correlation $\rho(x_t,x)$ of the true total score and the total score.

The difference score $x - s$ is the portion of the total test score that is not from the subscore. The true difference score is $x_t - s_t$, and the corresponding measurement error is $x_e - s_e$. It is assumed that if the reliability coefficients of the subscore and total score are both less than 1, then the measurement error of the difference score is uncorrelated with the measurement error of the subscore. This assumption is likely to hold in a test in which the subscore and the difference score depend on completely different test items. For example, in the language test, the items used to obtain the speaking subscore are not used in the reading, listening, or writing subscores. The assumption of uncorrelated errors of measurement of the subscore and difference score implies that the correlation $\rho(s_e,x_e)$ of the measurement error of the subscore and the measurement error of the difference score is the ratio $\sigma^2(s_e)/\sigma^2(x_e)$ of the variance of measurement of the subscore and the variance of measurement of the total score.

Table 3.2 *Variances and reliability coefficients*

Score	Variance			Reliability
	Observed	True	Error	
Listening	43.0	37.6	5.4	0.88
Reading	65.4	57.2	8.2	0.88
Speaking	10.5	9.0	1.5	0.85
Writing	10.0	7.3	2.7	0.73
Total	**342.8**	**325.0**	**17.8**	**0.95**

In practice, true scores and parallel-form test scores are not known; however, as discussed in Sections 3.8 and 3.9, inferences can be made concerning the variances of the true score and the measurement error. In this section and in Sections 3.3 to 3.7, we treat summary measures such as variances as though they are known, although in reality they are estimates based on samples.

As already noted in Chapter 1, in typical cases, subscores are less reliable than are total test scores. For example, consider Table 3.2 that applies to the language example. The reliability coefficient for writing is much smaller than any other reliability coefficient, and the reliability coefficient for the total score is much larger than any reliability coefficient of a subscore. Results for listening, reading, and speaking are roughly comparable. The larger reliability coefficient for the total score reflects the usual result that errors of measurement of distinct subscores are uncorrelated, so that the sum of the variances of measurement of the subscores is the variance of measurement of the total score, but the sum of the variances of the true subscores is much smaller than the variance of the true total score, and the sum of the variances of the subscores is much smaller than the variance of the total score.

The smaller reliability coefficients of subscores compared to the total score is usually encountered. For instance, in the Praxis example considered in Haberman (2008a), the total score is the sum of four subscores, each of which is the sum of 25 item scores. The subscores have reliability coefficients between 0.68 and 0.79, values considerably smaller than the reliability coefficient of 0.90 for the total score.

In almost all tests, combining subscores increases reliability. For example, consider a receptive subscore obtained by summation of reading plus listening. The variance of measurement for the receptive subscore is the sum of the variance of measurement of the reading score and the variance of measurement of the listening score. The variance of the receptive subscore is 185.2. We could also have a subscore for written communication equal to the sum of the reading and writing subscores. In this case, the reliability is 0.90. We do not claim that score users necessarily want these particular subscores, but we do note that aggregation of subscores is a possible approach to poor reliability.

The means and variances that determine the reliability coefficient are population dependent, so reliability coefficients are also population dependent. In the examples under study, the population consists of tests administered. Different variances apply to other populations. For example, all students who take SAT exams are not the same as admitted MIT students from that population.

3.3 Predicting the True Subscore

The Kelley estimate (Kelley, 1923) permits interpretation of the reliability coefficient in terms of proportional reduction in mean square error (PRMSE) from prediction of the true score by the score rather than by the mean score. For prediction of the true subscore s_t by the subscore s, the Kelley estimate

$$s_s = \left(1 - \rho_s^2\right) E(s) + \rho_s^2 s \qquad (3.1)$$

is the weighted average of the mean true subscore $E(s)$ and the subscore s. The weight assigned to the subscore is the reliability coefficient of the subscore. The Kelley estimate also applies to prediction of subscores for parallel-form tests. Thus, the predictor of the parallel-form subscore s' from the subscore s is s_s. Although we are primarily concerned with subscores, cases arise in discussion in which we use Kelley estimates for true total scores. In such cases, x replaces s in formulas.

With the Kelley estimate for the true subscore, the (residual) error $s_{sr} = s_t - s_s$, and the mean square error (MSE$_{sub}$) is now the residual variance

$$\sigma^2\left(s_{sr}\right) = \sigma^2\left(s_t\right)\left(1 - \rho_s^2\right). \qquad (3.2)$$

The mean square error from use of the mean score $E(s) = E(s_t)$ is $\sigma^2(s_t)$. If the reliability coefficient of the subscore is positive, then the proportional reduction in mean square error (PRMSE$_{sub}$) from use of the Kelley estimate rather than the mean expected true score is the difference

$$1 - \sigma^2\left(s_{sr}\right) / \sigma^2\left(s_t\right) = 1 - \sigma^2\left(s_t\right)\left(1 - \rho_s^2\right) / \sigma^2\left(s_t\right) = \rho_s^2. \qquad (3.3)$$

As in Sinharay (2013), application of the Kelley estimate to parallel-form scores yields larger mean square errors and lower proportional reductions in mean square error relative to corresponding results for true scores. For the parallel-form subscore s', the error $s'_{sr} = s' - s_s$, and the residual variance $\sigma^2(s'_{sr}) = \sigma^2(s)(1-\rho_s^4)$ is the mean square error MSE_{psub}, where ρ_s^4 is the square of the reliability coefficient of s. The mean square estimation error from use of the mean score $E(s) = E(s_t)$ is $\sigma^2(s)$, so the proportional reduction in mean square error $\text{PRMSE}_{\text{psub}}$ from use of the Kelley estimate rather than the mean expected true score is ρ_s^4.

In terms of mean square error and proportional reduction in mean square error, the Kelley estimate is superior to use of the score to predict either the true score or the parallel-form score. For the true subscore, the subscore has the conditional unbiasedness property that the true subscore is the conditional mean of the subscore given the true subscore; however, conditional unbiasedness has a cost. The mean square error MSE_{unb} is $\sigma^2(s_e) = \sigma^2(s)(1-\rho_s^2)$, $\sigma^2(s_t) = \sigma^2(s)\rho_s^2$ is the mean square error from prediction by the mean subscore $E(s)$, and the proportional reduction in mean square error $\text{PRMSE}_{\text{unb}}$ is $(2\rho_s^2 - 1)/\rho_s^2$ whenever the reliability coefficient $\rho_s^2 > 0$. The reliability coefficient ρ_s^2, which is also $\text{PRMSE}_{\text{sub}}$, exceeds $\text{PRMSE}_{\text{unb}}$ by $(1-\rho_s^2)^2 / \rho_s^2$. The difference between $\text{PRMSE}_{\text{sub}}$ and $\text{PRMSE}_{\text{unb}}$ from use of the conditionally unbiased estimate increases as the reliability decreases. If the reliability coefficient is not 1, then $\text{PRMSE}_{\text{unb}}$ is less than $\text{PRMSE}_{\text{sub}}$. If the reliability coefficient ρ_s^2 is 0.5, then $\text{PRMSE}_{\text{unb}}$ is 0, and $\text{PRMSE}_{\text{unb}}$ has a large negative value if the reliability coefficient ρ_s^2 is near 0. For the parallel-form subscore, the mean square error MSE_{punb} from prediction by the subscore is $2\sigma^2(s)(1-\rho_s^2)$, and the mean square error from prediction by the mean subscore $E(s)$ is $\sigma^2(s_s)$, so the proportional reduction in mean square error $\text{PRMSE}_{\text{punb}}$ is $2(1-\rho_s^2)$.

The improvement from use of the Kelley estimate rather than the subscore is an average improvement rather than an improvement for all population members. In general, the Kelley estimate is most effective if the true subscore is close to the mean true subscore and least effective if the true subscore is far from the mean true subscore.

Table 3.3 shows the impact of use of the subscore to estimate the true subscore in the language test. Results for the total score are included for comparison. Formulas for the subscore apply if the total score is regarded as a subscore that includes all items in the test.

For the total score, $\text{PRMSE}_{\text{unb}}$ in Table 3.3 is very close to the corresponding reliability coefficient in Table 3.2. The ratios of 0.97 and 0.98 indicate that the differences between the reliability coefficients of Table 3.2 and the PRMSE values of Table 3.3 are of modest size for the subscores other than writing. In the case of writing, the difference is much larger, as is evident

3.3 Predicting the True Subscore

Table 3.3 *PRMSE for conditionally unbiased estimation of true scores by scores*

Score	PRMSE$_{unb}$	PRMSE$_{unb}$/PRMSE$_{sub}$
Listening	0.86	0.98
Reading	0.86	0.98
Speaking	0.83	0.97
Writing	0.62	0.86
Total	**0.95**	**1.00**

from the ratio of 0.86. The comparisons between Tables 3.2 and 3.3 reflect a general result that the conditionally unbiased estimate of the true score is very unsatisfactory when reliability is low.

Figure 3.1 provides a plot of the Kelley estimate of the true total score by the total score, while Figure 3.2 provides a plot of the Kelley estimate of the true writing score by the writing score. In each figure, the Kelley estimate is given by the solid line, while the estimate of the true score by the score is given by the dotted line. In each plot, the line slope is the reliability coefficient, and the Kelley estimate and the score are the same at the mean score. The smaller the angle between the dotted and solid lines, the higher the reliability. Thus, the angle in Figure 3.1 is somewhat smaller than the one in Figure 3.2.

The Kelley estimate is very close to simple use of the score if the reliability coefficient is close to 1, as is the case for the total score in the language test, and the estimate is somewhat different than use of the score if the reliability coefficient is relatively low, as is the case for the writing subscore.

Although we emphasize PRMSE in this chapter, we do note that alternatives exist. For example, Dorans and Walker (2007) suggest a number of alternative versions of the reliability coefficient when this coefficient is positive. We will apply the signal-to-noise ratio (SNR) in Section 3.11 when we explore effects of changing test length. This measure is also the basis of the Brennan (2012) relative utility index. For a subscore, SNR is the ratio of the variance of the true subscore to the variance of measurement. Thus for the subscore s, SNR$_s$ is $\rho_s^2 / (1 - \rho_s^2)$. Whereas a reliability coefficient is nonnegative and does not exceed 1, the SNR can assume any nonnegative value.

A basic problem is to ascertain what is an acceptable reliability coefficient. Obviously higher is better than lower, and the use of the test result matters. The standard for a practice test may be different than the standard for a test to certify surgical skills. Nonetheless, some basic calculations can clarify matters. It is common for reported scores to have reliability coefficients of 0.9 or higher.

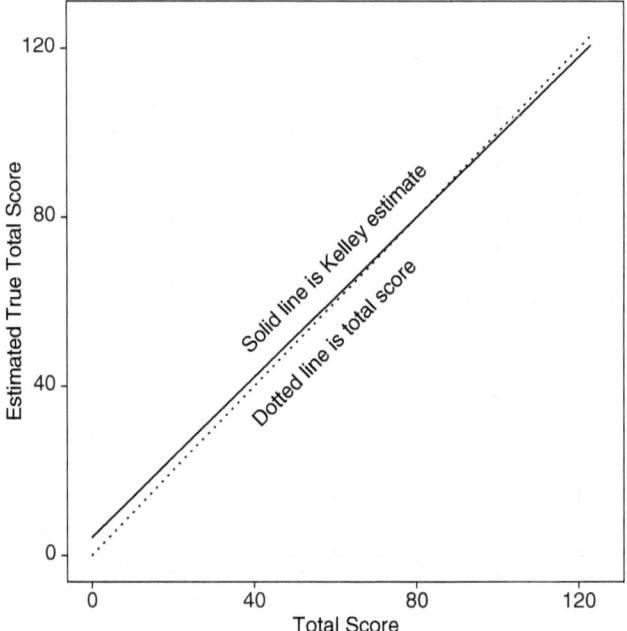

Figure 3.1 Kelley estimate of true total score by total score.

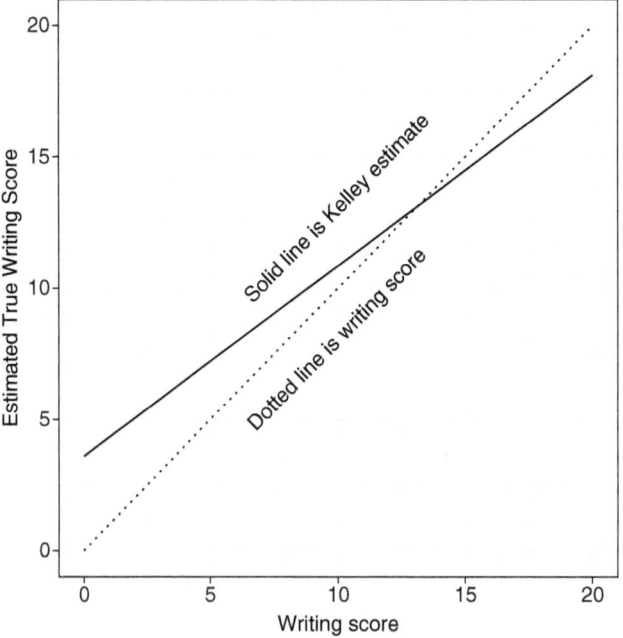

Figure 3.2 Kelley estimate of true writing score by writing score.

For example, Haberman (2008a) reports reliability coefficients for one form of the SAT I of 0.91 for the 78-item Verbal test and 0.92 for the 60-item Math test. The same paper reports a reliability coefficient of 0.90 for a form for the Praxis test Fundamental Subjects: Content Knowledge in which the test score is the sum of 100 item scores, each of which is either 0 (missing or incorrect) or 1 (correct). In the language test, the total test score, which is the sum of 84 item scores, has a reliability coefficient of 0.95.

At the other extreme, a test reliability coefficient of 0.5 corresponds to a test with variance of measurement as large as the variance of the true score. As an aid in interpretation of this coefficient, we apply the RiU measure of Dorans and Walker in which proportional reduction of root mean square error is considered. Here root mean square error is just the square root of mean square error. For a subscore, the standard deviation $\sigma(s_e)$ of the error of measurement is compared to the standard deviation $\sigma(s)$ of the subscore. This comparison has the virtue that root mean square errors are in the original unit of measurement, so they provide an indication of the reduction in error bounds for true subscores. In terms of the reliability coefficient for a subscore, RiU_s is

$$1-\sigma(s_e)/\sigma(s) = 1-\sqrt{1-\rho_s^2} = \rho_s^2 / \left(1+\sqrt{1-\rho_s^2}\right). \tag{3.4}$$

A reliability coefficient of 0.5 corresponds to a reduction of uncertainty of only 0.29 and an SNR of 1. Thus, a test score with a reliability coefficient of 0.5 is better than no test score at all – but not a lot better.

For an intermediate example, a reliability coefficient of 0.75 corresponds to an SNR of 3 and an RiU of 0.5, so the root mean square error from prediction of the score based on the true score is half as large as the root mean square error from prediction with the test mean without regard to data. This reliability coefficient thus indicates a test score that provides some useful information concerning the skill measured, although measurement error is a substantial issue.

These results concerning estimation of true subscores have immediate impact on the use of unreliable subscores. It is common for subscores provided to test users to be very unreliable when the subscores rely on only a few items. Reporting such subscores does not help anyone. Because such subscores are so unstable, they do not provide enough information for students to modify their studies, for instructors to modify their teaching, or for institutions to admit or place students. In addition to the interests of score users, an added consideration is the interests of score producers. As already noted, $\text{PRMSE}_{\text{psub}}$ is less than $\text{PRMSE}_{\text{sub}}$. For these predictions concerning parallel-form forms, $\text{PRMSE}_{\text{psub}}$ is 0.5 if the reliability coefficient is about

Table 3.4 *PRMSE for estimation of parallel-form scores by scores*

Score	PRMSE$_{psub}$
Listening	0.77
Reading	0.77
Speaking	0.73
Writing	0.53
Total	**0.90**

0.71. Thus, instability of results across repeated measurements is expected. Such instability may be a challenge for the test producer to justify. For results for the language test, see Table 3.4. Results for the total score correspond to a subscore equal to the total score. They are provided for comparison with subscore results. Results for writing indicate considerable instability for parallel-form forms. In general, it is clear that predicting a new score is much more challenging than predicting a true score.

A basic requirement for producers of test scores is to estimate their reliability and to publish the results, and a basic requirement for institutional score users is to insist that reliability estimates be available. As previously noted, reliability estimation will be considered in Sections 3.8 and 3.9. For test takers without statistical or psychometric training, responsible reporting of test accuracy is especially important. Intervals about score predictions can help, although the methodology presented so far in this chapter is not adequate for this purpose.

3.4 Predicting a True Subscore with a Total Score

Even if a subscore has acceptable reliability for its use, it may still be of little value. In many cases, by an approach similar to that used with the Kelley estimate of the true subscore, the total test score provides an estimate of the true subscore with a smaller PRMSE than can be achieved by predicting the true subscore by the Kelley estimate based on the subscore. Let ρ_s denote the square root of the reliability coefficient of the subscore and let ρ_x denote the square root of the reliability coefficient of the total score. For any variable X with mean $E(X)$ and positive standard deviation $\sigma(X)$, let its standardized value be $z(X) = [X - E(X)]/\sigma(X)$, so $z(X)$ has mean 0 and variance 1. For an additional variable Y with positive standard deviation $\sigma(Y)$, the correlation

3.4 Predicting a True Subscore with a Total Score

Table 3.5 $PRMSE_{tot}$ and VAR for language test

Score	$PRMSE_{tot}$	VAR
Listening	0.86	1.02
Reading	0.84	1.05
Speaking	0.64	1.33
Writing	0.89	0.82

$\rho(X,Y)$ of the variables X and Y equals the mean of $z(X)z(Y)$. Given these definitions, if both the subscore and total score have positive reliability coefficients, then the predictor of the true subscore s_t by the total score x is

$$s_x = E(s) + \sigma(s)\rho_s\rho(s_t, s_x)\rho_x z(x). \tag{3.5}$$

The estimation error is $s_{xr} = s_t - s_x$, the mean square error MSE_{tot} is

$$\sigma^2(s_{xr}) = \sigma^2(s_t)\left[1 - \rho^2(s_t, x)\right], \tag{3.6}$$

and the proportional reduction in error $PRMSE_{tot}$ is

$$\rho^2(s_t, x) = \rho_x^2 \rho^2(s_t, x_t). \tag{3.7}$$

The Brennan (2012) utility index is provided by Equation 3.7. As in Feinberg and Wainer (2014), the value-added ratio VAR, the ratio of $PRMSE_{sub}$ to $PRMSE_{tot}$ is

$$\rho_s^2 / \rho^2(s_t, x) = \rho_s^2 / [\rho_x^2 \rho^2(s_t, x_t)]. \tag{3.8}$$

Thus, a VAR that exceeds 1 indicates some gain from use of the Kelley estimate rather than the estimate based on the total score, while a VAR less than 1 indicates that use of the total score is more effective.

We will say that a subscore has added value if VAR exceeds 1 ($PRMSE_{sub}$ is greater than $PRMSE_{tot}$). We will make repeated use of the VAR criterion for added value in this and subsequent chapters.

As is evident from Table 3.5, the writing subscore does not have added value, but the other subscores do have at least some added value. The speaking subscore has much more added value than the subscores for listening or reading.

The results in Table 3.5 are not unusual. We, together with colleagues, have made numerous comparisons of PRMSE based on subscores or based on total scores (Haberman, 2008a; Sinharay, 2010; Feinberg & Wainer, 2014), and further comparisons appear in Chapter 4. Results have varied. Consider the Praxis example of Haberman (2008a) previously noted in Section 3.2. Here four subscores measure knowledge of four subjects relevant for prospective teachers in elementary school. The available subscores are for English language arts, mathematics, citizenship and social science, and science. Each subscore consists of 25 items scored as 1 for correct and 0 for not correct or omitted, and the total score is the sum of the four subscores. In the administration studied, only the first two subscores have added value, and the added value is negligible for English language arts.

When VAR is less than 1, reporting the subscore is deceptive. Reporting implies that the subscore provides information beyond the total score when no such conclusion is justified. If the subscore has an unsatisfactory reliability coefficient and VAR is less than 1, then reporting is inappropriate due both to the instability of the subscore and existence of a more accurate way to estimate the skill represented by the subscore. If the total score and the subscore both have low reliability coefficients, then the testing organization needs to reexamine the test, for no useful information at all is supplied.

As in the case of reliability of subscores, combining subscores may sometimes help in terms of the value-added ratio; however, gains are not guaranteed. For the receptive subscore considered in Section 3.2, $PRMSE_{tot}$ is 0.93, and the VAR is 1.00, so the receptive subscore is slightly worse by this criterion than either the listening or the reading subscore. For the subscore for written communication, $PRMSE_{tot}$ is 0.89 and VAR is 1.02. The result is better than for writing but worse than for reading, so the combination is not very helpful. In addition, the receptive subscore and the subscore for written communication share the reading subscore, a contribution to a correlation of true scores of 0.98. Thus, the attempt to combine subscores has not helped in this case.

In Sections 3.5 and 3.7, we examine augmented subscores in which true subscores are predicted by use of both the subscore and either the total score or other subscores. Augmented subscores warrant investigation whenever the total score has acceptable reliability.

3.5 Prediction by Subscore and Total Score

We can use both the subscore and the total score to predict the true subscore.[3] The resulting estimate of the subscore is the augmented subscore of Haberman

---

[3] Strictly speaking, the correlation $\rho(s,x)$ of the subscore and total score must not have absolute value 1. As a practical matter, this condition always holds.

3.5 Prediction by Subscore and Total Score

(2008a) examined in Sinharay and Haberman (2011). The procedure relies on standardized partial regression coefficients and partial correlation coefficients. If X, Y, and Z are variables with positive variances and the correlation $\rho(Y,Z)$ is neither 1 nor -1, then the standardized partial regression coefficient for prediction of X by Y given Z is

$$\beta(X|Y \cdot Z) = \frac{\rho(X,Y) - \rho(X,Z)\rho(Y,Z)}{1 - \rho^2(Y,Z)}, \qquad (3.9)$$

and the partial correlation coefficient of X and Y given Z is

$$\rho(X,Y|Z) = \frac{\rho(X,Y) - \rho(X,Z)\rho(Y,Z)}{\sqrt{\left[1 - \rho^2(X,Z)\right]\left[1 - \rho^2(Y,Z)\right]}}. \qquad (3.10)$$

The partial correlation coefficient $\rho(X,Y|Z)$ is the correlation of the residual error X_{Zr} from prediction of X by Z and the residual error Y_{Zr} from prediction of Y by Z. Thus, the partial correlation measures the relationship of X and Y not explained by Z. If the reliability of the subscore is positive, then the predictor of the true subscore based on both the subscore and the total score is the augmented subscore

$$s_{sx} = E(s) + \sigma(s_t)\left[\beta(s_t | s \cdot x)z(s) + \beta(s_t | x \cdot s)z(x)\right], \qquad (3.11)$$

and the proportional reduction in mean square error $PRMSE_{aug}$ for the augmented subscore is the squared multiple correlation coefficient

$$\begin{aligned}\rho^2(s_t | s,x) &= \rho_s^2 + \left(1 - \rho_s^2\right)\rho^2(s_t, x | s) \\ &= \rho^2(s_t, x) + \left[1 - \rho^2(s_t, x)\right]\rho^2(s_t, s | x)\end{aligned} \qquad (3.12)$$

of the true subscore, given both the subscore and the total score. If the reliability coefficient of the subscore is 0, then the predictor $s_{sx} = E(s)$. If the reliability coefficient of the subscore is positive, then $PRMSE_{aug}$ is at least as large as the maximum of $PRMSE_{sub}$ and $PRMSE_{tot}$. To examine the value of the augmented subscore, we consider two value-added ratios. $VAR_{aug/sub}$ is the ratio of $PRMSE_{aug}$ to $PRMSE_{sub}$, while $VAR_{aug/tot}$ is the ratio of $PRMSE_{aug}$ to $PRMSE_{tot}$. The relative sizes of the standardized partial regression coefficients indicate the relative importance of the subscore and total score as predictors of the true subscore. In the rare case that the reliability coefficient of the subscore is 1, then the predictor is just the subscore, and $PRMSE_{aug}$ is 1.

Results for the language test appear in Table 3.6. For all subscores except writing, augmented subscores provide modest added value over the original

Table 3.6 PRMSE$_{aug}$ and standardized partial regression coefficients for language test

Subscore	PRMSE$_{aug}$	$\beta(s_t\|s \cdot x)$	$\beta(s_t\|x \cdot s)$	VAR$_{aug/sub}$	VAR$_{aug/tot}$
Listening	0.91	0.53	0.44	1.04	1.06
Reading	0.90	0.60	0.36	1.03	1.07
Speaking	0.88	0.75	0.23	1.02	1.36
Writing	0.90	0.18	0.79	1.24	1.01

subscores. The improvement for writing is much larger, although the added value is limited compared to the total score. Relative to prediction by the total score, the augmented subscores provide very large added value for speaking and relatively modest added value for listening and reading. Consistent with the comparisons with prediction by just the subscore or prediction by just the total score, the standardized partial regression coefficients vary by subscore. In the cases of listening and reading, $\beta(s_t|s \cdot x)$ is larger than $\beta(s_t|x \cdot s)$, so the standardized subscore has higher weight that the standardized total score. For speaking, $\beta(s_t|s \cdot x)$ is much larger than $\beta(s_t|x \cdot s)$, so the standardized subscore has much higher weight than the standardized total score. For writing, $\beta(s_t|s \cdot x)$ is much smaller than $\beta(s_t|x \cdot s)$, so the standardized subscore has much lower weight than the standardized total score.

In the previously mentioned Praxis example in Haberman (2008a), there is a substantial gain for the first two subscores, but the gains for the latter two subscores are modest compared to use of just the best linear predictor of the true subscore by the total score. For none of these subscores was the subscore very effective nor even close to the best choice.

A rational argument can be made for routine use of augmented subscores. Results are never worse than from prediction by just the Kelley estimate and sometimes much better. In addition, such usage can avoid awkward choices in cases such as the language test in which three subscores are far more satisfactory than the writing subscore. Nonetheless, if PRMSE$_{aug}$ is unsatisfactory, then due to the inadequate quality of the prediction, no user should receive any estimate of the subscore.

A second possible issue when several subscores are reported is very high correlations of predictions based on the subscore and total score. Consider the language test. Table 3.7 provides correlation coefficients for the four subscores and the total score. These correlation coefficients and Table 3.6 permit computation in Table 3.8, for any pair of subscores, of the correlation coefficients of the corresponding augmented subscores s_{sx}.

Table 3.7 *Correlations of subscores and total scores*

Score	Listening	Reading	Speaking	Writing	Total
Listening	1.00				
Reading	0.73	1.00			
Speaking	0.68	0.54	1.00		
Writing	0.71	0.71	0.67	1.00	
Total	**0.91**	**0.91**	**0.77**	**0.85**	**1.00**

Table 3.8 *Correlations of augmented subscores*

Subscore	Listening	Reading	Speaking	Writing
Listening	1.00			
Reading	0.90	1.00		
Speaking	0.83	0.75	1.00	
Writing	0.96	0.95	0.86	1.00

The correlations in Table 3.8 are much higher than are corresponding correlations in Table 3.7, especially for other subscores with writing. Although the high correlations are simply a reflection of the data, testing organizations may need to explain this matter to score users.

3.6 Residual Subscores: Finding Areas of Special Strength or Weakness

We use residual subscores to identify areas of relative strength or weakness, say, whether in the language example a test taker is stronger or weaker in speaking than expected by the total score. This identification is challenging in practice due to the common phenomenon that subscores and total scores are positively correlated and corresponding correlations of true subscores and true total scores are even larger.

For instance, in the language test, correlations of true scores are even larger than the score correlations of Table 3.7, as is evident in Table 3.9. The latter table can be derived from Tables 3.2 and 3.7. For any two subscores, the correlation of their true scores is the ratio of the correlation of the subscores and the square root of the product of their reliability coefficients, a result that dates back at least to Spearman (1904). Because the error of measurement of the subscore and the error of measurement of the total score are correlated, the correlation of true subscore and true total score is

Table 3.9 Correlations of true subscores and total scores

Score	Listening	Reading	Speaking	Writing	Total
Listening	1.00				
Reading	0.83	1.00			
Speaking	0.79	0.63	1.00		
Writing	0.89	0.89	0.85	1.00	
Total	0.95	0.94	0.82	0.97	1.00

$$\rho(s_t, x_t) = \frac{\sigma(s)\sigma(x)\rho(s,x) - \sigma^2(s_e)}{\sigma(s)\sigma(x)\rho_s\rho_x}. \tag{3.13}$$

The correlations of true subscores and the true total score provides a useful index of the ability of the true total score to predict the true subscores. The proportional reduction of mean square error $\text{PRMSE}_{\text{tott}}$ for prediction of a true subscore s_t by the true total score x_t is $\rho^2(s_t, x_t)$. For the four subscores, the average proportional reduction of mean square error $\text{APRMSE}_{\text{tott}}$ is than 0.85. Thus, the preponderance of the variance of the four true subscores is explained by the true total score, but appreciable variance of these true subscores remains. Readers familiar with treatments of profiles of true scores such as Bulut et al. (2017) should note that the criterion there for variability of true subscores is somewhat different, for each standardized true score is compared to the average standardized true score. The average over the standardized true subscores of these deviations is the average correlation of the true subscores. In the language test, this average is 0.86, a value quite close to $\text{APRMSE}_{\text{tott}}$.

We can ask if the relatively limited variability of true subscores not explained by the true total permits practical use of residual subscores to identify areas of relative strength, say, whether a test taker is less proficient in speaking than expected based on overall fluency.

For the subscore s, the residual subscore

$$s_{rx} = s - E(s) - \sigma(s)\rho(s,x)z(x) \tag{3.14}$$

for prediction of the subscore by the total score provides the basis for estimation of the residual true subscore s_{rxt} for prediction of the true subscore by the true total score. Note that s_{rx} in (3.14) is not the same as $s_{xr} = s_t - s_x$ in (3.6). The residual true score is

$$s_{rxt} = s_t - E(s) - \sigma(s_t)\rho(s_t, x_t)z(x_t). \tag{3.15}$$

3.7 Combining Subscores: Alternatives to Total Scores

Table 3.10 $PRMSE_{res}$ in the language test

Subscore	$PRMSE_{res}$
Listening	0.48
Reading	0.60
Speaking	0.67
Writing	0.16

The means of the residual subscore and the residual true subscore are both 0, and the predictor of the residual true subscore by the subscore and total score is

$$s_{rsx} = \{\rho_s^2[1-\rho^2(s_t,x_t)]/[1-\rho^2(s,x)]\}s_{rx}. \quad (3.16)$$

The proportional reduction in mean square error $PRMSE_{res}$ relative to the trivial predictor 0 is $\rho_s^2[1-\rho^2(s_t,x_t)]/[1-\rho^2(s,x)]$.

Results for the language test appear in Table 3.10.

These low $PRMSE_{res}$ values are discouraging, especially for writing. All $PRMSE_{res}$ values are much lower than are any of the corresponding reliabilities of the subscores. Due to these low values, use of residual subscores in the language test is inappropriate. The reader should not infer that the true total score perfectly explains all true subscores. Instead, the conclusion should be that accurate measurement of residual true subscores is not possible because their variances are too small relative to the respective variances of measurement of their predictions.

Results for the language test are not unusual. In the SAT administration discussed in Haberman (2008a), if Math and Verbal are regarded as subscores and the total score is the sum of these two scores, the $PRMSE_{res}$ for each residual subscore is only 0.73 despite reliability coefficients for both Math and Verbal of at least 0.91.

3.7 Combining Subscores: Alternatives to Total Scores

In this section, we consider ways to combine subscores to provide alternatives to total scores. Two approaches are considered, principal-components analysis and canonical analysis.

3.7.1 Principal Components: How Distinct Are True Subscores?

In this section, analysis of principal components addresses the question of whether the true subscores are so highly correlated that they have little marginal value even if all subscores have very high reliability coefficients. We consider a profile of k standardized true subscores associated with subscores with positive reliability coefficients. We assume that more than one subscore is considered. For example, we can study the four standardized true subscores associated with the listening, reading, speaking, and writing subscores of the language test. Associated with these standardized true subscores are k uncorrelated principal components C_j with mean 0 and variance 1. Each principal component is a weighted sum of the standardized true subscores, and each standardized true subscore $z(s_t)$ is a weighted sum of the principal components. Each principal component is associated with an eigenvalue and eigenvector of the correlation matrix of the standardized true subscores. The eigenvalue associated with a principal component is the total of the proportional reductions in mean squared error from prediction of standardized true subscores by the principal component. The associated eigenvector is proportional to the vector of weights the principal component assigns to the standardized true subscores. The sum of the total proportional reductions in mean square error of the principal components is equal to the number of standardized true subscores. It is customary to order principal components by the size of the corresponding eigenvalues, so the first principal component C_1 corresponds to the largest eigenvalue of the correlation matrix, and the last principal component C_k corresponds to the smallest eigenvalue.

In the language test, the eigenvalues are 3.44, 0.38, 0.14, and 0.04. These numbers can be represented in a scree plot as in Figure 3.3[4] (Sinharay et al., 2011). The average proportional reduction of 0.86 = 3.44/4 in mean square error from use of the first principal component is slightly higher than the values noted in Section 3.6 from prediction by the true total score or by use of the profile analysis in Bulut et al. (2017). The difference is 0.09 for the prediction by the true total score and 0.02 for the profile analysis. With the first two principal components as predictors, the average proportional reduction in mean square error rises to 0.95 = (3.44 + 0.38)/4. The first principal component is almost equal to the standardized true total score, for their correlation is 0.99. In general, the correlations of standardized true subscores with components are summarized in Table 3.11. The modest gain from use of the second principal component appears to involve a contrast between reading and speaking. The first skill is receptive and concerns written communication. The second skill is productive and concerns oral communication. In conclusion, the main picture from the use of principle components is that the

---

[4] In Sinharay et al. (2011), the scree plot applies to standardized subscores rather than standardized true subscores, but the graphical procedure is unaffected.

3.7 Combining Subscores: Alternatives to Total Scores

Table 3.11 *Correlations of true scores with principal components*

Score	Component			
	C_1	C_2	C_3	C_4
Listening	0.95	0.03	0.32	−0.01
Reading	0.90	0.40	−0.13	−0.10
Speaking	0.88	−0.46	−0.09	−0.08
Writing	0.98	0.02	−0.11	0.17
Total	**0.99**	**0.10**	**0.02**	**−0.03**

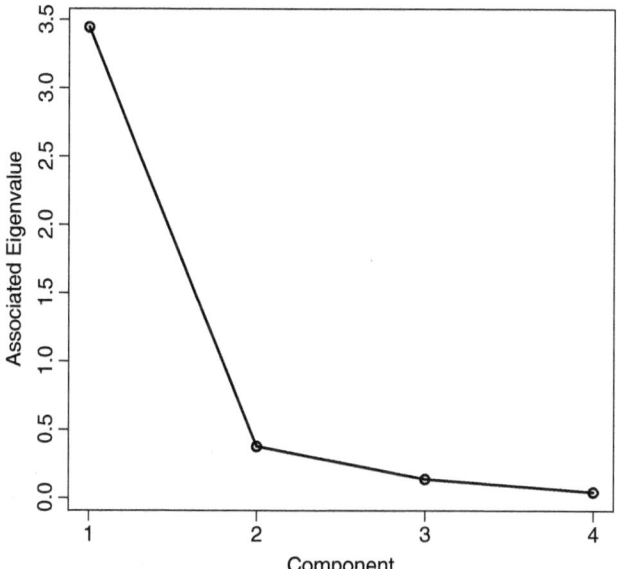

Figure 3.3 Scree plot of true subscores.

standardized true subscores primarily reflect a single variable, which might perhaps be regarded as general fluency. A limited amount of further information is provided by the true subscores.

3.7.2 Canonical Analysis: Using All Subscores to Predict a True Subscore

Canonical analysis (Haberman et al., 2009) considers prediction of a true subscore by all subscores rather than prediction of a true subscores by just the corresponding subscore and the total score. In canonical analysis, both standardized subscores and standardized true subscores are considered. The k canonical scores S_j are weighted sums of the k standardized subscores. The canonical scores are uncorrelated and have means of 0 and variances of 1. In addition, the true canonical scores are also uncorrelated. We order canonical scores g by their reliability coefficients so that the first canonical score has the highest reliability coefficient and the last canonical score has the smallest reliability coefficient. The reliability coefficient of the first canonical score h is the maximum possible reliability coefficient of a linear combination of the subscores, and the reliability coefficient of the last canonical score is the minimum possible reliability coefficient of a linear combination of the subscores. For a subscore s, the Wainer-augmented subscore[5] of Wainer et al. (2000) is the linear predictor s_w of the true subscore s_t from the k subscores. This predictor is equal to the subscore mean $E(s)$ plus the sum of the products $\sigma(s_t)\rho(s_t, S_j)S_j$. The corresponding proportional reduction in mean square error $PRMSE_{waug}$ is the sum of the squared correlations of s_t and S_j. In all cases, $PRMSE_{waug}$ is at least as large as the $PRMSE_{sub}$.

For the language test, PRMSE results from canonical analysis are nearly the same as for prediction by the subscore and total score. To the accuracy in the PRMSE values in Table 3.6, the only change is that the PRMSE for writing increases from 0.90 to 0.91. The reliability coefficients of the canonical scores S_j are 0.95, 0.70, 0.47, and 0.13. The first reliability coefficient is nearly the same as the reliability coefficient of the total score, so a different weighting of the subscores to yield a composite score cannot yield a composite score with an appreciably higher reliability coefficient than that achieved for the total score. The other reliability coefficients of the canonical scores are not large, although, as is evident in Figure 3.4, they decrease more slowly than in Figure 3.3. The reliability coefficient of 0.70 for the second canonical score indicates that no linear combination of subscores uncorrelated with the first canonical score can have better than a modest reliability, a result that is consistent with those for residual subscores. The correlations of true subscores and true canonical scores are provided in Table 3.12. The first canonical score is the dominant one, although the second canonical score has some influence on reading and speaking. In this example, use of augmentation based on total scores and subscores is reasonable in terms of simplicity and in terms of a consistent approach to the four subscores. The gain in this case from Wainer augmentation is negligible. Of course, different examples can yield different outcomes.

---

[5] The definition of s_w in Wainer et al. (2000) is algebraically equivalent to the definition here, but s_w is defined there without recourse to eigenvalues or eigenvectors.

Table 3.12 *Correlations of true subscores with canonical principal components*

Score	Component			
	S_1	S_2	S_3	S_4
Listening	0.87	0.00	0.19	0.00
Reading	0.83	−0.30	−0.09	−0.01
Speaking	0.78	0.37	−0.09	−0.01
Writing	0.81	0.00	−0.07	0.06

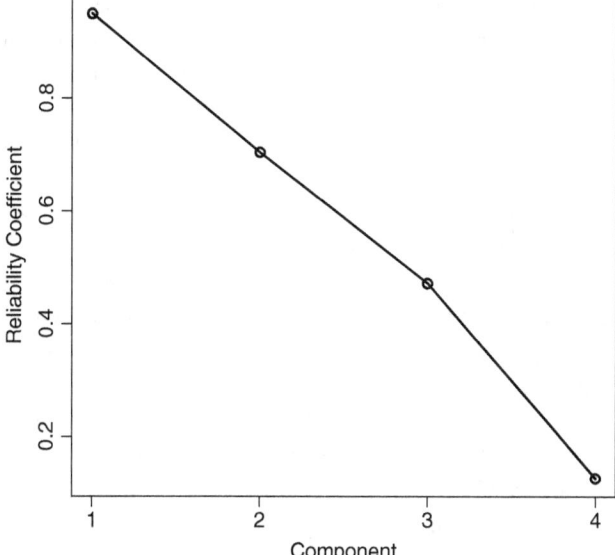

Figure 3.4 Scree plot of reliability coefficients of canonical scores.

3.8 Estimation

In typical cases, estimates required in this chapter rely on samples of test takers who took the assessment under study. Usually, we treat the test takers as a random sample from a population of test takers with similar characteristics. This population is often hypothetical. For scores, sample means, variances, standard deviations, and correlations provide estimates for the population of score means, variances, standard deviations, and correlations. In addition, because the true score has the same mean as the score, the sample mean of the score provides an estimate of the mean of the true score.

To estimate variances, standard deviations, and correlations associated with true scores requires much more effort than for the corresponding scores, although simple approximations based on Cronbach's alpha and stratified alpha are remarkably helpful in typical cases. These applications require a rather specific test structure in which the total score x is the sum of several subscores s and each subscore is the sum of $k \geq 2$ item scores. These conditions hold in the language test and in the SAT and Praxis examples, but, as emphasized in Section 3.9 in the discussion of item-response theory, they do not hold for all cases of interest. In the language test, the total score is the sum of the listening, reading, speaking, and writing subscores. The listening subscore is the sum of 34 item scores, the reading subscore is the sum of 42 item scores, the speaking subscore is the sum of 6 item scores, and the writing subscore is the sum of 2 item scores. In addition, we require that each item score be the sum of a true item score and an item measurement error and all item measurement errors be uncorrelated with each other and with all true item scores. This last assumption can fail in tests with multiple items based on a single stimulus such as a reading passage, a listening passage, or a series of extremely similar items. The assumption can also fail if a test is speeded so that many test takers cannot complete the assessment in the allotted time.

Under the assumptions made in this section, the variance of measurement of a subscore is the sum of the variances of measurement of the item scores associated with the subscore, and the variance of measurement of the total score is the sum of the variances of measurement of the subscores.

In this section, we begin with Cronbach's alpha, the most common tool for reliability estimation for subscores. We then apply Cronbach's stratified alpha, a simple extension of Cronbach's alpha needed for the reliability estimation of total scores when the subscores may have some value. We then explore the relationship of the Cronbach alpha and stratified alpha to reliability estimation based on repeated tests and half tests. In Section 3.9, comparisons are made with reliability estimation based on item-response theory.

3.8.1 Cronbach's Alpha

To obtain Cronbach's alpha, we apply the following definitions. For each subscore s, let $\sigma^2(I)$ be the sum of the variances of the item scores associated with the subscore with k items. Then Cronbach's approximation to the reliability coefficient ρ_s^2 is

$$\alpha_s = \frac{k}{k-1} \frac{\sigma^2(s) - \sigma^2(I)}{\sigma^2(s)}. \tag{3.17}$$

3.8 Estimation

Table 3.13 *Standard errors of estimated reliability coefficients*

Score	Standard error
Listening	0.0017
Reading	0.0017
Speaking	0.0026
Writing	0.0058
Total	**0.0007**

Under the assumptions concerning the item scores, α_s never exceeds the reliability coefficient of the subscore s. In practice, the difference between Cronbach's alpha approximation and the reliability is generally small, especially if the number of items involved is large. The difference is 0 in the special case in which the variances of the true scores of the associated items are all equal and the correlations of the item true scores are all 1. Cronbach's alpha and the variance of the subscore then provide variances of the true subscore and the measurement error of the subscore. Because Cronbach's alpha depends on variances of observations, substitution of sample variances for population variances provides an estimate of alpha. The resulting estimated reliability coefficient for the total score is then an example of Cronbach's stratified alpha. Although not a common problem, it should be noted that use of Cronbach's alpha can lead to impossible estimates in analysis of subscores. For example, in the case of two items with item scores that have a negative sample correlation, the estimated Cronbach's alpha is negative. Such cases require examination of data and of summary statistics to explore what problem exists.

Open-source software packages provide some of the computations considered in this chapter. Dai et al. (2017) review R packages available for computations in this chapter. The package *subscore* uses the estimate of α_s to estimate the reliability coefficient of the subscore s and applies the estimates to s_s, s_x, and s_{sx} and to associated proportional reductions in mean square error. Its use is illustrated in Figure 5.5 of Chapter 5. The package *sirt* includes *subscore*. A Fortran 90 program *SQE* and associated SAS macro appear in Yao et al. (2014).

The estimates in this section have standard errors that can be approximated by resampling methods. Because simple formulas are available for recomputing sample means, variances, and correlations after removal of an observation, jackknifing is an attractive option (Sinharay & Haberman, 2014). For the language test, where the sample size is 9,617, standard errors are very small, as is evident in Table 3.13 for estimates of reliability coefficients.

3.8.2 Repeated Tests and Half Tests

Alternatives to Cronbach's alpha exist, but their application is generally difficult. One simple option involves repeated tests. In the ideal case, a random sample is available of test takers who take two equivalent but different tests. This procedure corresponds to the assumptions in Section 3.2 used to develop reliability. The model assumes that the true scores for the same person on the two tests are the same and, given the common true scores, measurement errors for the two administrations are independent and have the same distributions. Thus, the two tests yield subscores s and s' with common true score s_t and total scores x and x' with common true score x_t. The measurement errors $s_e = s - s_t$ and $s'_e = s' - s_t$ have the same variance, the correlations of the measurement errors s_e are 0 for distinct subscores, the correlations of the measurement errors s'_e are 0 for distinct subscores, and the correlations of the measurement errors are 0 for subscores from different tests. Then $\sigma^2(s_e) = \sigma^2(s-s')/2$ and $\sigma^2(x_e) = \sigma^2(x-x')/2$. This information permits estimation of the reliability coefficients of the subscores and total scores by use of sample variances of observations.

Unfortunately, the desired random sample rarely exists. Test takers usually do not repeat tests unless they are discontented with initial results, and taking a test once often affects preparation for the next text. Use of real samples of repeat test takers requires elaborate procedures to adjust for biased samples (Haberman et al., 2015; Haberman & Yao, 2015). In practice, estimation of variances and correlations of true scores are usually not based on repeat test taking. However, as in the case of the referenced papers, cases can arise in which alternative estimation methods are not available due to special subpopulations under study, use of numerous test administrations, or subscores with only one item.

Nonetheless, the concept of repeating tests does play a role in other common approaches to estimating reliability that do not require anyone to take a test twice. The basic notion is to split one test into two similar half tests, which we call half-test 1 and half-test 2. To half-test j equal 1 or 2 correspond half-test subscores s_j such that the subscore s for the complete test is the sum of the half-test subscores s_1 and s_2. In addition, half-test total scores x_1 and x_2 have a sum equal to the total score x of the full test. For half-test j, the sum of the half-test subscores yields the half-test total score. This division of a full test into two half tests applies to the language test. The 34 listening items are divided into two sets of 17 items, the 42 reading items are split into two sets of 21 items, the 6 speaking items are split into two sets of 3 items, and the two writing items are split into two sets of 1 item. For illustration, one half test consists of even-numbered items and the other half test consists of odd-numbered items. Thus in the list of 84 items, one half test includes, among other items, the second,

Table 3.14 *Half-sample estimates of variances and reliability coefficients*

Score	Variance			Reliability
	Observed	True	Error	
Listening	43.0	38.0	5.0	0.88
Reading	65.4	57.3	8.1	0.88
Speaking	10.5	9.0	1.5	0.85
Writing	10.0	7.3	2.7	0.73
Total	**342.8**	**325.6**	**17.2**	**0.95**

fourth, and sixth items. The other half test includes, among other items, the first, third, and fifth items. It is assumed that all correlations of measurement errors are 0 for subscores for distinct half tests, all correlations of measurement errors are 0 for distinct subscores from each half test, and all correlations of measurement errors of subscores and true subscores are 0. The variance of measurement of the subscore s for the full test is no greater than the variance of the difference $s_1 - s_2$ of the subscores s_1 and s_2 from the half tests. For the total score x, its variance of measurement is no greater than the variance of the difference $x_1 - x_2$ of the total scores x_1 and x_2 from the half tests. Results are exact if true subscores for corresponding half tests are equal. To illustrate results, compare Table 3.2 and 3.14. Clearly, results are very similar. Indeed, the variances of measurement and the variances of true scores of Table 3.2 are the averages of results for all possible half tests with equal numbers of items for listening, reading, speaking, and writing.

Half tests can be preferable to use of Cronbach's alpha and stratified alpha when items are sorted by some criterion; however, such use is relatively uncommon.

3.9 Item-Response Theory

Item-response theory provides many tools for analysis of subscores. For application of multidimensional item-response theory to subscores, see Haberman and Sinharay (2010). In addition, for virtually all computations in this chapter that involve item-response analysis, we use the program *mirt* described in Haberman (2013) in computations.[6]

---

[6] The program is available in the repository https://github.com/EducationalTestingService/ MIRT. All files in this repository are freely available under an Apache 2.0 license. Source files in the subdirectory *Source* require compilation with a current *gfortran* compiler.

The advantages and disadvantages of item-response theory are closely linked. Predictors of true scores considered so far in this chapter are best linear predictors rather than best predictors. Estimation of these predictors and of the corresponding proportional reductions of mean square error require only sample means, sample variances, and sample correlations, so routine statistical software suffices for all computations. Indeed, essentially all computations so far other than graphs have been implemented with the *base* package of *R* without use of added packages such as *subscore*. In theory, item-response theory can provide better predictors of true scores by use of much more restrictive models than those required so far in this chapter. We emphasize that theoretical advantages do not necessarily result in practical gains. Item-response theory for the models required in this section requires far more computation than do the linear predictors applied in previous sections. For analysis of subscores and total scores derived from sums of item scores, we have generally found little practical gain from use of item-response theory beyond verification that we have achieved little practical gain. In addition, because the models in item-response theory are restrictive, risks exist that model error will distort inferences. Another problem is that estimation procedures for item-response models for subscores become unstable when subscores are nearly redundant. On the other hand, item-response theory permits many kinds of inferences that are otherwise unavailable. This situation is notable for analysis of scaled scores and cut scores.

3.9.1 Multidimensional Item-Response Models

To illustrate possibilities, we employ one possible multidimensional model for the language test. In the model, we assume the existence of four latent variables with a joint multivariate normal distribution. The latent variables correspond to the four skills listening, reading, speaking, and writing. Each latent variable has mean 0, and 1 is its conditional variance, given the other latent variables. We assume a between-items model (Adams et al., 1997) based on a slightly modified generalized partial credit model (Muraki, 1992). In this model, for any item associated with a subscore, the logarithm of the ratio of the conditional probabilities given the latent variable corresponding to the subscore of the item is h rather than g is a linear function of the latent variable with slope being a multiple of the difference $h-g$ as long

---

Documentation is in the subdirectory *Documents*, and examples are in the subdirectory *Examples*. Within *Examples*, analyses in this chapter are based on the file *fourskilll.txt*. The repository provides an update of the program described in Haberman (2013).

Table 3.15 $PRMSE_{irt}$ for prediction of latent variable and true subscore by item-response theory

Subscore	Latent variable	True subscore
Listening	0.91	0.92
Reading	0.91	0.91
Speaking	0.88	0.88
Writing	0.89	0.89
Total	**0.95**	**0.95**

as both h and g are possible item values. Different linear functions apply to different items. In addition, for the same h and g, the slope is the same multiple of $h-g$ for both writing items. The last assumption is required for stable estimates when only two items are in a subscore. Under this model, we use maximum-likelihood estimation to predict the latent variables and the corresponding true subscores from the 84 item responses. The resulting predictions are not functions of the four subscores. The proportional reductions in mean square $PRMSE_{irt}$ for the subscores appear in Table 3.15. The total latent variable is the sum of the four latent variables. The *mirt* program permits predictions of both the latent variables and the true subscores. The true subscores are the same true subscores as in Table 3.6. The proportional reductions in mean square error for this case are virtually the same in Tables 3.6 and 3.7, so item-response theory supports the previous results but does not improve upon them. Another notable feature of Table 3.15 is that proportional reductions in mean square error for the latent variable and true subscore are nearly the same even though the true subscore is not a simple function of the latent variable.

Given Table 3.15, the reader may wonder why item-response theory should be considered at all. As suggested at the beginning of this section, the answer involves the flexibility of item-response theory. The methods of item-response theory required to produce the predicted latent variables in Table 3.15 can be employed in cases in which items are selected at random for different test takers or in which the assessment is adaptive so that the items presented to the test taker at any point in the test depend on the preceding responses of the test taker. In some cases, the test is scored with item-response theory, so subscore reporting may need to fit into this framework.

A further feature of item-response theory is applicability to issues such as scaled scores and cut scores. These uses are explored in the next two subsections.

3.9.2 Scaled Scores

With item-response theory, we can also consider the use of scaled subscores. This approach helps verify inferences that were based on Cronbach's alpha. We used two transformations, a normal approximation and a two-category transformation. In the case of the normal approximation, for each subscore s, we sought a scaled score $g(s)$ with an approximate normal distribution with mean 10 and standard deviation 4 such that all scaled scores had integer values from 0 to 20. For the total score x, we also sought a scaled score $h(x)$ with an approximate normal distribution with mean 10 and standard deviation 4 such that all scaled scores were integers from 0 to 20. All scaled scores were required not to decrease if the score increased. The procedure used for subscores and total scores was essentially the same, so we will just describe the case for subscores. For any possible value i of the subscore, $g(i)$ is the closest integer between 0 and 20 to the number $q(h)$ such that the probability that a normal random variable with mean 10 and standard deviation 4 is less than $q(i)$ is the average of the probability that the subscore is less than i and the probability that the subscore is less than or equal to i. The two-category transformation considers whether test takers are above average or not for a particular skill. The transformed subscore $c(s)$ is defined to have values 0 and 1, with $c(i)$ equal to 0 if i is less than the median subscore and $c(i)$ equal to 1 otherwise.

Table 3.16 provides the PRMSE$_{irt}$ for prediction of each true transformed subscore. For the normal approximation, the PRMSE$_{irt}$ is very close to the PRMSE$_{irt}$ in Table 3.15 for the true subscore. This result corresponds to a general finding that scaled scores that are close to continuous functions of sums of item responses yield proportional reductions in mean square error that are close to proportional reductions in mean square error for sums of item scores. For the two-category case, there is a moderate decrease in PRMSE$_{irt}$ compared to the normal approximation. This decrease in PRMSE$_{irt}$

Table 3.16 *PRMSE$_{irt}$ for prediction of true transformed subscore by item-response theory*

Subscore	Normal approximation	Two categories
Listening	0.92	0.89
Reading	0.91	0.88
Speaking	0.88	0.83
Writing	0.89	0.87
Total	**0.95**	**0.91**

is typical when reported scores assume only a very small number of categories. Thus, scaled scores with few values can in some cases result in a significant decrease in reliability.

With item-response theory, we can report accuracy of test results at an individual level. Many options exist, with choices dependent on reasonable expectations concerning what a score user will understand. To illustrate results, we consider some options for listening for the first test taker in the file. With the normal approximation, *mirt* provides for this test taker the predicted transformed listening subscore of 14.5 and the corresponding standard error of 1.1. For all test takers, the mean prediction is 10.0, and the standard deviation of predictions is 3.2. The mean true transformed subscore is also 10.0, and the corresponding standard deviation is 3.7. With a normal approximation for the distribution of the conditional distribution of the transformed true listening subscore given the data for the test taker under study, we can provide an interval from 13.4 to 15.6 that includes the transformed true listening subscore with probability of about 0.68. The interval may be easier for many test takers to understand than the standard deviation. Another alternative is to apply the ratio of the mean deviation to the standard deviation of the normal distribution to indicate that 0.9 is the average difference between the predicted and actual true transformed subscore.

3.9.3 Cut Scores

Two-category scale scores have numerous applications to cut scores. In many cases, institutions that use tests for certification or admissions have cut scores such that a test taker must achieve a minimum score to pass the assessment. In some cases, institutions use cut scores with subscores as well as total scores. For example, as of this writing, the IELTS requirements for visas for the United Kingdom include cutoffs for a total score and four subscores:

www.ielts.org/en-us/about-ielts/ielts-for-migration/united-kingdom/ielts-used-for-uk-visa-applications

Responsible use of cut scores requires considering the reliability of the decision based on the cut score; that is, the reliability of a two-category scaled score such as the one used in the TC transformations in Table 3.16 in which a value of 1 corresponds to passing and a value of 0 corresponds to failing. As is evident from Fleiss (1975), the reliability coefficient for this case is the same as the kappa coefficient for the agreement of the decision value for the score and parallel-form score. For the language test, results are provided in Table 3.17. The reliability coefficients are much smaller than are the corresponding proportional reductions in mean square error in Table 3.16, for Table 3.17 examines the correlation of the cut scores for parallel forms. Of

Table 3.17 *Reliability of cut scores in the language test*

Subscore	Reliability	Squared reliability
Listening	0.71	0.51
Reading	0.71	0.50
Speaking	0.66	0.44
Writing	0.54	0.29
Total	**0.81**	**0.65**

greater note is the squared reliability, which is the proportional reduction in mean squared error from prediction of the parallel-form cut-score decision. These values are sufficiently low that the decision for the subscore is not an effective predictor of the decision for the parallel-form subscore, especially in the case of the writing score. *Thus, decisions on subscores based on these cut scores are unsatisfactory.*

In two ways, the example with individual cut scores is much more favorable than many other possible cases. Cut scores further from the median can be expected to lead to even lower reliability coefficients. For example, the reliability of the cut-score decision for total score drops to 0.76 if the cut is set so that only about 17% of test takers pass, and the reliability of the cut-score decision for the writing score drops to 0.48 if the cut is set so that about 14% of test takers pass.

Simultaneous use of cut scores requires great scrutiny. In the example, only 31% of test takers meet cut scores for all subscores. With an alternative analysis based on item-response theory, 34% of test takers pass. In this analysis, the cut decision is to pass if the conditional probability is at least one half that all latent variables are at least 0. The reliability is only 0.66.

This computation is the only one in this section not easily derived from the *mirt* program by use of the correct control statements. In this case, the program was used to find the estimated conditional joint distribution for each observation of the latent variables given the data. The results were then read into R to complete the analysis. For each observation i, we estimated the conditional probability p_i that all latent variables were positive and we estimated the cut decision c_i. Here c_i is 1 if p_i is greater than 0.5, and c_i is 0 otherwise. The estimated variance of measurement is the average over the observations i of $p_i(1-p_i)+(c_i-p_i)^2$, and the estimated variance of the cut decision is $\bar{c}(1-\bar{c})$, where $\bar{c}$ is the average of c_i. The reliability estimate is 1 minus the ratio of the estimated variance of measurement to the estimated variance of the cut decision.

For now, we strongly advise that institutions not apply cut scores to subscores unless required by law or unless the subscores are very reliable. We do note that composite scores can be created that increase emphasis on portions of a test that are of increased interest to the score user. For example, an institution can double the weight assigned to the speaking section if speaking is of great interest.

3.10 The Effect of Test Length on Subscore Usage

An important feature that follows from the reliability bound from Cronbach's alpha is that, in typical cases, as the number of items in a subscore becomes large, the reliability coefficient of the subscore increases. When the reliability coefficient of a subscore is low, this result provides an estimate of the number of items required to achieve a reliability coefficient at least equal to a specified value less than 1. A traditional tool is the prophecy formula of Spearman (1910) and Brown (1910). Recall the signal-to-noise ratio of Section 3.3. The reliability coefficient is the ratio of the signal-to-noise ratio SNR to SNR + 1. The prophecy formula implies that multiplying the number of items by a constant multiplies the SNR by the same constant. The result can be exact. For example, in the hypothetical ideal case of repeat tests, a new test can be created by combining the two test results. In this case, the SNR is doubled. Thus, a reliability of 0.9 for one test leads to an SNR of 18 for the combined tests and a reliability of 18/19 that is about 0.95.

As an illustrative example, we apply the prophecy formula to Table 3.1. Figure 3.5 shows the projected reliability coefficients for listening, reading, speaking, and writing for numbers of items from 2 to 60, while Table 3.18 indicates the minimum number of items needed for a projected reliability coefficient of 0.8 or 0.9. For the same sample size, projected reliability coefficients are much larger for speaking and writing than for listening and reading. Thus, 5 items suffice for the 0.8 standard in speaking, and 4 items suffice for the 0.8 standard in writing, whereas the same standard requires 19 listening items and 24 reading items. The graph shows another important feature of reliability coefficients. The rate of improvement of the reliability coefficient with an increasing number of items decreases rapidly.

To achieve the 0.8 standard for reliability for each subscore entails a total of 52 items, while the 0.9 standard requires a total of 115 items. With the current test that has 84 items and with prediction with both score and subscore, all subscores have a $PRMSE_{aug}$ of at least 0.88, and the subscores other than speaking have a $PRMSE_{aug}$ of at least 0.90. Given the assumption that the

Table 3.18 *Number of items needed for reliability of 0.8 and 0.9*

Score	Reliability	
	0.8	0.9
Listening	19	44
Reading	24	54
Speaking	5	10
Writing	4	7

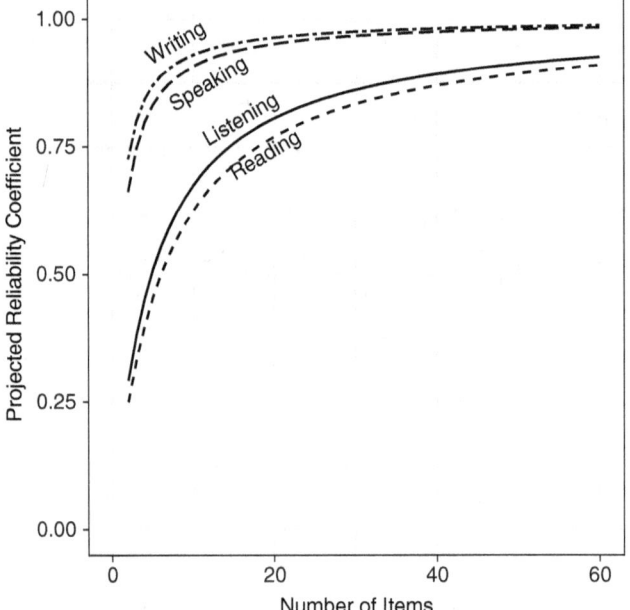

Figure 3.5 Projected reliability coefficients for different numbers of items.

true subscore and true total score have correlation less than 1, it is true that a sufficient increase in the number of items does lead eventually to a case in which PRMSE$_{sub}$ exceeds PRMSE$_{tot}$; however, the number of items required may not be practical, given cost and time limitations that affect tests. A similar issue affects prediction of the true subscore by both the subscore and total score. With sufficiently many items, PRMSE$_{aug}$ becomes increasingly similar to PRMSE$_{sub}$. Once again, the number of items for similar results may be excessively large. In addition to considerations of cost, an excessively long test may begin to measure endurance rather than proficiency. In most cases, tests are not intended to measure stamina.

To some degree, cost–benefit analysis to inform decisions concerning test length are difficult to quantify; however, some basic issues should be noted. Test length affects the time required for the test. Test takers' time has economic value, and this value is highly variable. Presumably the time per hour of neurosurgeons is much more costly than the time per hour of students in kindergarten. Testing time affects facility cost and cost of proctoring. Producing test items entails significant cost, and scoring tests has variable costs that depend on whether scoring is automated or requires human judgment. The cost of human judgment is also highly variable. Scoring may require an undergraduate degree in education or board certification in cardiology. The importance of the accuracy of results is also highly variable. A practice examination in middle school on knowledge of fractions does not have the same consequences as a certification test to enable pilots to fly commercial passenger planes. Unfortunately, it is easier to evaluate the direct economic costs of testing than the costs of variation in test results, a challenge that is often encountered in discussions of statistics and public policy (Spencer, 1997; Wainer & Robinson, 2023). As discussed in the next section, a further consideration involves validity.

3.11 Incremental Validity

So far in this chapter, we have provided conditions under which subscores provide some information above what is provided by the total score; however, we have not explored whether the subscores are useful. To explore the utility of subscores, we must examine their validity and incremental validity. A rather detailed discussion of validity issues for subscores is provided by Haladyna and Kramer (2004) in the context of an examination program for dentists; however, the discussion is more widely applicable. They note requirements for construct definition, survey of needs of the profession, establishment of test specifications, item development, procedures for item development and analysis, test design, consideration of the structure of item responses, and subscore reports. The consideration of professional needs may be substituted in cases involving academic programs for needs of the programs. They also note the need to establish that subscores are distinct.

These aspects of validity evidence do not address incremental predictive validity. For example, a graduate admissions program in the United States often receives applicants whose first language is not English. There is a general wish to verify that the applicants have sufficient fluency in English to participate in a graduate program. A specific issue is whether the applicant can speak English sufficiently well to serve as a teaching assistant who must speak to students. Thus, the institution may well want a subscore for fluency in spoken English. Similar considerations may be relevant to candidates from outside the United States who seek positions as pharmacists, nurses, or physicians. Here institutions and certifying agencies need to know that the subscore helps evaluate the expected candidate performance in the relevant task and that any such help from the subscore goes beyond help provided by the total score. Evaluation of the incremental predictive validity of the subscore requires demonstration by empirical study that the subscore contributes to prediction of an external validity criterion for the skill the subscore measures beyond the prediction provided by the total score. For instance, an external validity criterion for the speaking score might involve student reviews of their satisfaction with the spoken English of the teaching assistant. The question would be the extent the speaking subscore contributes to prediction of satisfaction beyond the contribution of the total score. We note that such empirical study is challenging and not often undertaken. Selection effects arise because only candidates with adequate performance are likely to have the positions in question. For example, evaluation of the teaching assistant takes place only if the student has been accepted based on adequate test performance.

In some cases, the claim of the testing organization is that the subscore results can help learners see where they need to improve their skills. Such a claim is useless without evidence that the information provided in fact does improve overall performance. Such evidence can be obtained only via empirical study. Thus, reporting subscores requires not just evidence that they have adequate reliability coefficients and predict the measured skill better than the total score. Subscore value also entails validity study that includes empirical evidence.

As in Haberman (2008b), reliability of residual subscores limits incremental validity. Consider a subscore s, a total score x, and an external validity variable v. For instance, in Davison et al. (2015), the validity variable is college grade-point average, the subscores are SAT section scores, and the total score is the sum of the SAT section scores. Incremental validity is limited by the reliability of the residual s_{rx} from prediction of the subscore from the total score. The predictor of the validity variable from the total score is v_{sx}, and the proportional reduction of mean square error PRMSE_{vtot} is $\rho^2(v,x)$. With both the total score and the subscore, the predictor is v_{sx}, and the proportional reduction of mean square error PRMSE_{vaug} is $\rho^2(v,x) + \rho^2(v, s_{rx})$. The

Table 3.19 *Reliability coefficients of residual subscores*

Subscore	Reliability
Listening	0.48
Reading	0.60
Speaking	0.67
Writing	0.16

incremental validity measure $\rho^2(v, s_{rx})$ is the difference between $\text{PRMSE}_{\text{vaug}}$ and $\text{PRMSE}_{\text{vtot}}$. In typical cases, the validity measure itself has measurement error, so $\rho^2(v, s_{rx})$ is the product of the reliability coefficient of v, the reliability coefficient of s_{rx}, and the square of the correlation of the true score v_t of v and the true score of s_{rx}. In practice, the problem encountered in Section 3.7 for prediction of s_{rxt} is repeated, although the PRMSE in that section is slightly different than the reliability coefficient of the residual subscore. For instance, the reliability coefficients in Table 3.19 are virtually the same as the PRMSE values in Table 3.10. No difference exceeds 0.0007. Clearly, an incremental validity measure for writing must be quite small no matter how reliable v may be and no matter how highly correlated are the true scores of v and the residual subscore. For other subscores, restraints on incremental validity are much less extreme.

Even when internal study of a test indicates that a subscore might have appreciable incremental validity for its intended use, the burden of proof is on the testing organization to demonstrate that empirical evidence justifies use of the subscore.

3.12 Aggregate-Level Subscores

The methods developed in this chapter can be modified to apply to average scores of groups of test takers rather than to individual test takers (Haberman et al., 2009; Longford, 1990). Groups can be schools, classes, counties, states, or whole countries. The total scores and subscores may be published by testing organizations; by countries, as is done for TOEFL on an annual basis; or by states, as is done by the National Assessment for Educational Progress. State educational systems may analyze school results obtained by state assessments of individual students. As in the case of individual test takers, there is a question of whether subscores are useful to report for such groups. Analysis is very similar to the previously presented analyses, except that variance estimation and reliability deal with variations associated with groups and with individuals within groups. In practice, the number of test takers in a group has a major impact. It can be far easier to identify the value of a subscore when a group has many members. In particular, a subscore may provide useful information concerning the group even though the subscore is not useful at an individual level. On the other hand, no guarantee exists that a subscore is useful at a group level for a relevant group of realistic size. For examples, see the cited paper (Haberman et al., 2009).

The needed analysis requires a decomposition of a subscore s into a group mean s_g and an individual component $s_i = s - s_g$. The total score x is also decomposed into a group mean x_g and an individual component $x_i = x - x_g$. The individual components are uncorrelated with the group means. The individual subscore component has positive variance $\sigma^2(s_i)$, while the individual component of the total score has positive variance $\sigma^2(x_i)$. The subscore group mean has positive variance $\sigma^2(s_g)$, while the group component of the total score has positive variance $\sigma^2(x_g)$. The correlation of the subscore mean and mean of the total score is $\rho(s_g, x_g)$, while the correlation of the individual subscore component and the individual component of the total score is $\rho(s_i, x_i)$.

Groups in this analysis include variable numbers of individuals. For a group with n individuals, we consider the sample group subscore mean $\bar{s}$ and the sample mean $\bar{s}_i$ of the individual subscore component. The sample group mean total score is $\bar{x}$, and $\bar{x}_i$ is the sample mean of the individual component of the total score. The group subscore mean has estimate $\bar{s}$ with variance given the group of $\sigma^2(s_i)/n$. The group mean total score has estimate $\bar{x}$ with variance given the group of $\sigma^2(x_i)/n$. The sample group subscore mean then has reliability

$$\rho_{\bar{s}g}^2 = \sigma^2(s_g) / \left[\sigma^2(s_g) + \sigma^2(s_i)/n\right], \qquad (3.18)$$

and the sample group mean for the total score has reliability

$$\rho_{\bar{x}g}^2 = \sigma^2(x_g) / \left[\sigma^2(x_g) + \sigma^2(x_i)/n\right]. \qquad (3.19)$$

The correlation of the group subscore mean and the sample group mean of the total score is

$$\rho(s_g, \bar{x}_g) = \rho(s_g, x_g) \rho_{\bar{x}g}. \qquad (3.20)$$

These equations, together with the population means of the subscore and total score, suffice to obtain versions of the Kelley estimate for the subscore group mean based on the sample subscore group mean, the linear predictor of the subscore group mean based on the sample group mean of the total score, and the linear predictor of the subscore group mean based on the sample subscore group mean and the sample group mean of the total score. In addition, proportional reductions of mean square error and value-added ratios may be computed. As long as the sample size for the group is sufficiently large, the version of the Kelley estimate for the group mean has a larger proportional reduction in mean square error than the estimate based on the sample group mean of the total score.

Use of sample data to estimate the required variances and correlations is less straightforward than in the applications to individuals because samples of test takers within groups involve both subscores and total scores. One essentially has an unbalanced one-way multivariate analysis of variance, and some possibility exists for impossible estimates. We refer the reader to Haberman et al. (2009) for details.

3.13 Conclusions and Recommendations

The basic challenge in decisions regarding reporting of subscores involves whether value-added ratios are less than 1 and whether augmented scores help improve the accuracy of predictions of true subscores sufficiently to justify their use. In addition to examples cited in Section 3.4, further examples of value-added ratios for different subscores value appear in Chapter 4 and in references cited in Section 3.4 and Chapter 4. Recommendations on what subscores to report and how to report them must consider testing organizations, institutional score users, and test takers. Testing organizations have a professional obligation to provide information concerning the reliability of any score they provide and concerning the correlations of all scores on the same test. They also need to provide data on incremental validity of subscores, although we recognize that such data will not exist when a testing program begins. It is far more likely that institutional score users rather than test takers have the ability to use this information to inform their decisions on how to utilize or not utilize all scores they receive. This situation is most likely for large universities with professional staff with the expertise to conduct validity studies and to analyze test results. In addition, testing organizations such as the College Board have services to help academic institutions study validity. Institutions should not take on faith that testing organizations have justified use of the subscores they provide. They should demand that testing organizations provide the information needed to evaluate the quality of their test scores.

Test takers or their representatives should also have access to information concerning the value of the test scores provided, although such information should be presented to them in a manner appropriate to their expected education. Information for parents of students in elementary school is likely to differ from information for associate actuaries.

Unless required by law, subscores based on only subscore items should not be provided at all unless they predict their true scores better than can be accomplished by a total score. Providing such subscores is misleading, for the testing organization implicitly or explicitly suggests that the subscores give useful information. To be sure, there are two levels of questionable subscores to consider. An unreliable subscore is far worse than a reliable subscore that still predicts its true score less well than does the total score. The damage is even higher if the user of the score has no indication that the subscore reported has little relationship to what it claims to measure.

Even subscore estimates based on subscores and total scores should not be used unless the gain over use of a single total score is appreciable. The value of an increase of PRMSE from 0.90 to 0.91 is limited.

Decisions to use or not to use item-response theory involve considerations of transparency and technical skill. Scores that involve multidimensional item-response theory may be difficult to explain to score users. In addition, the required software and methodology may not be familiar to many psychometricians with testing organizations. On the other hand, multidimensional item-response theory may be necessary in many complex tests with features such as adaptive testing or simultaneous delivery of multiple test forms, and item-response theory can also assist in linking test forms and in providing information for individuals concerning the accuracy of results. In addition, item-response theory is important in examining the effects of test scaling and the use of cut scores.

For all approaches to subscores, special precautions are required when multiple items are derived from a single reading passage or listening passage, for passage effects may distort common methods of item analysis.

We emphasize that the issue of subscores is not simply whether the correlation of the true subscore and subscore is less than 1 or whether the correlations of all true subscores are less than 1. For example, in the language test, the subscores do not appear to measure exactly the same skill. Nonetheless, the correlations, except for speaking, are so high that the value of the other subscores is quite limited for a test of reasonable length. We do recommend scree plots of correlation matrices of true scores to appreciate this issue.

Our basic plea is that score producers and score users evaluate subscores to assess their features and consider what should be reported and what information should be provided. We want to avoid a false sense of knowledge based on faith rather than facts. We note a comment attributed in *Harper's Weekly* on May 29, 1869, to the American humorist Josh Billings: "I honestly believe it is better tew (to) know nothing than tew (to) know what ain't (is not) so."

4
A Survey to Explore the Conditions under Which Subscores Have Added Value

> In God we trust. All others must bring data.
> *W. Edwards Deming (1986)*

In Chapter 3, we described the requirements, in terms of psychometric characteristics such as reliability, correlation, PRMSE, and value-added ratio for subscores to have added value. You may wonder what those requirements translate to in practice and whether they are too restrictive for operational tests. Two relevant questions in this regard are: "To what extent are the requirements stipulated in Chapter 3 satisfied for operationally reported subscores?" and "For subscores that do satisfy those requirements, what are their features that lend themselves to added value?" Inspired by Deming's sensible demand, we respond to those questions using a survey of data from 36 operational tests.

4.1 The 36 Data Sets

Table 4.1 includes key information for the 36 data sets that we surveyed. The seven entries in each row of the table provide (1) the name or type of the test that the corresponding data set originated from, (2) the number of subscores, (3) the number of subscores that had added value according to the PRMSEs and value-added ratios discussed in Chapter 3, (4) the average number of items comprising the subscores (referred to as "average length"), (5) the average reliability (Cronbach's alpha) of the subscores, (6) average disattenuated correlation among the subscores, and (7) the source or reference of the test data set (the sources are provided as acronyms that are elaborated in a note below the table). The rows of the table are sorted first according to the decreasing

Table 4.1 Details of some tests illustrating how the reliability of and dependence among subscores influence their likelihood of having added value

The test	Number of subscores	Number of subscores with added value	Average length	Average reliability	Average disattenuated correlation	Source of data
NBME Part I Exam	7	7	136	0.83	0.70	FJ17
Swedish Scholastic Aptitude Test	5	4	24	0.78	0.71	Ly09
Examination for dentists	4	3	100	0.93	0.89	HK04
State English language proficiency exam	5	3	24	0.83	0.73	LP18
SAT I	2	2	69	0.92	0.76	H08a
Test of mastery of a language I	2	2	43	0.90	0.75	SH08
Test of achievement in a discipline I	3	2	67	0.87	0.82	SH08
GRE Psychology	6	2	34	0.80	0.83	LRYM18
Educators' content knowledge	4	2	25	0.72	0.78	H08a
Test of achievement in a discipline II	3	1	68	0.85	0.90	SH08
Test of mastery of a language II	2	1	44	0.85	0.90	SH08
LT for teachers of Spanish	4	1	29	0.80	0.80	PSHL10
LT for teachers in elementary school	4	1	30	0.74	0.79	PSHL10
LT for paraprofessionals	3	0	24	0.85	0.89	PSHL10
A large-scale French Language test	2	0	32	0.83	0.93	LL20
SAT I Verbal	3	0	26	0.79	0.95	H08a
Preliminary ACT English	2	0	25	0.79	0.95	HH91
SAT I Math	3	0	20	0.78	0.97	H08a
TOEIC Listening Comprehension	4	0	25	0.78	0.95	W00

(continued)

Table 4.1 (cont.)

The test	Number of subscores	Number of subscores with added value	Average length	Average reliability	Average disattenuated correlation	Source of data
Delaware State Mathematics (8th Grade)	4	0	19	0.77	1.00	SYZL10
State Reading (5th Grade)	2	0	37	0.72	0.92	AS09
Preliminary ACT Mathematics	2	0	20	0.71	0.94	HH91
Test of school & individual student progress I	4	0	15	0.70	0.98	SH08
Test of school & individual student progress II	6	0	13	0.70	1.00	SH08
TOEFL Primary Reading	3	0	10	0.70	0.90	CP20
TIMSS eighth-grade mathematics	4	0	8	0.65	0.86	DSW17
LT for teachers of social studies	6	0	22	0.63	0.87	PSHL10
LT for teachers of mathematics	3	0	16	0.62	0.95	PSHL10
Large-scale physics test	6	0	12	0.58	0.96	LL20
MFT Business	7	0	17	0.56	0.85	Li12
Assessing knowledge on test theory	2	0	17	0.55	0.98	MBTBA17
TOEFL Primary Listening	4	0	8	0.52	0.98	CP20
LT for principals and school leaders	4	0	15	0.48	0.85	PSHL10
LT for teachers of special educ programs	3	0	19	0.46	0.96	PSHL10
Test of cognitive and technical skills	7	0	11	0.42	1.00	SH08
LT for beginning teachers	4	0	19	0.38	1.00	PSHL10

Note: educ = Education; LT = Licensure Test; NBME = National Board of Medical Examiners; AS09 = Ackerman and Shu (2009); CP20 = Choi and Papageorgiou (2020); DSW17 = Dai, Svetina, and Wang (2017); FJ17 = Feinberg and Jurich (2017); H08a = Haberman (2008a); HK04 = Haladyna and Kramer (2004); HH91 = Harris and Hanson (1991); LL20 = Lim and Lee (2020); Li12 = Ling (2012); LP18 = Longabach and Peyton (2018); LRYM18 = Liu, Robin, Yoo, and Manna (2018); Ly09 = Lyren (2009); MBTBA17 = Meijer, Boeve, Tendeiro, Bosker, and Albers (2017); PC18 = Papageorgiou and Choi (2020); PSHL10 = Puhan, Sinharay, Haberman, and Larkin (2010); SH08 = Sinharay and Haberman (2008); SYZL10 = Stone, Ye, Zhu, and Lane (2010); W00 = Wilson (2000).

order of the number of subscores with added value and then by the decreasing order of average reliability. Extra spaces between the rows of the table separate the tests with no value-added subscores from the tests with one value-added subscore, the tests with one value-added subscore from those with two value-added subscores, and so on. The appendix provides further details of the tests and the corresponding data sets.

In the following eight subsections, we describe several critical insights – regarding added value of subscores – that we gained from analyses of the 36 data sets.

4.2 Subscores Rarely Have Added Value in Practice

Table 4.2 shows a frequency table summarizing the number of subscores that have added value for each of the 36 tests. Table 4.3 converts the numbers

Table 4.2 *The number of subscores that have added value for the 36 tests that we surveyed*

Number of subscores with added value	Number of tests
0	23
1	4
2	5
3	2
4	1
7	1

Table 4.3 *The percentage of subscores that have added value for the 36 tests that we surveyed*

Percentage of subscores with added value	Number of tests
0	23
25	2
33	2
50	2
60	1
67	1
75	1
80	1
100	3

in the second column of Table 4.2 into percentages. Interestingly, 23 out of 36 tests that we surveyed had zero subscores with added value. The percentage of subscores that have added value is 50 or less in 6 of the 13 remaining tests. Considering the increasing demand for subscores and the fact that the subscores on many of these tests are used to make important remedial and instructional decisions, the frequencies and percentages in Tables 4.2 and 4.3 are surprising and point to a problem in operational practice that requires rectification. We take an in-depth look at the data sets below, trying to tease out the factors that separate the 13 tests with at least one value-added subscores from the remaining 23 tests.

4.3 Required Minimum Subtest Length: 24 Items

Figure 4.1 graphically represents how the average length of the subtests on a test affects the number of subscores that have added value. The figure includes, for each of the 36 aforementioned tests, a circle that represents the average length of the subtests on the test (shown along the X axis) and the number of subscores that have added value on the same test (along the Y axis). For convenience of viewing, the X axis is scaled logarithmically. The circle for a test is an empty circle (with and without a dot at its center) or a solid black circle depending on whether the number of subscores with added value for the test is zero or not. The figure shows that a subscore is more likely to have added value when its average length is larger. A vertical and dashed line is drawn at average length = 23. All the solid black points fall to the right of the line. The location of the line indicates that a test has at least one value-added subscore only when the average subtest length is 24 or larger. However, the figure also shows that the average length is 24 or larger for 6 tests (that are shown using empty circles with a dot at its center[1]) for which no subscore had added value. We will revisit these six tests later. The names of all the tests with at least one value-added subscore and some of the tests with no value-added subscores are shown next to the circles.[2]

---

[1] Two such tests have an average length of 25 – so the plotting points for them are overlapping, giving the impression that there are five such tests in the figure.

[2] The figure does not show all test names to avoid congestion. We tried our best to make it clear which circle corresponds to which test. In case of confusion, Table 4.1 should be helpful in figuring out the test to which a circle corresponds. For example, while it is difficult to figure out which circle corresponds to the TOEIC Listening test from Figure 4.1, Table 4.1 shows that the average length for the test is 25 and the test has no value-added subscore – so the circle for the test is the one with X coordinate = 25 and Y coordinate = 0.

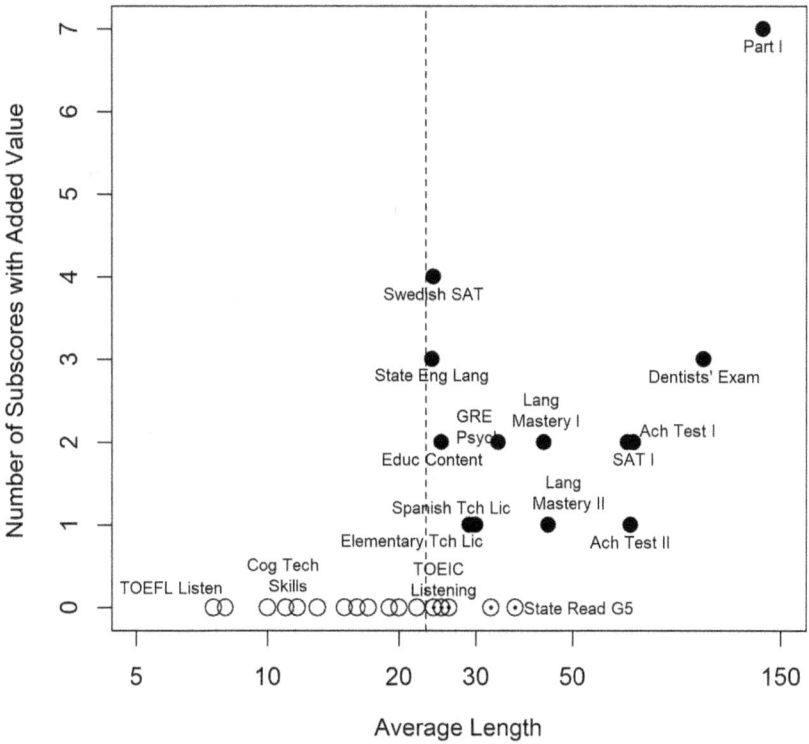

Figure 4.1 Plot showing how average length influenced the number of subscores with added value for the 36 data sets that were surveyed. Plotting symbols are empty circles (with or without a dot at the center; a dot at the center of a circle indicates that the average length is larger than 23 for the corresponding test) for the tests that had no value-added subscores, or solid circles for the tests that had one or more value-added subscores.[3]

Figure 4.2 is another graphical representation of how the average length of the subscores on a test affects the percentage of the subscores that have added value for the test. The figure shows – like Figure 4.1 does – the average length

---

[3] The names of some of the tests are shown next to the plotting symbols (Ach Test I & II = test of achievement in a discipline I & II; Cog tech skills = test measuring cognitive and technical skills; Dentists' Exam = examination for dentists; Educ Content = educators' content knowledge; Elementary Tch Lic = LT for teachers in elementary school; GRE Psych = GRE Psychology; Lang Mastery I & II = test of mastery of a language I & II; Paraprof Lic = LT for paraprofessionals; Part I = National Board of Medical Examiners Part I Examination; Spanish Tch Lic = LT for teachers of Spanish; State Eng Lang = state English language proficiency examination; State Read G5 = State Reading [5th Grade]; Swedish SAT = Swedish Scholastic Aptitude Test; TOEFL Rdg = TOEFL Primary Reading; TOEIC Listening = TOEIC Listening Comprehension; LT = licensure test).

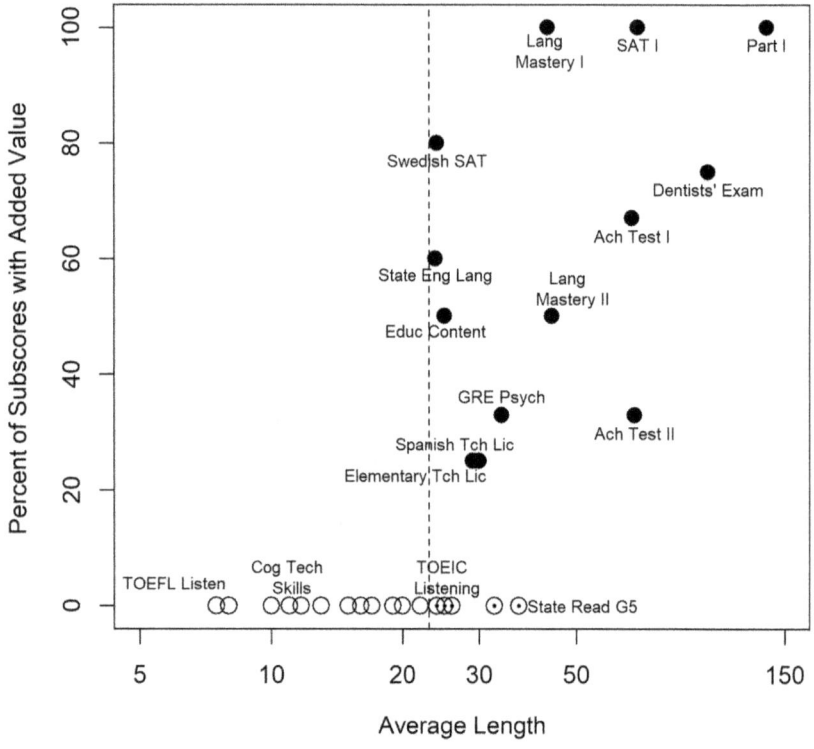

Figure 4.2 Plot showing how average length influenced the percentage of subscores with added value for the 36 data sets that were surveyed. Plotting symbols are empty circles (with or without a dot at the center; a dot at the center of a circle indicates that the average length is larger than 23 for the corresponding test) for the tests that had no value-added subscores, or solid circles for the tests that had one or more value-added subscores.[4]

of the subtests along the X axis on a logarithmic scale but shows the percentage of value-added subscores along the Y axis. The plotting symbols in Figure 4.2 have the same meanings as in Figure 4.1. The pattern formed by the circles

---

[4] The names of some of the tests are shown next to the plotting symbols (Ach Test I & II = test of achievement in a discipline I & II; Cog tech skills = test measuring cognitive and technical skills; Dentists' Exam = examination for dentists; Educ Content = educators' content knowledge; Elementary Tch Lic = LT for teachers in elementary school; GRE Psych = GRE Psychology; Lang Mastery I & II = test of mastery of a language I & II; Paraprof Lic = LT for paraprofessionals; Part I = National Board of Medical Examiners Part I Examination; Spanish Tch Lic = LT for teachers of Spanish; State Eng Lang = state English language proficiency examination; State Read G5 = State Reading (5th Grade); Swedish SAT = Swedish Scholastic Aptitude Test; TOEFL Rdg = TOEFL Primary Reading; TOEIC Listening = TOEIC Listening Comprehension; LT = licensure test).

in the figure is similar to that in Figure 4.1, especially toward the left. That is because the percentage of value-added subscores for a test is zero when the number of value-added subscores for the test is zero – so the points for these tests are plotted in the same coordinates in Figures 4.1 and 4.2. However, the top right corner of Figure 4.2 is more crowded than Figure 4.1 that has only one circle (that corresponding to the National Board of Medical Examiners Part I examination) in the top right quadrant. This result is an outcome of the number of value-added subscores (=7) for the National Board of Medical Examiners Part I examination being considerably larger than that for any other data set (ranging between 0 and 4). The percentage for the examination (=100), however, is matched by the SAT I and the test of mastery of a language I and is only slightly larger than that for Swedish Scholastic Aptitude Test (=80) and the examination for dentists (=75). Figure 4.2 indicates, like Figure 4.1 does, that the subscores are more likely to have added value when the corresponding subtests are longer, and that average subtest length of 24 is the minimum that is required for a test to have any value-added subscores.

4.4 Required Minimum Subscore Reliability: 0.71

Figure 4.3 shows – as does Figure 4.1 – the number of subscores that have added value for the 36 tests along the Y axis, but shows the average reliability of the subscores for the tests (instead of average length) along the X axis. The plotting symbols in Figure 4.3 have the same meanings as in Figure 4.1. A vertical and dashed line at 0.71 in Figure 4.3 indicates that a test had any value-added subscores only when the average reliability was larger than 0.71. The figure shows that once the threshold of 0.71 is crossed, a subscore is more likely to have added value when its reliability is larger. Thus, Figure 4.3 provides strong evidence that average subscore reliability of about 0.71 is the minimum that is required for a test for its subscores to have added value.

You may wonder why there is a need of both (1) a condition based on subtest length and (2) another condition based on subtest reliability, especially given that the Spearman–Brown formula (see Section 3.10 of Chapter 3) probably gives you the impression that subtest length and subtest reliability are perfectly related. However, such a perfect relationship may hold for a set of tests that are similar to each other (except for the length) in nature, but it does not hold for our 36 data sets.

Figure 4.4 shows the average reliabilities of the subscores versus the average subtest lengths for the 36 data sets using plotting symbols as in Figures 4.1

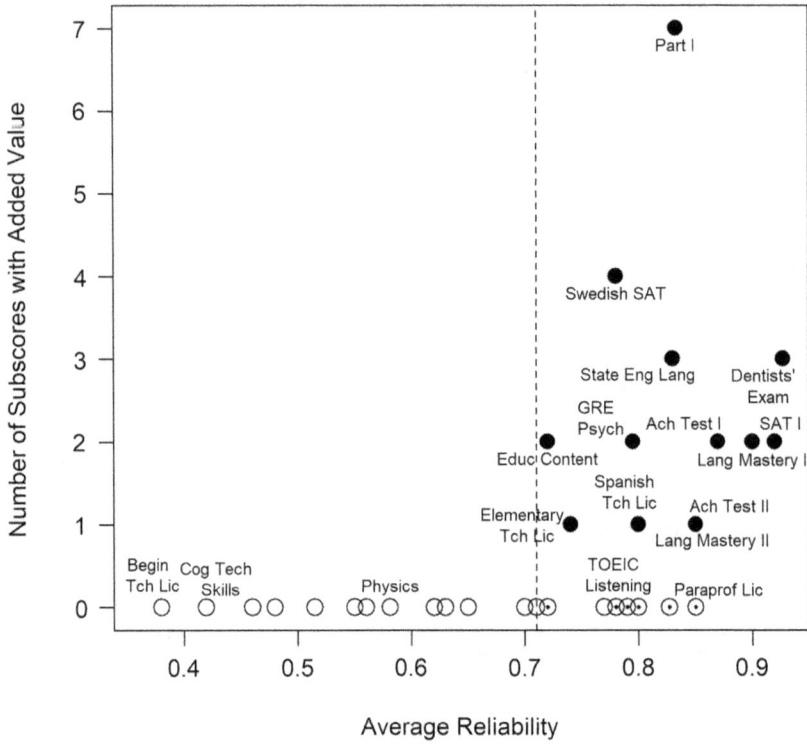

Figure 4.3 Plot showing how average reliability influenced the number of subscores with added value for the 36 data sets that were surveyed. Plotting symbols are empty circles (with or without a dot at the center; a dot at the center of a circle indicates that the average length is larger than 23 for the corresponding test) for the tests that had no value-added subscores, or solid circles for the tests that had one or more value-added subscores.[5]

to 4.3. The X axis in the figure is scaled logarithmically. The figure also shows a dotted line that represents the linear regression of average reliability on the logarithm of average subtest length from the 36 tests. The figure shows that

---

[5] The names of some of the tests are shown next to the plotting symbols (Ach Test I & II = test of achievement in a discipline I & II; Begin Tch Lic = LT for beginning teachers; Cog tech skills = test measuring cognitive and technical skills; Dentists' Exam = examination for dentists; Educ Content = educators' content knowledge; Elementary Tch Lic = LT for teachers in elementary school; GRE Psych = GRE Psychology; Lang Mastery I & II = test of mastery of a language I & II; Paraprof Lic = LT for paraprofessionals; Part I = National Board of Medical Examiners Part I Examination; Physics = large-scale physics test; Spanish Tch Lic = LT for teachers of Spanish; State Eng Lang = state English language proficiency examination; Swedish SAT = Swedish Scholastic Aptitude Test; TOEIC Listening = TOEIC Listening Comprehension; LT = licensure test).

4.4 Required Minimum Subscore Reliability

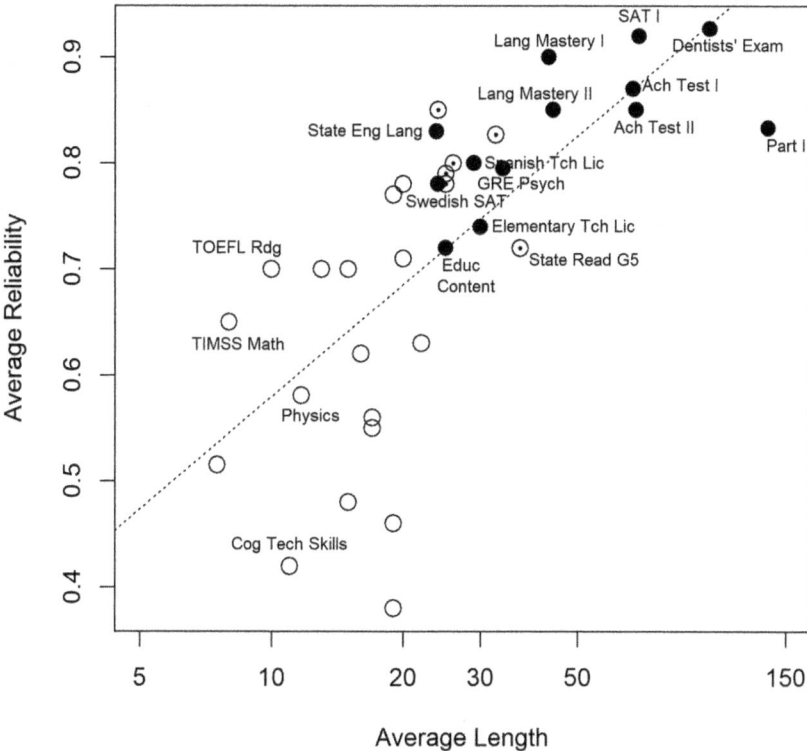

Figure 4.4 Plot showing how average subtest length influenced the average subscore reliability for the 36 data sets that were surveyed. Plotting symbols are empty circles (with or without a dot at the center; a dot at the center of a circle indicates that the average length is larger than 23 for the corresponding test) for the tests that had no value-added subscores, or solid circles for the tests that had one or more value-added subscores.[6]

the relationship between average subtest length and average subtest reliability is not perfectly linear – the simple correlation coefficient between the two variables is only 0.57.

---

[6] The names of some of the tests are shown next to the plotting symbols (Ach Test I & II = test of achievement in a discipline I & II; Cog tech skills = test measuring cognitive and technical skills; Dentists' Exam = examination for dentists; Educ Content = educators' content knowledge; Elementary Tch Lic = LT for teachers in elementary school; GRE Psych = GRE Psychology; Lang Mastery I & II = test of mastery of a language I & II; Paraprof Lic = LT for paraprofessionals; Part I = National Board of Medical Examiners Part I Examination; Physics = large-scale physics test; Spanish Tch Lic = LT for teachers of Spanish; State Eng Lang = state English language proficiency examination; State Read G5 = State Reading (5th Grade); Swedish SAT = Swedish Scholastic Aptitude Test; TIMSS Math = TIMSS eighth-grade mathematics; TOEFL Rdg = TOEFL Primary Reading).

4.5 Required Maximum Disattenuated Correlation: 0.91

Figure 4.5 is similar to Figure 4.1 and shows the number of value-added subscores along the Y axis but shows the average disattenuated correlation among the subscores – instead of average length – along the X axis, where the disattenuated

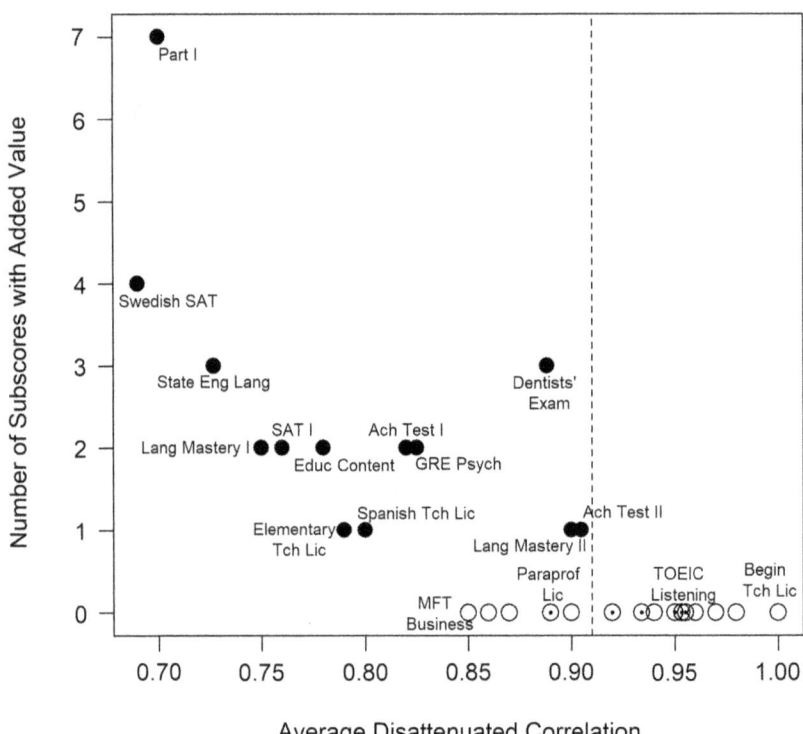

Figure 4.5 Plot showing how average disattenuated correlation affects the number of subscores with added value for the 36 data sets. Plotting symbols are empty circles (with or without a dot at the center; a dot at the center of a circle indicates that the average length is larger than 23 for the corresponding test) for the tests that had no value-added subscores, or solid circles for the tests that had one or more value-added subscores.[7]

---

[7] The names of some of the tests are shown next to the plotting symbols (Ach Test I & II = test of achievement in a discipline I & II; Begin Tch Lic = LT for beginning teachers; Cog tech skills = test measuring cognitive and technical skills; Dentists' Exam = examination for dentists; Educ Content = educators' content knowledge; Elementary Tch Lic = LT for teachers in elementary school; GRE Psych = GRE Psychology; Lang Mastery I & II = test of mastery of a language I & II; Paraprof Lic = LT for paraprofessionals; Part I = National Board of Medical Examiners Part I Examination; Spanish Tch Lic = LT for teachers of Spanish; State Eng Lang = state English language proficiency examination; Swedish SAT = Swedish Scholastic Aptitude Test; TOEIC Listening = TOEIC Listening Comprehension; LT = licensure test).

correlation between two subscores is the ratio of the simple (Pearson productmoment) correlation between the subscores divided by the product of the square roots of the reliabilities of the subscores. The disattenuated correlation between two subscores is essentially the correlation between them after correcting for their unreliability (e.g., Lord & Novick, 1968, p. 137). The plotting symbols in this figure have the same meaning as in Figures 4.1 to 4.4. A vertical and dashed line at 0.91 in Figure 4.5 indicates that a test had any value-added subscores only when the average disattenuated correlation was smaller than 0.91. The figure also shows that once the threshold of 0.91 is crossed, a subscore is more likely to have added value when its disattenuated correlation is smaller. The figure indicates that the aforementioned six tests (the six circles, with dots at their centers, for these tests lie in the bottom right part of the figure) did not have any subscore with added value in spite of having average subtest length of 24 or more, primarily because their average disattenuated correlation was large (0.90 or larger). So the subscores on these six tests were reliable but not distinct enough for the PRMSE-based method to designate them as those with added value. Interestingly, five of these six tests were language or reading tests and include the SAT I Verbal test, Preliminary ACT English (Harris & Hanson, 1991), a state reading test, and the TOEIC Listening Comprehension test.

4.6 Importance of Satisfying Both the Reliability and Correlation Requirements

Figure 4.6 shows how average lengths of the subtests and the disattenuated correlations among the subscores jointly influence the added value of subscores. In the figure, the X axis corresponds to the average length of the subscores, and the Y axis corresponds to the average disattenuated correlation among the subscores. The X axis is scaled logarithmically. The figure includes, for each test, a circle (either empty, empty with a dot at its center, or partially filled) at the point (x, y), where x is the average length of the subtests and y is 100 times the average disattenuated correlation for the test. As an example, the subscores for the dentists' examination discussed in Haladyna and Kramer (2004) comprise 100 items on average, and the average disattenuated correlation among the subscores is 0.89. Hence, Figure 4.5 includes a (partially filled) circle at the point (100, 89). As in Figures 4.1 to 4.4, for each test that has no value-added subscore, the plotting symbol is an empty circle if the average subtest length for the test is up to 23 and is an empty circle with a dot at its center if the average subtest length is 24 or larger. The circles corresponding to the tests that have at least one value-added subscore are partially filled; the percentage filled

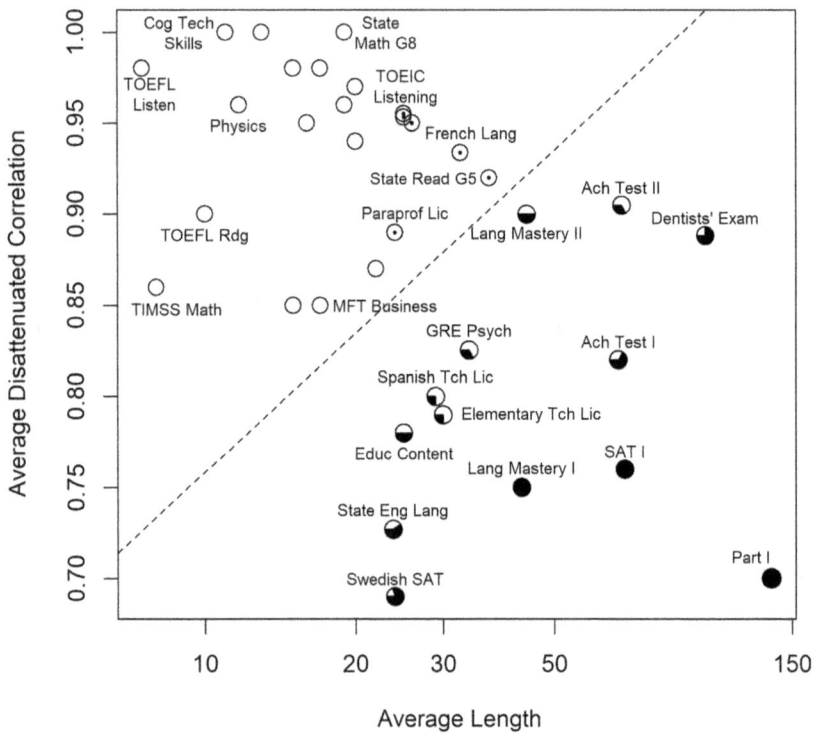

Figure 4.6 Plot showing how length and distinctness (expressed as disattenuated correlations) of subscores jointly affect their likelihood of having added value for the 36 data sets. Plotting symbols are empty circles (with or without a dot at the center; a dot at the center of a circle indicates that the average length is larger than 23 for the corresponding test) for the tests that had no value-added subscores, or partially filled circles for the tests that had one or more value-added subscores.[8]

---

[8] The names of some of the tests are shown next to the plotting symbols (Ach Test I & II = test of achievement in a discipline I & II; Begin Tch Lic = LT for beginning teachers; Cog tech skills = test measuring cognitive and technical skills; Dentists' Exam = examination for dentists; Educ Content = educators' content knowledge; Elementary Tch Lic = LT for teachers in elementary school; French Lang = a large-scale French language test; GRE Psych = GRE Psychology; Lang Mastery I & II = test of mastery of a language I & II; Paraprof Lic = LT for paraprofessionals; Part I = National Board of Medical Examiners Part I Examination; Physics = large-scale physics test; Spanish Tch Lic = LT for teachers of Spanish; State Eng Lang = state English language proficiency examination; State Math G8 = Delaware State Math (8th Grade); State Read G5 = State Reading (5th Grade); Swedish SAT = Swedish Scholastic Aptitude Test; TIMSS Math = TIMSS eighth-grade mathematics; TOEFL Listen = TOEFL Primary Listening; TOEFL Rdg = TOEFL Primary Reading; TOEIC Listening = TOEIC Listening Comprehension; LT = licensure test).

4.6 Importance of Reliability and Correlation Requirements 101

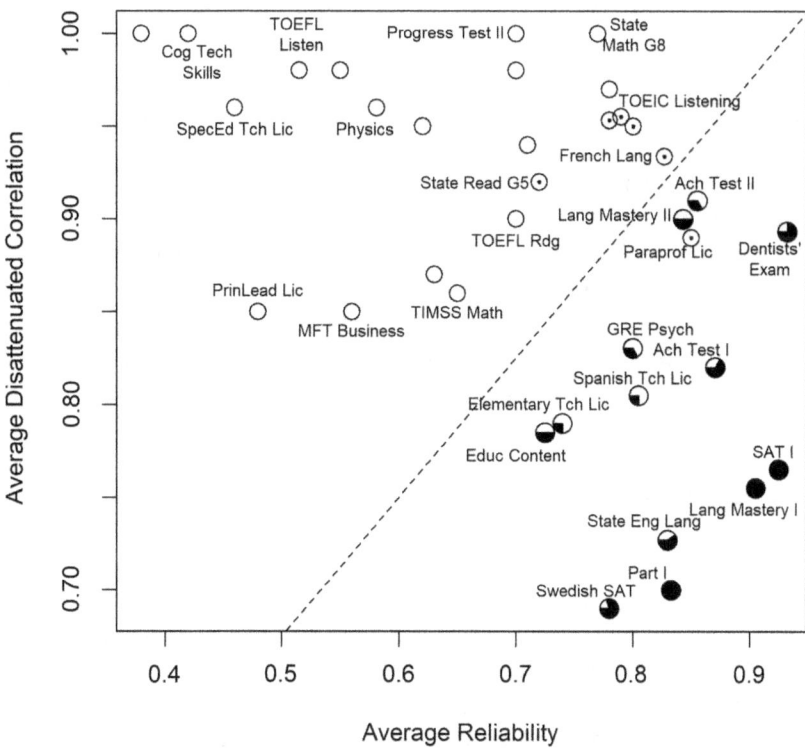

Figure 4.7 Plot showing how reliability and distinctness (expressed as disattenuated correlations) of subscores jointly affect their likelihood of having added value. Plotting symbols are empty circles (with or without a dot at the center; a dot at the center of a circle indicates that the average length is larger than 23 for the corresponding test) for the tests that had no value-added subscores, or partially filled circles for the tests that had one or more value-added subscores.[9]

---

[9] The names of some of the tests are shown next to the plotting symbols (Ach Test I & II = test of achievement in a discipline I & II; Begin Tch Lic = LT for beginning teachers; Cog tech skills = test measuring cognitive and technical skills; Dentists' Exam = examination for dentists; Educ Content = educators' content knowledge; Elementary Tch Lic = LT for teachers in elementary school; French Lang = a large-scale French language test; GRE Psych = GRE Psychology; Lang Mastery I & II = test of mastery of a language I & II; Paraprof Lic = LT for paraprofessionals; Part I = National Board of Medical Examiners Part I Examination; Physics = large-scale physics test; PrinLead Tch Lic = LT for principals and school leaders; Progress Test II = test of school and individual student progress II; Spanish Tch Lic = LT for teachers of Spanish; SpecEd Tch Lic = LT for teachers of special education programs; State Eng Lang = state English language proficiency examination; State Read G5 = State Reading (5th Grade); Swedish SAT = Swedish Scholastic Aptitude Test; TIMSS Math = TIMSS eighth-grade mathematics; TOEFL Listen = TOEFL Primary Listening; TOEFL Rdg = TOEFL Primary Reading; TOEIC Listening = TOEIC Listening Comprehension; LT = licensure test).

is equal to the percentage of subscores that have added value for the test. For the dentists' examination (Haladyna & Kramer, 2004), the circle is 75% filled because three out of four subscores (or 75% of the subscores) have added value for the test. Figure 4.6 also includes a bold dotted line roughly dividing the plot into two regions in which the percentages of value-added subscores are zero or nonzero. This line is not unique and was drawn after a visual examination of the points in the plot, not using any mathematical formula.

Figure 4.7 is similar to Figure 4.6 but shows average subscore reliability instead of average subscore length along the X axis.

In Figures 4.6 and 4.7, as one goes from the top left corner to the bottom right corner (i.e., as the average length or average reliability increases and the average disattenuated correlation decreases), the subscores show an increasing tendency to have added value. The subscores that have added value satisfy minimum average subtest length (of 24) and reliability (0.71) and maximum correlation (0.91) conditions. More importantly, Figures 4.6 and 4.7 also show that once the minimum and maximum conditions are satisfied, the percent of subscores with added value is determined by the interaction between subtest length and disattenuated correlation; in other words, for a given value of average subtest length or average subscore reliability, the percentage of subscores that have added value depends on the correlations among the subscores. The smaller the correlation (or the more unique/distinct are the subscores), the greater is the percentage of the subscores that have added value.

Figures 4.6 and 4.7 promise to be valuable tools to test practitioners, especially for tests that do not have any value-added subscores, because they show what the subscores lack – reliability or distinctness or both – that causes them to not have added value. Also, the distance of a circle from the dashed lines in these figures provides guidance regarding how far the subscores are from having added value. If a circle is close and to the left of the dashed line, then this would imply that if the corresponding test is revised to a slightly longer test, then the subtests would involve a larger number of items and the circle for the revised test would possibly fall below to the right of the dashed line, and, consequently, the subscores on the revised test would most likely have added value. On the other hand, if a circle for a test is far to the left of the dashed line, the test length has to be increased substantially for the subscores on the revised test to have added value.[10]

---

[10] These results are predicated on the fact that if a test is made longer (while ensuring that the subtests measure the same skills as the original test), then the disattenuated correlations among the subscores for the revised test would be close to those for the original test (both of these two sets of correlations would be close to the correlations among the underlying true scores or true examinee abilities).

4.7 Prediction of the Chance of a Subscore Adding Value

The increasing tendency of subscores to have added value as one goes from the top left to the bottom right of Figures 4.6 and 4.7 indicates that it is possible to go one step further and fit a statistical model to predict the chance of a subscore having added value from average subtest length/reliability and average disattenuated correlation. Consequently, we fitted a logistic regression model to the data shown in Table 4.2 to predict the probability of a subscore having added value from average test length and average disattenuated correlation. We fitted another logistic regression model to the same data to predict the probability of a subscore having added value from

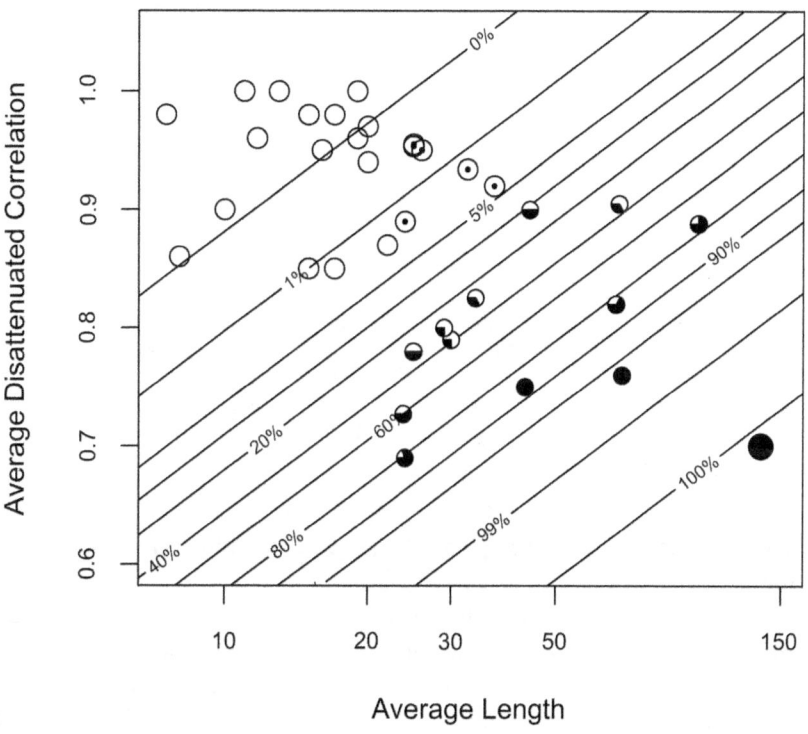

Figure 4.8 Contour lines showing the approximate chance of subscores having added value for various combinations of test length and disattenuated correlations. Superimposed are 36 circles that correspond to the 36 data sets. as in the previous figure, circles are empty for the tests that had no value-added subscores or partially filled for the tests that had one or more value-added subscores.

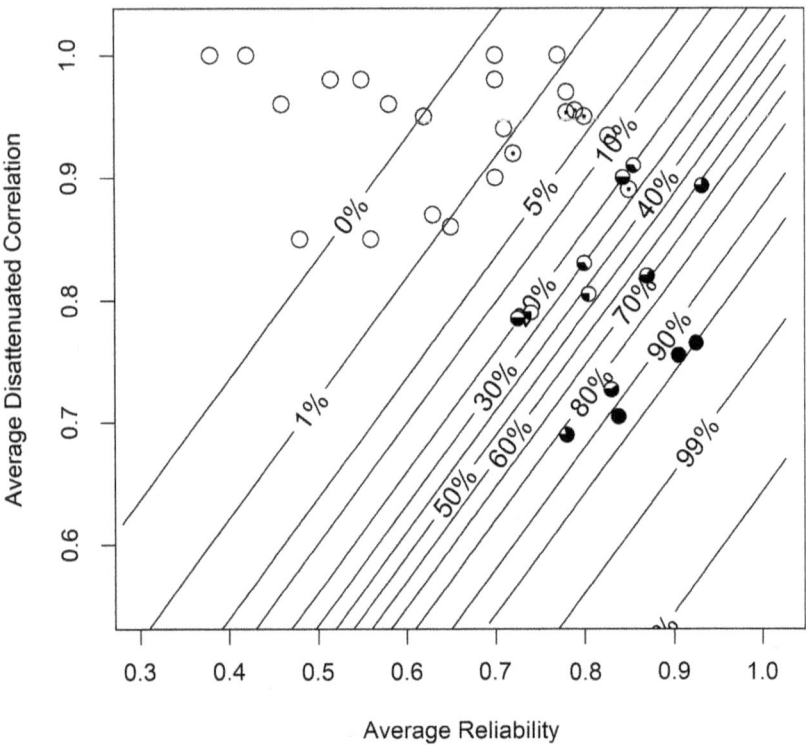

Figure 4.9 Contour lines showing the approximate chance of subscores having added value for various combinations of average subscore reliability and average disattenuated correlations. Superimposed are 36 circles that correspond to the 36 data sets. As in the previous three figures, circles are empty for the tests that had no value-added subscores or partially filled for the tests that had one or more value-added subscores.

average reliability and average disattenuated correlation. The models were found to fit the data satisfactorily.[11]

Figures 4.8 and 4.9 show the *contour lines* (e.g., Paolino, 2020) or *isarithms* (e.g., Bertin, 1983, p. 385) that are lines along which the predicted percentage of subscores with added value is constant (and is equal to one of 0, 1, 5, 10, 20, ..., 90, 95, 99, and 100 after rounding to the nearest integer).

---

[11] McFadden's pseudo R^2 (McFadden, 1974; Theil, 1970), like the PRMSE measures discussed in Chapter 3, is a one-number summary of the quality of prediction of a logistic regression model, lies between 0 and 1, is close to 1 when the model fits the data well, and performed quite accurately in a comparison study in Menard (2000). The values of McFadden pseudo R^2 were 0.81 and 0.76 for the two logistic regressions that we performed.

The X axes of the two figures correspond to the average subtest length and average reliability of the subscores, respectively, whereas the Y axes of both figures correspond to the average disattenuated correlation among the subscores. The X axis is scaled logarithmically for Figure 4.8. The percentages, which were computed from the aforementioned logistic regression model, are printed along the contour lines. As an example, the line toward the bottom right of Figure 4.8 with *100%* written along it indicates that for all combinations of average subtest length and average disattenuated correlation along the line, the predicted probability of the subscores to have added value is 100%. Thus, you would expect all subscores to have added value for a test with average subtest length = 50 and average correlation = 0.6 as well as for a test with average subtest length = 150 and average correlation = 0.7. The circles corresponding to the 36 tests are also shown in Figures 4.8 and 4.9. To avoid congestion, the test names are not shown in Figures 4.8 and 4.9.[12] We believe that these two figures may help test publishers to build new test forms by allowing them to estimate the chance of the subscores on a new test having added value, as long as they have a rough idea of the subtest lengths and the disattenuated correlations among the subscores.

Figure 4.4 may be helpful to practitioners who have some idea of their subtest lengths and simple correlations among subscores and want to utilize Figure 4.8 or 4.9 but have no clear idea about the reliabilities or disattenuated correlations for the subscores – Figure 4.4 would allow them to estimate the subscore reliabilities that, in turn, would allow them to estimate the disattenuated correlations[13] and consequently to use Figure 4.8 or 4.9.

4.8 Uniqueness of the Value-Added Subscores

A quick look at the top few rows of Table 4.1 – these rows correspond to the tests that involve the largest number of value-added subscores in our survey – reveals that they correspond to tests of a wide variety, including the National Board of Medical Examiners Part I Examination, the Swedish Scholastic Aptitude Test, a state English language proficiency test, two tests of mastery of languages, two tests of achievement in a discipline, the SAT I test, an educators' content knowledge test, and two other licensure tests. Thus, our survey

---

[12] However, one can easily figure out the test names using Table 4.2 or Figures 4.6 and 4.7 because Figure 4.9 is essentially Figure 4.7 with the contour lines added, and Figure 4.8 is essentially Figure 4.6 with the contour lines added.

[13] As the disattenuated correlation is the ratio of the corresponding simple correlation and the product of the square roots of the reliabilities.

results may be frustrating to those who expect certain types of tests to be more likely to involve value-added subscores.

Subscores typically cannot have any added value unless that value was built in by the test developers originally. Intuitively, one would expect the subscores to have added value for a test that was built to capture multiple skills or was built to be multidimensional. In a listing of sources of validity evidence for supporting a subscore interpretation or use provided by Haladyna and Kramer (2004), a major source is construct definition. At the beginning of the test development process, a test developer should assert how the content of the test was constructed to purposely yield either a unidimensional or multidimensional structure. If a test developer claims that the content is intended to be multidimensional and/or thought that subdomains are useful instructional targets for training and provides empirical evidence to support those claims, only then are the subscores originating from the test likely to have added value. Haladyna and Kramer (2004) also emphasized the importance of defining the construct and linking the definition to the test via a survey of the profession referred to as *practice analysis* or *job analysis*. When a practice analysis is created and conducted, the content domain and its subdomains are identified (Raymond, 2001), and test specifications that identify these subdomains are created. Item development is also based on these subdomains. The identification of content subdomains, the practice analysis, the test specifications, and the design of the test all speak to the idea that the test is multidimensional because you have well-defined categories of content subdomains. Test development activities proceed with the idea that each item reflects one of these different subdomain content categories. The abovementioned types of validity evidence are referred to as logical and procedural evidence.

Now, turning to Part I of the examination for dentists that was considered by Haladyna and Kramer (2004), the test developers intended the test to measure four subdomains of basic biomedical science, and, consequently, the test consisted of four content domains as determined from the practice analysis, the item development effort, the test specifications, and the test design. Similarly, as described in Swanson et al. (1991) and Margolis, Clauser, Winward, and Dillon (2010), extensive logical and procedural evidence exists in favor of the multidimensional nature of the National Board of Medical Examiners Part I test considered in Feinberg and Jurich (2017). Therefore, it is not a surprise that all but one of the subscores combined over the two tests had added value.

On the other hand, information on logical and procedural evidence in favor of the subscores is unavailable for the other tests considered in our survey. In addition, experts such as Brennan (2012) noted that the subscores are often an afterthought in the sense that the test developers did not originally plan for them and, consequently, the specifications for test development do not control for subscores nearly as well as for the total score. Therefore, the occurrence of the several tests in Table 4.1 with exactly 0 subscores with added value should have been expected.

4.9 Reading Tests Rarely Have Value-Added Subscores

The locations of the circles with dots at their centers in Figures 4.1 to 4.9 indicate that it is notoriously difficult to have value-added subscores for tests that measure essentially only one language skill (like reading only or listening only). These circles correspond to tests for which the average subtest length (and hence average reliability) was quite respectable, and yet, the subscores did not have added value, primarily because of high correlations among the subscores. Note that other researchers have also found language tests to essentially measure one language skill; von Davier (2008) found a unidimensional item response theory model to fit the data from each of the Reading and Listening sections of the TOEFLi BT adequately, and Wilson (2000) used factor analysis to find the TOEIC listening comprehension test essentially measures one overall skill.

4.10 Discussion

In this chapter, we analyzed 36 operational data sets, with the goal of finding the factors that may lead to the added value of subscores. The review and analysis lead to the finding that it is rare to find subscores that have added value. The results from the survey support the claim of Wainer and Feinberg (2017) that most operationally reported subscores are "substandard," that is, they do not satisfy professional standards in the sense that they are either not reliable enough or are not distinct from each other or both. There are exceptions such as the National Board of Medical Examiners Part I examination (Swanson et al., 1991) and the examination for dentists (Haladyna & Kramer, 2004), which involved subscores that were based on a large number of items and also were sufficiently distinct from each other. The content covered by subscores from these tests was supported by logical and procedural evidence (such as that collected from a practice analysis) in favor of the multidimensionality of the subscores. Roughly speaking, the subscores have to comprise at least 20 items and have to have disattenuated correlation of at most 0.9 with each other to have any hope of having added value. From our experience, several practitioners believe that subscores consisting of a few items may have added value if they are sufficiently distinct from each other. However, Figure 4.6 provides evidence that is contrary to that belief, at least for the types of data set that you will typically encounter. The average disattenuated correlation between two tests (MFT business and licensure test for principals and school leaders) was 0.85, yet neither of the two tests had any value-added subscores. Further, Sinharay (2010) found from a detailed simulation study that subscores comprising 10 items were not of any added value even for a realistically extreme (low) disattenuated correlation of 0.7.

It should be noted that the results of the survey performed in this chapter apply only to tests with mostly dichotomous or short constructed-response items. Specifically, results for long constructed-response items may be entirely different. Sawaki and Sinharay (2018) found the TOEFL Speaking section score to have added value even though the score is based on only six constructed-response items,[14] each of which is scored as an integer between 0 and 4. All 36 tests that we considered had nonoverlapping subscores; in other words, no item contributed to more than one subscore in any of these tests. Thus, the results from this chapter apply only to tests that involve nonoverlapping subscores, and one would have to use other methods to evaluate the quality of overlapping subscores. The correlation between any two overlapping subscores would be large (because of some items contributing to both of them) – so they would be more likely (than nonoverlapping subscores) to not satisfy professional quality standards.

The method based on PRMSE and value-added ratio that we endorse only indicates whether subscores have the potential to add value. While we found out that the value-added ratio is larger than 1 for the subscores from the aforementioned examination for dentists (Haladyna & Kramer, 2004), they truly add value only if score users were able to make decisions that improved instruction and remediation for the examinees. If not, then the subscores are not satisfying the purpose for which they are being reported in spite of having added value. Unfortunately, there is a severe lack of demonstration of utility of value-added subscores for instructional and remedial benefits to examinees. Therefore, we recommend that test publishers perform validity studies where those with low scores on a specific subtest may be offered targeted remedial lessons on that subarea and the results on a subsequent test compared to that of a control group who are given more general lessons (possibly covering the whole test). The

---

[14] Currently, the section includes four items, each scored on a 0 to 4 scale and yet, the reliability is around 0.85 (e.g., ETS, 2020).

practical value of the specific subscore would thus be confirmed if the group who received lessons on the subarea improved more than the control group.

A more thorough analysis would involve the study of how various psychometric characteristics of the subscores influence the extent to which they are valid for certain purposes. However, while the issue of the validity of subscores has been examined by Davison, Davenport, Chang, Vue, and Su (2015); Haberman (2008b); and Haladyna and Kramer (2004), validity evidence is unavailable for the tests that were surveyed in this chapter. Therefore, we could only examine the influence of various characteristics of the subscores on their added value, which, as argued in Chapter 3, is a necessary condition for their validity for their intended purposes.

5

What to Do When Subscores Do Not Have Added Value

Augmentation, No Subscore Reporting, and Some Other Options

> Few wish to assess others.
> Fewer still wish to be assessed.
> But everyone wants to see the scores.
> *Paul W. Holland (2001)*

It has been more than 20 years since our illustrious colleague, Paul Holland, made the above observation. Given the ever-increasing demand for more information from educational and psychological tests (Huff & Goodman, 2007), we can safely make the broader claim that everyone wants to see the subscores too. For example, Pub.L. 114-95 § 1005, which amends the Every Student Succeeds Act (Every Student Succeeds Act, 2015) imposes the challenging requirement that state tests should produce interpretive, descriptive, and diagnostic reports regarding achievement of individual students on such assessments. States address the requirement through the reporting of subscores for multiple subdomains such as the number system, geometry, and algebraic reasoning in mathematics, and the US Department of Education has signed off on this approach for more than 20 years.

However, as we learned in Chapters 3 and 4, subscores often do not satisfy professional standards and do not provide added empirical evidentiary value. The survey in Chapter 4 revealed that no subscore had added value (and thus did not satisfy professional standards regarding reliability and distinctness) for 23 out of the 36 tests that we surveyed. Consequently, measurement researchers and practitioners often face the question "When subscores do not satisfy professional standards and hence cannot, in good conscience, be provided, what alternative options are ethically and scientifically available regarding the reporting of information in addition to the total score?" We discuss some such alternative options in this chapter.

We assume that test publishers want to satisfy ethical standards in any decision they make on the reporting of any information based on the test. One option with subscores of poor psychometric quality involves turning a blind eye to the results from the value-added analysis (or not performing such an analysis at all) and reporting them anyway; however, such a course of action is unethical and can never be recommended.

In the remainder of the chapter, we first describe our recommended strategy regarding the steps that can be taken when subscores do not have added value. The strategy involves several approaches – these approaches are described and demonstrated using a data set in Sections 5.2 to 5.9.

5.1 Our Recommended Strategy

We recommend, based on our long experience of working with subscores and with those who are interested in subscores, that when subscores do not have added value, you should consider augmented subscores as the first alternative and proceed to examine the quality of these subscores. If you find that the augmented subscores have added value, that is, their PRMSEs are substantial improvements over $PRMSE_{sub}$ and $PRMSE_{tot}$,[1] then by all means, go ahead and report them.[2]

If neither the subscores nor the augmented subscores have added value for a test, our preference is not to report any subscore or diagnostic score and instead perform a scale anchoring or item-mapping study and perhaps consider a quality check using the outlier approach described by Haberman (2008c). Test publishers should also consider redesigning the test in such a case if they want to report some type of subscores.

Test publishers may face a situation in which some type of diagnostic scores are mandated for a test (e.g., when confronted by unremitting legal requirements such as the Every Student Succeeds Act) for which neither the subscores nor the augmented subscores have added value. In such a situation, we believe that the use of augmented subscores provides a relatively harmless way of conforming to the requirements of the situation while at the same time avoiding the potential damage caused by suggesting examinee deficiencies when there is little or no supporting evidence. Reporting augmented subscores for such a test is very much like reporting the total score multiple times, albeit under the

---

[1] Where $PRMSE_{sub}$ and $PRMSE_{tot}$ were defined in Chapter 3.
[2] A further rigorous step would be to establish evidence of the validity of the augmented subscores (see Chapter 3 for a discussion on validity of subscores) before reporting them.

112   *What to Do When Subscores Do Not Have Added Value*

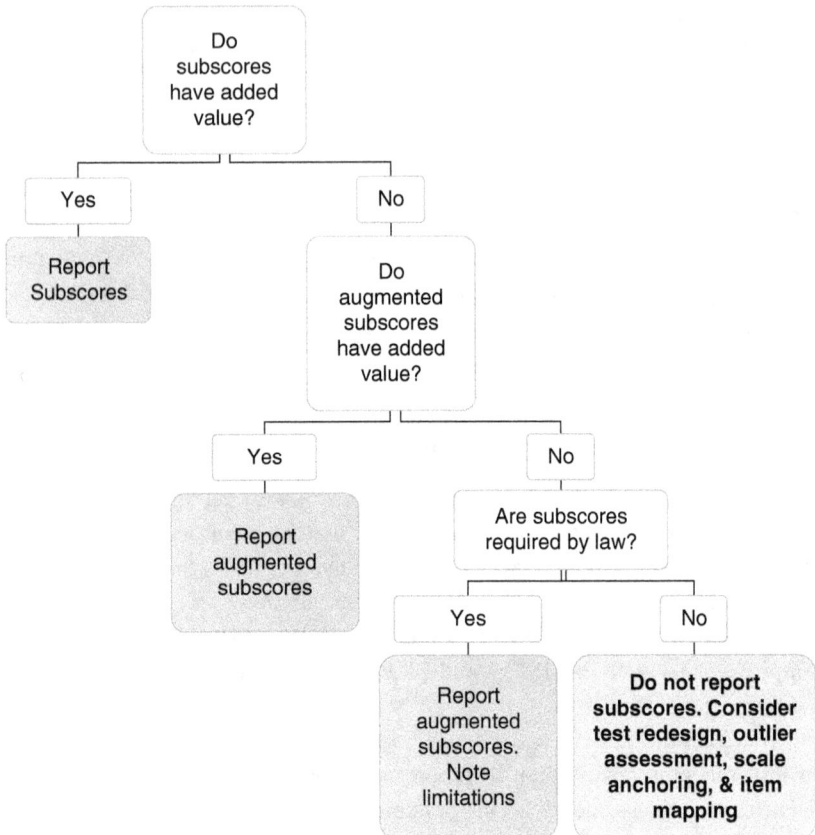

Figure 5.1 A flow chart showing our recommend strategy for the case when subscores do not have added value.

names of subscores; this is a reasonable strategy because the lack of any added value of the subscores for the test indicates that the total score is a better predictor than the actual subscore of the underlying true subscore.[3] If, however, the PRMSEs of the augmented subscores are too small for the purposes of subscore use (that would typically happen if the reliability of the total test score is unsatisfactory), then reporting subscores may cause harm if they generate needless expense by being used for instructional and remedial purposes. In such a case, we strongly recommend a test redesign to improve the reliability of both the total test score and the subscores to satisfactory levels. Figure 5.1 graphically summarizes the aforementioned strategy.

---

[3] Thus, this strategy will lead the score users to take any remedial/instructional decision based, essentially, on the total score.

Table 5.1 *The four subtests and the corresponding mean scores and reliabilities*

Subtest	Mean score	Reliability
Mathematics	19	0.85
Science	17	0.72
Language Arts/Reading	25	0.71
Social Studies	17	0.67

You may have noticed that in making our recommendations, we mentioned several options (like reporting of augmented subscores, no reporting, outliers, etc.) even though we have not provided any details about those options. Consequently, in the following subsections, we discuss some alternatives to subscores that we recommended above and some alternatives that researchers have suggested. To illustrate some of the alternative methods, we will employ a data set that includes item scores of more than 23,000 examinees on one form of the Elementary Education: Content Knowledge test. The test is designed for prospective teachers of children in primary through upper elementary school grades (Educational Testing Service, 2008)[4] and covers the following four subareas: (1) mathematics, (2) science, (3) language arts/reading, and (4) social studies. A subscore is reported for each of the four subareas. The test form that is considered in this chapter contained 30 multiple-choice, dichotomously-scored items for each of the four subareas.

Table 5.1 shows the average subscores, rounded to the nearest integer, where the averages are computed over all the examinees in the data set, and the reliability coefficients (Cronbach's alpha) of the subscores. The subscores have been sorted according to decreasing order of reliability. The table shows that the subscore reliabilities range between 0.85 and 0.67 and that the average language arts/reading subscore is considerably larger than the other three subscores. Table 5.1 also shows the PRMSE for prediction of the true subscore by the total score (denoted $PRMSE_{tot}$) – a comparison of these and the subscore reliabilities indicate that only the mathematics subscore has added value according to the PRMSE-based criterion introduced in Chapter 3.

---

[4] The Elementary Education: Content Knowledge test that is the source of the data set used in this chapter was later replaced by a very similar test that also has the same name but a slightly different composition (Educational Testing Service, 2021). Any results discussed below have implications for the former version of the test and do not have any implications for the current version of the test. Sinharay (2010) and Sinharay, Puhan, and Haberman (2011) analyzed the data set used in this chapter.

5.2 Reporting of Augmented Subscores

Subscores almost always correlate moderately or highly with each other, as can be seen from Table 4.1 and Figure 4.5. Therefore, it is reasonable to assume that each of the science, reading, and social studies subscores of an examinee provides some information about the mathematics subscore of the same examinee on the Elementary Education: Content Knowledge test. Consequently, Wainer et al. (2000) defined an examinee's *augmented subscore* on a particular subscale (e.g., mathematics) as a linear combination of that examinee's scores on the items formally in that subscale as well at that examinee's scores on the remaining subscales (e.g., science, reading).[5] An augmented subscore thus *borrows information* from the other subscores of the same examinee. The subscales that have the strongest correlation with, say, the mathematics subscale have larger weights and have more influence on the augmented mathematics subscore. The augmented subscores can be considered an extension, to the case of multiple scores, of the Kelley estimate (for one score) defined in Equation 3.1.

Haberman (2008a) suggested a special case of the augmented subscore that is a linear combination of the subscore and the total score. This version of the augmented subscore is defined in Equation 3.11 and can be expressed as

$$\text{Augmented Subscore} = \mu_s + a(s - \mu_s) + b(x - \mu_x), \tag{5.1}$$

where a and b are regression coefficients[6] that depend on the reliabilities and standard deviations of the subscore (s) and the total score (x) and the correlations between the subscores, and μ_s and μ_x, respectively, are the mean of the subscore and the total score. It can be mathematically proved that the augmented subscore (either the one defined by Wainer et al., 2000, or the one by Haberman, 2008a) is very close to the actual subscore if the subscore is highly reliable and very close to the average subscore if the subscore is not reliable. The two versions of augmented subscores are very close (in the sense of being correlated above 0.99 in all data sets that we analyzed), and

---

[5] The mathematical formula for the vector of augmented subscores is obtained as the linear regression of the true subscore vector on the actual subscore vector and is given by $\bar{x} + B(x_i - \bar{x})$, where x_i is the actual subscore vector, $\bar{x}$ is the vector of sample means of all subscores, and $B = S^{\text{true}}(S^{\text{obs}})^{-1}$, where S^{obs} is the variance–covariance matrix of the actual subscores and S^{true} is the estimated variance–covariance matrix between the true subscores. The concept of augmented subscore is borrowed from empirical Bayes methods (e.g., Casella, 1985).

[6] Corresponding to the linear regression of the true subscore on the actual subscore and actual total score.

5.2 Reporting of Augmented Subscores

Table 5.2 *Subscores and additional information for Maya*

	Mathematics	Science	Reading	Social studies
Actual Subscore	12	16	19	6
Augmented Subscore	12	13	20	10
Objective				
Performance Index	12	16	19	6
Percentile Rank	12	41	6	0
Subscore Reliability	0.85	0.72	0.71	0.67
$PRMSE_{aug}$	0.87	0.83	0.80	0.79
$PRMSE_{tot}$	0.76	0.79	0.72	0.74
Sample Average	19	17	25	17
Sample SD	5.8	4.5	3.3	4.2
Values of a	0.62	0.30	0.39	0.29
Values of b	0.11	0.15	0.09	0.14
Category				
Performance Indicator	Nonsig	High	Nonsig	Nonsig
Standardized Residual	−0.3	2.0	−0.9	−2.6
Residual-based	Non	Extremely	Non	Extremely
Indicator	Extreme	High	Extreme	Low
DINA Estimate	Non-M	Non-M	Non-M	Non-M

Note: DINA = deterministic-input, noisy and gate; Non-M = nonmaster; Nonsig = nonsignificant; SD = standard deviation; $PRMSE_{Aug}$ = PRMSE for the augmented subscore; $PRMSE_{Tot}$ = PRMSE for prediction from total score.

the term *augmented subscore* will henceforth refer to that of Haberman (and is provided by Equation 5.1).

The first row of numbers in Table 5.2 shows the actual subscores of an examinee on the aforementioned form of the Elementary Education: Content Knowledge test. Let us refer to this examinee as Maya. Maya's total score on the test is 53, which is the sum of her four subscores.[7] For the data set, μ_x is equal to 78.4, and the values of μ_s, a, and b for the four subscores are provided in Table 5.2, which also includes the standard deviations (SD) of the subscores computed from the data set and Maya's percentile ranks for each subscore. Consequently, Equation 5.1 indicates that Maya's augmented social studies subscore is equal to

---

[7] In practice, this total score is converted to a scaled score before reporting, but we will confine our discussion to the total score.

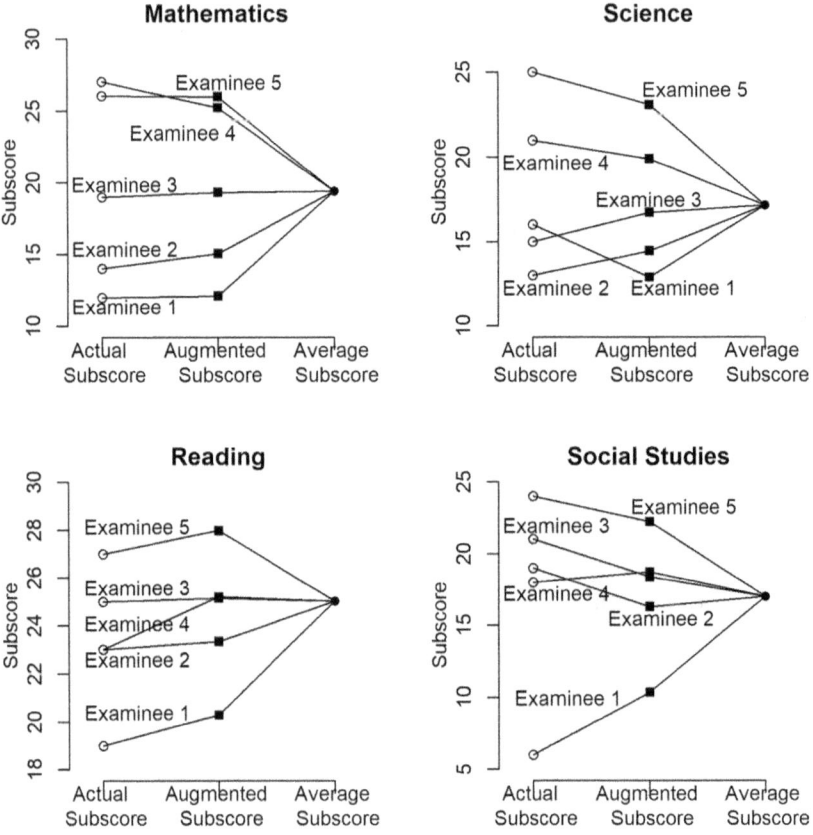

Figure 5.2 The actual and augmented subscores of five examinees and the average subscore for each subtest on the Elementary Education: Content Knowledge Test.

$$17.0 + 0.29(6.0 - 17.0) + 0.14(53.0 - 78.4) = 10.3,$$

which lies between the estimate based on her actual subscore (i.e., the Kelley estimate provided in Equation 3.1 and that has a value of 9.6 for Maya) and the estimate based on her observed total score (provided by Equation 3.5 and that has a value of 11.9 for Maya). The second row of numbers in Table 5.2 provides Maya's augmented subscores on all the subareas (rounded to the nearest integer).

Figure 5.2 demonstrates how the augmented subscores are related to the actual subscores for five examinees for the aforementioned data set from the Elementary Education: Content Knowledge test. The total scores of these five examinees – 53, 69, 80, 89, and 102 – are the 5th, 25th, 50th, 75th, and 95th percentiles of the distribution of the total scores of all the examinees for the data set.

The examinees are henceforth referred to as Examinees 1, 2, 3, 4, and 5, respectively. Note that Maya is Examinee 1. For each subscore, a panel in Figure 5.2 shows the actual subscores (the five hollow circles along a vertical line in the left side of each panel) and the augmented subscores (the five solid squares along a vertical line in the middle of each panel) for the five examinees. Each panel also shows the average of the corresponding subscore (averaged over all examinees in the data set) as a solid circle on the right. A solid line joins the actual subscore and the augmented subscore for each examinee, and another solid line joins the augmented subscore for each examinee and the average subscore. The figure shows that for each subarea, the augmented subscores are less spread out (or closer overall to the average subscore) than are the actual subscores. The augmented subscores are closest to the actual subscores for the mathematics subscore, which has the largest reliability, and the furthest from the actual subscores for the social studies subscore, which has the smallest reliability. Figure 5.2 also shows that whenever an examinee obtained a subscore that is substantially different – in the sense of being unexpectedly small or unexpectedly large – compared to their other subscores, the corresponding augmented subscore differs considerably from the subscore. Examinee 4 performed considerably worse on reading compared to the other subareas, to the extent that the reading subscores of Examinees 4 and 2 (whose percentile ranks based on the total score are 75 and 25, respectively) are the same; consequently, the augmented reading subscore of Examinee 4 is considerably larger than the examinee's actual reading subscore. The figure also shows that the augmented subscores, unlike the actual subscores, order examinees in the same manner as do their total scores. For example, for each subtest, the augmented subscore of Examinee 5 is larger than that of Examinee 4, that of Examinee 4 is larger than that of Examinee 3, and so on. In contrast, the actual subscores often do not order the examinees as do their total scores. The same ordering of augmented subscores and total scores is an outcome of the augmented subscores borrowing information from the total score (see Equation 5.1). The more unidimensional the test, the greater is the similarity of the ordering of augmented subscores and total scores.

Figure 5.3 shows the standardized actual subscores (top panel) and standardized augmented subscores (bottom panel) of Examinees 1 through 5 and thus provides another look at the relationship between the subscores and the augmented subscores. The figure is essentially a *profile plot* (e.g., McDermott, Glutting, Jones, Watkins, & Kush, 1989), or a plot of the subscore profiles, the starting point of *profile analysis*[8] that is popular in the

---

[8] *Profile analysis* is a multivariate data analysis technique for distinguishing the shapes and patterns of scores between groups of test takers (e.g., Stanton & Reynolds, 2000).

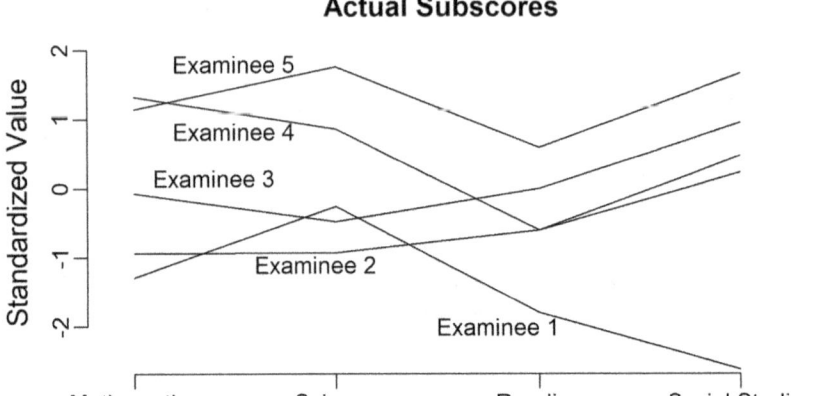

Figure 5.3 The actual and augmented subscores of five examinees on the Elementary Education: Content Knowledge Test.

psychology literature. The top panel of the figure shows that high-scoring examinees (like Examinees 4 and 5) generally obtain high scores, and low-scoring ones generally obtain low scores on all subtests. However, there is a considerable amount of jiggling around – the science subscore of Examinee 1 is larger than that of Examinees 2 and 3, but the social studies subscore of Examinee 1 is much smaller than that of the other four. The bottom panel, which shows the augmented subscore profiles for Examinees 1 through 5, reveals much less jiggling than in the top panel. The profiles in the bottom panel do not cross over at all, in sharp contrast to the multiple cross-overs in

5.2 Reporting of Augmented Subscores

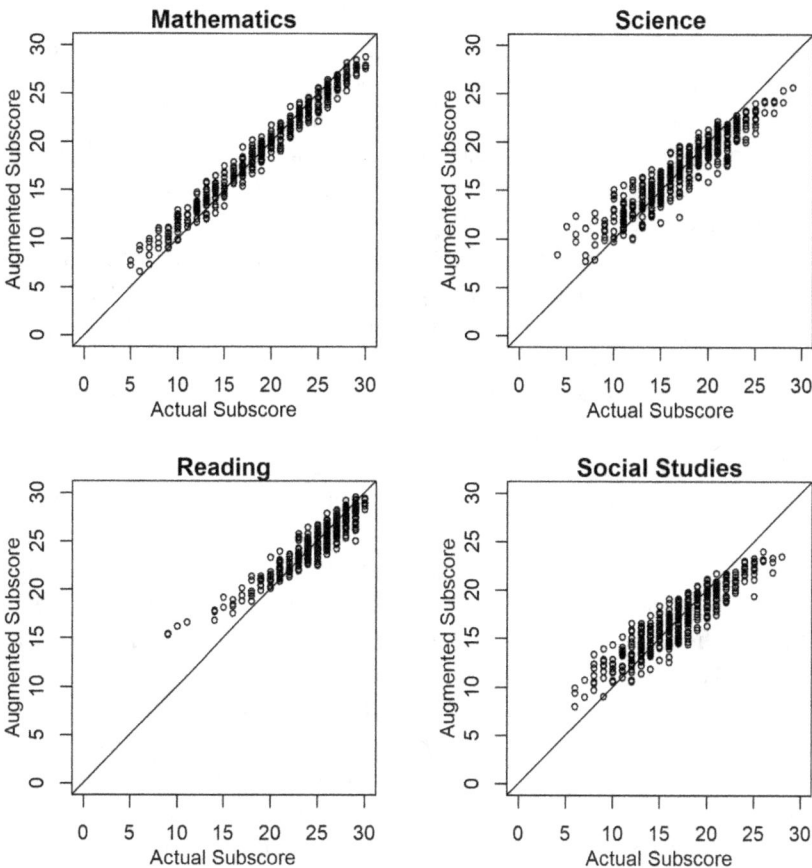

Figure 5.4 Scatter-plots of the actual versus augmented subscores of all examinees for each subtest for the Elementary Education: Content Knowledge Test.

the top panel, which points to the improved stability of the augmented subscores compared to the actual subscores. The extent of jiggling in augmented subscore profiles is typically small for more unidimensional tests, and the augmented subscore profiles of the examinees will be mostly parallel to each other for essentially unidimensional tests.

Figure 5.4 provides scatter-plots of the actual subscores (along the X axis) versus the augmented subscores (Y axis) for all the examinees in the data set for all four subtests. Each hollow circle represents an examinee in each panel of the figure. The ranges of the X and Y axes are the same in each panel. A diagonal line is shown in each panel for convenience. A substantial number of circles above the diagonal in the left side and below the diagonal in the right side of each panel implies that the augmented subscores for low-scoring examinees are not as low and those for high-scoring examinees are not as high as the original subscores, which was also observed in Figure 5.2.

As discussed in Chapter 3, whether augmented subscores have added value over the subscores and the total score can be judged by evaluating if their PRMSE, computed using Equation 3.12 and denoted as $PRMSE_{aug}$, is substantially larger than both $PRMSE_{sub}$ and $PRMSE_{tot}$. For the Elementary Education: Content Knowledge test, $PRMSE_{aug}$ (shown in the fourth row of numbers in Table 5.1) is substantially larger than the other two PRMSEs (also shown in the table) for each subtest. Therefore, the augmented subscores for the data set have added value according to the criterion of Haberman (2008a).

Several researchers (e.g., Edwards & Vevea, 2006; Liu, Robin, Yoo, & Manna, 2018; Puhan et al., 2010; Sinharay, 2010; Skorupski & Carvajal, 2010; Wainer et al., 2000, 2001; also see Chapter 4 of this book) have reported that augmented subscores are substantially more reliable than the actual subscores and often have added value over the actual subscores and the total score. Sinharay, Haberman, and Wainer (2011) showed that augmented subscores predict the corresponding parallel-form subscores better than do the actual subscores. Thissen (2013) commented, citing Haberman and Sinharay (2010), that subscore augmentation is useful in a narrowly defined window, one in which the correlations between the underlying true subscores are between about 0.8 and the low 0.9s. Wang, Svetina, and Dai (2019), in a detailed simulation study on exploring the factors that affect the added value of subscores, found results that support Thissen's conjecture. Haberman and Sinharay (2013) and Sinharay and Haberman (2014) showed that another benefit of augmented subscores is that the function providing the augmented subscore and the added value of augmented subscores is invariant over relevant population subgroups.[9]

Augmented subscores may be difficult to explain to the general public, who may not like the idea that a reported reading subscore is based not only on the observed reading subscore but also on the observed writing subscore (and may find it even more puzzling if it was also based on the observed math score). You may, however, consider several approaches for explaining augmented subscores to their potential users. One is that the augmented subscore better estimates examinee proficiency in the content domain represented by the subscore than does the subscore itself. You can discuss this result in terms

---

[9] Haberman and Sinharay (2013) also recommended against the use of any subgroup membership information to compute augmented subscores because of the potential unfairness of such a practice.

of prediction of performance on an alternative test. You can also discuss the issue in terms of common cases in which information is customarily combined. One such common case is the insurance industry, where premiums for automobile insurance reflect not just the driving experience of the policy holder but also related information (such as education and marital status) that predicts future driving performance. In most cases, the difficulty in explaining the augmented subscores is more than compensated for by their larger PRMSEs (i.e., more precision).

Stone et al. (2010) and Skorupski and Carvajal raised questions about the validity of augmented subscores because they found their intercorrelations to be very close to 1 for a few unidimensional tests. However, Sinharay, Haberman, and Wainer (2011) argued that if a test is unidimensional, then high intercorrelations between augmented subscores do not indicate a problem with the augmented subscores but instead point to a problem with the test or with the investigation that attempts to extract something (distinct subscores or some function of them) that simply does not exist for the test. The correlations are substantially smaller than 1 for nonunidimensional tests. One such test is the Elementary Education: Content Knowledge test, for which the correlation between the augmented mathematics subscore and the other three augmented subscores are between 0.86 and 0.88, while the three correlations among the other three augmented subscores range between 0.90 and 0.94 – these numbers agree with the result (see Table 5.2) that only the mathematics subscore has added value among the four subscores. The *R* package *subscore* (e.g., Dai, Wang, & Svetina, 2019) can be used to compute augmented subscores.

Several experts think that a predecessor of augmented subscores is the objective performance index, which we describe next.

5.3 Objective Performance Index

An approach aimed at enhancing a subscore by borrowing information from other parts of the test, in the same spirit as the augmented subscores, is the use of the *objective performance index* (Yen, 1987). This approach involves the use of a combination of item-response theory and Bayesian methodology. You fit a unidimensional item-response model to the data to compute an estimated subscore of each examinee based on the examinee's overall test performance and then use a χ^2-type statistic to determine if the estimated subscore differs significantly from the actual subscore. You then set the objective performance index equal to the actual subscore or to a weighted average of the actual subscore and the estimated subscore depending on whether the estimated subscore differs significantly (according to the value of the aforementioned χ^2-type statistic) from the actual subscore. An example of an operational score report that includes the objective performance indices of an examinee on the TerraNova test (CTB/McGraw-Hill, 2001) is provided in Figure 19 of Goodman and Hambleton (2004). These indices, because of the use of a unidimensional item-response model in their computation, are accurate estimates of true subscores when the test is truly unidimensional. However, for tests that are not unidimensional, a unidimensional item response model does not fit the data well, and, consequently, the objective performance indices often provide inaccurate estimates of the true subscores (e.g., Dwyer, Boughton, Yao, Steffen, & Lewis, 2006). The R package *subscore* (e.g., Dai, Wang, & Svetina, 2019) can be used to compute objective performance indices.

We computed the objective performance indices for the data from the Elementary Education: Content Knowledge test. For the four subscores, the respective correlations between the augmented subscores and the corresponding objective performance index were 0.94, 0.98, 0.93, and 0.95. The χ^2-type statistic indicated that Maya's estimated subscores do not differ significantly from the actual subscores – so Maya's objective performance indices are equal to her actual subscores. The χ^2-type statistic indicated that the estimated subscores of Examinee 2 considered in Figure 5.2 differ significantly from the actual subscores – the objective performance indices, the actual subscores, and augmented subscores for this examinee are shown in Table 5.3.

Figure 5.5 shows, for each subscore for the data from the Elementary Education: Content Knowledge test, the augmented subscore (along the X axis) versus the objective performance index (Y axis) for all examinees in the data set. The examinees for whom the objective performance indices are equal to the actual subscores (because the χ^2-type statistic indicated that the estimated subscores of the examinee differ significantly from the actual subscores) are represented using vertical lines, and other examinees are represented using horizontal lines. The figure indicates that the objective performance indices closely agree with the augmented subscores (and are pooled toward the mean) when the former are not equal to the actual subscores. However, when the objective performance indices are equal to the actual subscores for an examinee, the augmented subscores are pooled toward the mean subscore and are different from the objective performance indices that are not allowed to be pooled toward the mean by their definition; consequently, the objective performance indices differ substantially from the augmented subscores for these examinees – the vertical lines far from the diagonal lines represent these examinees in the figure.

5.3 Objective Performance Index

Table 5.3 *Subscores, augmented subscores, and objective performance indices of Examinee 2*

	Mathematics	Science	Reading	Social Studies
Actual Subscore	14	13	23	19
Augmented Subscore	15	14	23	16
Objective Performance Index	16	15	24	16

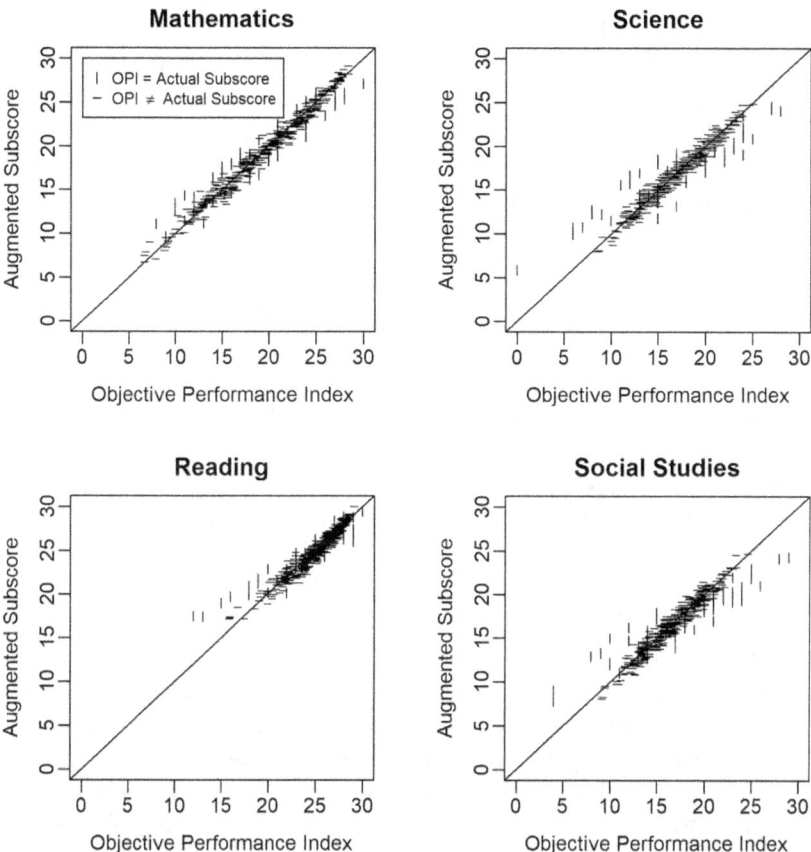

Figure 5.5 Graphical demonstration of how the objective performance indices for each subarea are related to the corresponding augmented subscores for the data from the Elementary Education: Content Knowledge Test.

In Section 5.1 and Figure 5.1, we provide several options for the case when neither the subscores nor the augmented subscores have any added value. Those options are described next.

5.4 No Reporting of Subscores

You can definitely choose not to report any form of subscores for a test for which neither subscores nor augmented subscores have added value. While psychometrically rigorous, this option may be politically impractical for reasons that include the test administrators being contractually obligated to report subscores (possibly because of acts such as the Every Student Succeeds Act). In addition, the test-score users may have legitimate needs for subscores. The National Council of Bar Examiners eliminated subscore reporting on the Multistate Bar Exam in 2014 (Albanese, 2014) but eventually decided to restore some subscore information for failing candidates (Pieper Bar Review, 2017) because of negative responses from the stakeholders. Test administrators may support their choice of not reporting the subscores by demonstrating how the subscores, if reported, may harm – rather than benefit – the test-score users.

5.5 Divert Attention Away from Subscores and Consider Alternatives

Demand for subscores typically originates from score-users' hunger for more information; they hope subscores will provide more information than is available in a single overall score. If subscores do not have added value, it is often sensible to suggest alternative types of additional information instead of reporting the subscore.

One such alternative is item-level feedback. Such feedback, taking the form of disclosed test questions and correct answers, has been found to improve performance and retention (e.g., Pashler, Cepeda, Wixted, & Rohrer, 2005) but may be too costly an option for large-scale assessments. Feinberg and Clauser (2016) discussed providing item-level feedback in the form of *item-level keywords* (or *educational objectives*) that are brief statements indicating the underlying competency of a particular item and that are typically provided to both individual examinees and program directors. As an example, the keyword for an item measuring anatomy knowledge could be *femoral nerve block anatomy*. You can provide such keywords to examinees for each question to which they responded incorrectly or, at the program level, all keywords may be provided along with the percentage who responded correctly. However, as Feinberg and Clauser (2016) found out, there is no guarantee that item-level feedback will be useful to the examinees.

5.5 Divert Attention Away from Subscores

A second alternative is information obtained from *scale anchoring* (e.g., Beaton & Allen, 1992) that involves making claims about what examinees at different score points know and can do. The idea underlying scale anchoring is similar to that for the Degrees of Reading Power test (e.g., Kibby, 1981) that measures students' abilities to process and understand English prose passages written at increasing levels of difficulty or readability, facilitating the determination of the level of reading material that a student can comprehend. Scale anchoring processes typically involve the following four steps:

- Select a few dispersed points (that are referred to as *anchor points*) on the score scale that will be *anchored*.
- Find examinees whose total score is close to each anchor point.
- Examine each item to see if it discriminates between successive anchor points, that is, if most of the examinees at the higher score levels answered the item correctly and most of the examinees at the lower level did not.
- Review the items that are found to discriminate between adjacent anchor points to find out if specific tasks or attributes that they include can be generalized to describe the level of proficiency at the anchor point. The outcome from this review is a description of what examinees at the anchor points know and can do.

A scale anchoring procedure for the aforementioned Elementary Education: Content Knowledge test may lead to statements such as "Those who received scaled scores of 150 can determine how changes to dimensions change area and volume" or "Those who received scaled scores of 180 can make inferences from a text and support them with appropriate evidences."[10]

A third alternative to subscore reporting is *item mapping* (e.g., Zwick, Senturk, Wang, & Loomis, 2001) that involves the use of exemplar items to characterize what examinees at particular score points know and can do. Investigators place (or *map*) an item at a point on the score scale where examinees are RP% likely to give successful responses to it. The value of RP (an acronym for *response percent* or *response probability*) varies between 50 and 80 in practical applications of item mapping. The first few steps in scale anchoring can be considered to constitute an item mapping procedure. In the context of the Elementary Education: Content Knowledge test, an item mapping procedure may lead to statements such as[11]

---

[10] Note that these statements are hypothetical examples and are not based on an actual scale anchoring study.

[11] The statements are hypothetical and are not based on an actual item mapping procedure for the test. The items are taken from the official study companion for the current version of the Elementary Education: Content Knowledge test (Educational Testing Service, 2021).

An item that characterizes test takers with a scaled score of 140 so that test takers with a scaled score of 140 are at least 50% likely to answer the item is:

How many phonemes are in the word "ball"?

(A) 1
(B) 2
(C) 3
(D) 4

and

An item that characterizes test takers with a scaled score of 180 so that test takers with scaled score of 180 are at least 50% likely to answer the item is:

Which of the following is an example of the commutative property of addition?

(A) $5 \times 3 = 3 \times 5$
(B) $(1+7) + 4 = 1 + (7+4)$
(C) $6 \times (4+2) = (6 \times 4) + (6 \times 2)$
(D) $8 + 9 = 9 + 8$

Large-scale assessments such as the National Assessment of Educational Progress and the National Adult Literacy Survey (e.g., Kolstad et al., 1998) have employed scale anchoring and item mapping procedures, which are closely related to standard setting procedures (e.g., Zieky, Perie, & Livingston, 2008) that are widely used in large-scale assessments. However, neither scale anchoring nor item mapping provides any information about the examinees' performance on the subtests and thus may disappoint score users who demand such information.

5.6 Reporting of Outliers or Conditional Subscores

Haberman (2008c) suggested a procedure to investigate if an examinee's subscore is an outlier, that is, is much larger or smaller than expected given the other subscores. The procedure is based on a linear regression of a subscore on the other subscores. A subscore for an examinee is considered an outlier if the corresponding standardized residuals or externally studentized residuals from the linear regression (e.g., Draper & Smith, 1998, pp. 207–208) are too large or too small. Haberman recommended that test administrators use these outliers for quality assurance and possibly request a hand examination of the original answer sheet, an image of the answer sheet, or a full list of responses stored in a database for the examinees with outlying subscores to detect possible scanning errors, accidental omission of all or part of a section, or errors

5.6 Reporting of Outliers or Conditional Subscores

in gridding. Consider an examinee who omitted an entire section by accident or marked the answers for an entire section in the wrong column of the answer sheet. If this particular section is mostly associated with one specific subscore, the examinee would receive an unexpectedly small subscore (leading to a statistically significant and negative externally studentized residual) on this particular subarea and may benefit if the test administrator notifies them of the mistake.

Feinberg and von Davier (2020) recommended for tests for which subscores do not have added value the reporting of *category performance indicators* depending on whether an examinee's subscores are significantly larger or smaller compared to their overall performance on the test. The steps in the computation of category performance indicators are:

- Fit the Rasch model (e.g., Rasch, 1966) to the data and compute item-parameter estimates for all items and examinee-ability estimates ($\hat{\theta}$) for each examinee.
- For each examinee, use the Lord–Wingersky procedure (Lord & Wingersky, 1984), along with the item-parameter estimates and the examinee's $\hat{\theta}$, to compute the discrete probability distribution for each subscore.
- Report category performance indicators of *low*, *high*, or *nonsignificant* for each subscore to the examinees depending on if their observed/actual subscores are in the lower tail, upper tail, or middle of the discrete probability distribution computed in the previous step. Feinberg and von Davier defined the two tails so that they have probabilities of 0.025.

While Haberman (2008c) did not claim that outliers provide any information about examinees' strengths and weaknesses, Feinberg and von Davier (2020) claimed that their category performance indicators indicate areas of relative strength/weaknesses.

One issue with the reporting of outliers (Haberman, 2008b) and category performance indicators (Feinberg & von Davier, 2020) is that given their definition and the way they are computed, only a small percentage of examinees would be labeled outliers or would receive a category performance indicator of low or high on a subarea and consequently would receive feedback. The users of score reports may perceive such a practice as a double standard, as some examinees would receive feedback while some others would not, and hence this may not be received well by the test-score users. A second issue, especially with category performance indicators, is that a small percentage of examinees would be outliers or would receive a category performance indicator of low or high on a subarea because of the random nature of the scores involved. Figure 4 of Feinberg and von Davier (2020) shows that 5% of examinees will have low or high category performance indicators even for essentially unidimensional tests (for which the correlations between the subscores are very close to 1) for which subscores are essentially *less reliable versions of the total score* (as noted by Longford, 1990, p. 92), and it would not be justified to claim that these indicators point to examinees' relative strengths/weaknesses.

We computed the category performance indicators for the abovementioned data from the Elementary Education: Content Knowledge test. For the same data, we also performed an outlier analysis as recommended by Haberman (2008b) and computed standardized residuals (e.g., Draper & Smith, 1998, p. 207) from a linear regression of each subscore on the other three subscores (that led to four regressions in all). We then converted the standardized residuals into a set of category indicators (henceforth referred to as *residual-based indicator*) that have values of *extremely low*, *extremely high*, or *nonextreme* depending on whether the standardized residual is significantly smaller than −1.96 (2.5th percentile of the standard normal distribution), significantly larger than 1.96 (97.5th percentile of the standard normal distribution), or between −1.96 and 1.96.

Figure 5.6 shows a plot of the reading subscore (along the Y axis) versus the total score (X axis), where the plotting symbol is a plus sign, circle, or triangle depending on whether the residual-based indicator is extremely high, nonextreme, or extremely low. A solid line in the figure represents the regression line of the reading subscore on the total score. The figure shows that the further the reading subscore is from the regression line, the more likely it is for the residual-based indicator to be extremely low or extremely high.

We found that there is a high rate of agreement between the category performance indicators and residual-based indicators for each of the four subscores. Tables 5.4a and 5.4b show the cross-tabulation of the two sets of indicators for

Table 5.4a *The cross-tabulation between the category performance indicators and residual-based indicators (numbers)*

Residual-based indicators	Category performance indicators			Total
	Low	Nonsignificant	High	
Extremely low	484	374	0	858
Nonextreme	111	22,069	113	22,293
Extremely high	0	25	242	267
Total	**595**	**22,468**	**355**	**23,418**

5.6 Reporting of Outliers or Conditional Subscores

Table 5.4b *The cross-tabulation between the category performance indicators and residual-based indicators (percentages, rounded to the nearest integer)*

Residual-based indicators	Category performance indices			Total
	Low	Nonsignificant	High	
Extremely low	2%	2%	0%	**4%**
Nonextreme	0%	94%	1%	**95%**
Extremely high	0%	0%	1%	**1%**
Total	**2%**	**96%**	**2%**	**100%**

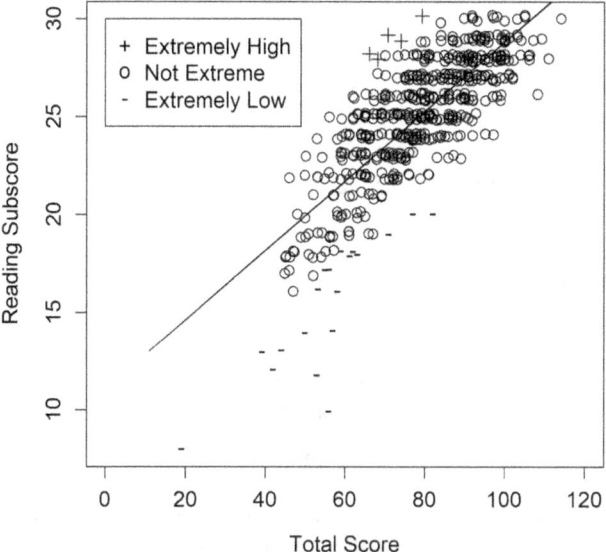

Figure 5.6 Graphical Demonstration of when standardized residuals from the regression of the reading subscore on the other subscores are too small or too large for the data from the Elementary Education: Content Knowledge Test. The plotting symbols represent the categorized standardized residuals; a symbol of plus sign, circle, or minus sign represent a standardized residual that is extremely high, not extreme, or extremely low, respectively.

the reading subscore. The numbers in the table represent the number of examinees (Table 5.4a) and the corresponding percentages (Table 5.4b) for each combination of the two indicators.

The percent agreement between the two sets of indicators is 97.3%, which is primarily due to the diagonals of the tables being much larger than the off-diagonals. A similarly high extent of agreement was found for the other three subscores as well. As an example, for Maya, the category performance indicator is high, and the residual-based indicator is extremely high for the science subscore. The reason is that Maya performed much worse than average on the other three subtests but performed close to the average on science; in other words, her performance on science was significantly better compared to the other subtests. The category performance indicator is nonsignificant, but the residual-based indicator is extremely low for the social studies subscore for Maya. So even though Maya performed comparatively worse on this subarea, the two sets of indicators do not agree. This difference is likely an outcome of the Rasch model not fitting the data adequately.[12] All of Maya's category performance indicators and residual-based indicators are shown in Table 5.2.

The reliability of the category performance indicators and residual-based indicators has not been investigated, although it is possible to compute the reliability or consistency of these indicators using measures such as Goodman and Kruskal's lambda, tau, and gamma (e.g., Goodman & Kruskal, 1954) – this is a potential area for future investigation.

5.7 Change the Test Structure and/or Combine Subareas

Another alternative option is to redesign the test by applying a technique such as *evidence-centered design* that is a framework for the design and development of assessments that ensures consideration and collection of validity evidence from the onset of the test design (e.g., Mislevy, Steinberg, & Almond, 2003) or *assessment engineering* that involves the use of engineering-based principles to direct the design and development as well as the analysis, scoring, and reporting of assessment results (e.g., Luecht, 2013).

But if test publishers cannot find a viable approach to redesign a test, they may combine some subareas to obtain subscores that have higher reliability and are more likely to satisfy professional standards.[13] Choi and Papageorgiou (2020), in their analysis of subscores for the Reading section of the TOEFL Primary test that included items of six types, combined some item types (those for which the investigators were able to employ the general theory of target language development and the framework of the test to obtain a clear rationale of combining) to end up with three more reliable subscores for the section.

---

[12] A format statistical model fit procedure revealed that the Rasch model did not fit the data adequately. The detailed results from the model-fit procedure are omitted and can be obtained from the authors.

[13] Although combining subareas might make the definition of the subscore overly broad.

5.8 Report Subscores Whose Categories Are Defined Using Psychometric Approaches

Experience shows that subtests created using only content blueprints do not guarantee that the subscores are distinct enough to add value. Reckase and Xu (2014) demonstrated that the use of content blueprints together with psychometric approaches as a basis of constructing subtests may yield more useful subscores. They suggested an approach based on multidimensional item-response theory (e.g., Reckase, 2009) and hierarchical cluster analysis (e.g., Everitt, 2011) to successfully construct subtests for the *Pearson Test of English Academic* (Pearson Longman, 2010) that measures nonnative English speakers' proficiency in listening, reading, speaking, and writing English. The number of subtests varied between six and eight for the six data sets from the English test that they considered. Two subtests that they identified are (a) listening and oral production and (b) writing and listening comprehension. They also found the corresponding subscores to be reliable and distinct. A possible drawback of the approach is that the use of psychometric-based approaches may lead to subscores that would be difficult to interpret. In addition, variation in the number of and definition of subscores over different test forms may create confusion among the users of test scores.

Given the popularity of cognitively diagnostic models and diagnostic scores produced by these models over the last 20 years, any treatment of subscores would be incomplete without some discussion of them. Therefore, these concepts are discussed next.

5.9 Report Diagnostic Scores Obtained from a Cognitive Diagnostic Model

It is possible to employ a psychometric model such as a *cognitive diagnostic model* or a *diagnostic classification model* (e.g., DiBello, Roussos, & Stout, 2007; Leighton & Gierl, 2007; Rupp, Templin, & Henson, 2010) to compute diagnostic scores and report them when subscores do not have added value. Diagnostic classification models involve the assumptions that

- Solving each test item requires the mastery of one or more skills
- For each examinee–skill combination, there exists a discrete latent skill parameter denoting mastery or lack of mastery of the examinee on the skill
- The probability that an examinee will answer an item correctly is a mathematical function of (1) the skills the item requires, (2) the latent skill parameters of the examinee, and (3) the item parameters

After a diagnostic classification model is fitted to a data set, the estimated values of the skill/mastery parameters are the diagnostic scores that may be reported. Examples of such models are the rule space model (Tatsuoka, 1983), the attribute hierarchy method (Leighton, Gierl, & Hunka, 2004), the *deterministic-input, noisy and gate* model (Junker & Sijtsma, 2001), the general diagnostic model (von Davier, 2008), and the reparameterized unified model (Roussos et al., 2007).

There has been substantial research on diagnostic classification models, and many measurement researchers incorrectly believe that these models can provide useful information even for unidimensional tests for which subscores

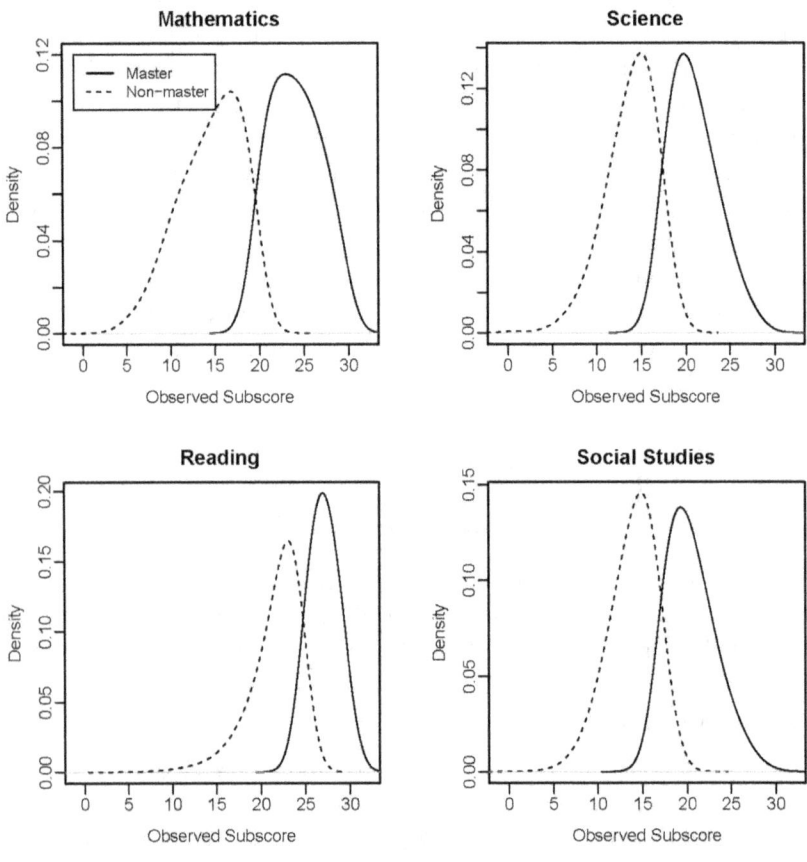

Figure 5.7 Graphical demonstration of how estimated diagnostic scores on each subarea are related to the corresponding subscores for the data from the Elementary Education: Content Knowledge Test.

typically do not have added value. However, as Rupp and Templin (2009) acknowledged, there has not been a very convincing case that unequivocally illustrates how the added parametric complexity of these models, compared to simpler measurement models, can be justified in practice. In addition, there have been few empirical illustrations that the diagnostic scores produced by these models are reliable and valid (see, e.g., Haberman & von Davier, 2007; Sinharay & Haberman, 2008), especially for unidimensional tests.

We fitted the deterministic-input, noisy and gate model (Junker & Sijtsma, 2001) to the data from the Elementary Education: Content Knowledge test using the *CDM* package in *R* (e.g., George, Robitzsch, Kiefer, Gross, & Uenlue, 2016) under the assumption that the test measures four skills, one corresponding to the subareas of mathematics, science, reading, and social studies. The estimated proportions of masters for the four subareas were 0.63, 0.51, 0.48, and 0.47, respectively.

Figure 5.7 demonstrates how the estimated diagnostic scores of the examinees are associated with their subscores. The figure shows, for each subarea, two smoothed density plots[14] of the distribution of the (actual) subscores of the examinees whose estimated diagnostic classification was "master" (solid line) and of the examinees whose estimated diagnostic classification was "nonmaster" (dashed line). The density plot for the nonmasters is always situated to the left of that of the masters for each subscore, indicating that examinees are highly likely to be classified as masters if their subscores are large and vice versa. However, for each subscore, there is a range of values so that an examinee with a subscore in that range could be estimated to be a master or a nonmaster. The results indicate that Maya is estimated to be a nonmaster of all the four subareas (as shown in the last row of Table 5.2), and Examinee 2, represented in Figure 5.2, is estimated to be a master only of social studies.

5.10 Discussions and Recommendations

In this chapter, we provided some guidance regarding several alternative options that have been suggested for the case when subscores are demanded but do not have satisfactory psychometric quality. Figure 5.8 shows some *R* code for performing some of the computations discussed in this chapter.

We deliberately did not include "report scores obtained from a multidimensional item response model" as an option because we have found these scores to be highly correlated with augmented subscores (Haberman & Sinharay, 2010)

---

[14] The plots were created using the function *density* in the *R* software (R Core Team, 2022).

```
> library(subscore)
> D=read.table("ElmEd.dat")
> colnames(D)=paste("I",1:120,sep="")
> ElmEd.d=data.prep(D, c(4,rep(30,4)) , c("Reading","Math","SS",
  "Sci","Total"))
> Output = CTTsub(ElmEd.d,method="Haberman") #Compute various
  PRMSEs
> SHAug=subscore.sx(ElmEd.d)$subscore.sx #Compute augmented
  subscores
> OPIs=Yen.OPI(ElmEd.d)$OPI*30 #Compute objective performance
  indices (OPIs)
> Subscores = Output$subscore.original[,1:4] # Extract the actual
  subscores
> colnames(Subscores)=paste("S",1:nsub,sep="")
**** Compute the Residual-based indicators (RBI) of Haberman (2008c)
> RBI=matrix(0,nrow(D),4)
> for (j in 1:4)
> {frla=as.formula(paste("S",j,"~.",sep=""))
  L=lm(frla,dat=SM)
  r=rstandard(L)
  RBI[,j]=ifelse(r<qnorm(0.025),-1,ifelse(r>qnorm(0.975),1,0))}
* Compute Diagnostic Scores from Deterministic-input, Noisy and
  Gate (DINA) Model
> library(CDM)
> qm=matrix(0,120,4) # qm= "Q-matrix" denoting which items
  require which skill
> qm[1:30,1]=1
> qm[31:60,2]=1
> qm[61:90,3]=1
> qm[91:120,4]=1
> colnames(qm)=paste("alpha",1:4,sep="")
> EE.dina <- din(data = D,q.matrix = qm, rule = "DINA",progress
  = TRUE)
> SP=IRT.factor.scores(EE.dina, type = "MLE")#SP=Estimated
  Mastery Parameters
```

Figure 5.8 R Code (using R packages **subscore** and **CDM**) for computing augmented subscores, Objective performance indices, residual-based indicators, and estimated diagnostic scores for the data set from the Elementary Education: Content Knowledge Test.

that are much easier to compute and also because several computer programs would not produce any estimates (because of the algorithm not converging) when one tries to fit a multidimensional item response model to unidimensional test data for which subscores do not have added value. We also did not include the option of reporting a subscore classification where the classifications relate student performance to state expectations, such as state achievement levels (e.g., Basic, Proficient, Advanced). Tanaka (2023) found several states reporting only subscore classifications (and not the subscores themselves). As discussed in

5.10 Discussions and Recommendations

Chapter 3 and shown in Sinharay (2014), the subscore classifications are of poor psychometric quality (in the sense of lacking accuracy and precision) if subscores for a test do not have added value, and the reporting of the classifications is not a viable option.

There are additional options, including reporting subscores based on types of incorrect answers chosen by students (e.g., Biancarosa et al., 2019), temporal efficiency in giving correct answers (e.g., Biancarosa et al., 2019), and information from multiple-choice distractors (e.g., Luecht, 2007), but these options need further examination.

The different options that we suggested in this chapter involve different amounts of work and hence different costs. It is easiest to not report subscores and relatively straightforward to compute augmented subscores. On the other hand, it is difficult and time-consuming to perform a scale anchoring or item mapping study. The choice of one of these options will most likely depend on the time and resources that are available to the test administrators. The choice of an option may also be an outcome of a conversation between the test administrators and score users focusing on questions like "What kind of information is needed?", "At what level of granularity?", and "How will the information be used?" None of the options suggested in this chapter is likely to make all test-score users happy all the time, but some of these may make some users happy some of the time.

6
Coda

Lessons Learned, Conclusions, and Recommendations

6.1 Introduction

In September of 1921, the legendary track coach Sam Mussabini (1867–1927) shared one of the basic criteria he used for deciding who he would be willing to train when he pointed out to Harold Abrahams (1899–1978) that "you can't get out what God hasn't put in." Serendipitously, this parallels (without the need to invoke any deity) the same message that we want to convey about subscores.

It is the unfortunate result of essentially all serious research into the efficacy of subscores that despite what are often the heartfelt and earnest desires of many users of test results, extracting useful subscores from tests is extraordinarily unlikely unless the capacity for such subscores is built into the tests from their very beginnings.

Modern evidence-centered test design (e.g., Almond et al., 2002; Mislevy et al., 2003) holds that test developers must begin test construction with a list of claims that they want to make, a list they obtain from the audience for the test scores.[1] Immediately following this enumeration is a parallel list of what they would consider to be evidence that would support those claims. This evidence must have obvious and direct relevance to the claims (the validity of the evidence), and there must be enough evidence to support the claims solidly, without much wobbling (reliability). The test is viewed simply as an instrument built to generate the evidence to support the claims.

As we pointed out in Chapter 1, the amount of time required to take a course exam (often one hour), an admission test (usually two to three hours),

---

[1] This attitude of the role of test development means that the first step in building a test is to survey the potential users about what claims they will want to make. Such a survey often involves negotiation between the users and the developers to balance what is desired with what is practical, or even possible.

or a licensing test (a whole day or more) seems like a lot of work to generate only a single number, especially if that number is just a binary decision (pass/fail, admit/reject). As we noted in Chapter 3, binary decisions require more reliability, not less. This issue really comes home to roost when examinees are required to pass each subtest (see Section 6.5.6). Thus, it is natural for users of test scores to demand of test developers more detailed performance information. Sometimes it is to aid examinees in remediating weaknesses in subject-matter mastery and/or to aid institutions (e.g., schools) in remediating weaknesses in instruction. But if these subscores are used to make consequential decisions about each examinee, the reliability of each of those subscores must be increased apace. This has the unfortunate consequence of requiring what may be profound increases in test length. For such practical reasons, the demand for meaningful subscores outstrips their supply, and so sadly, we find most subscores yield no added value over the total test score.

In earlier chapters, we reviewed the evidence for these conclusions and provided rigorous procedures to determine whether the extent of the value that the subscores provided exceeds that of merely using the total test score.

6.2 Brief Summaries of the Other Chapters: What Did We Learn?

- In Chapter 2, we discussed how subscores are reported by various testing organizations. We included the reporting's goals but did not comment on the efficacy, the content, or the format of the displays. Later in this chapter, we will suggest some improvements in both content and format. Our suggestions are not meant to be complete but only representative of the mind-set required on the path toward the improvement of such reports.
- Chapter 3 is the most technical chapter. It makes the strong, but obvious, recommendation (almost a commandment) that test administrators must evaluate the quality of subscores before reporting them. It then describes in detail the various empirical measures that can be used to do such an evaluation.
- Chapter 4 reported the results of a reasonably extensive survey of the psychometric quality of subscores for a broad variety of tests. The results of this survey yield two important benefits: Inferences about the characteristics of those rare tests that yield value-added subscores can help test developers in building future tests, and it should also make all potential users of subscores cautious.

- Chapter 5 provided guidance on what can be legitimately reported when we find that the psychometric quality of some, or all, of the claims to be made from the subscores are not adequately supported.

6.3 Recommendations for the Practitioners

> If we have data, let's look at the data.
> If all we have is opinion, let's go with mine.
>
> *Jim Barksdale*

Shown in Figure 6.1 is a version of a flow chart describing the step-by-step process through which the developers of test scores can construct tests that would yield high-quality subscores that can legitimately be reported. It is meant as an adjunct to the process depicted previously in Figure 5.8. What follows is a narrative explaining and expanding on the flow chart.

The process begins with a survey of the users of test scores to determine what claims they want to make and how the scores from a test can support

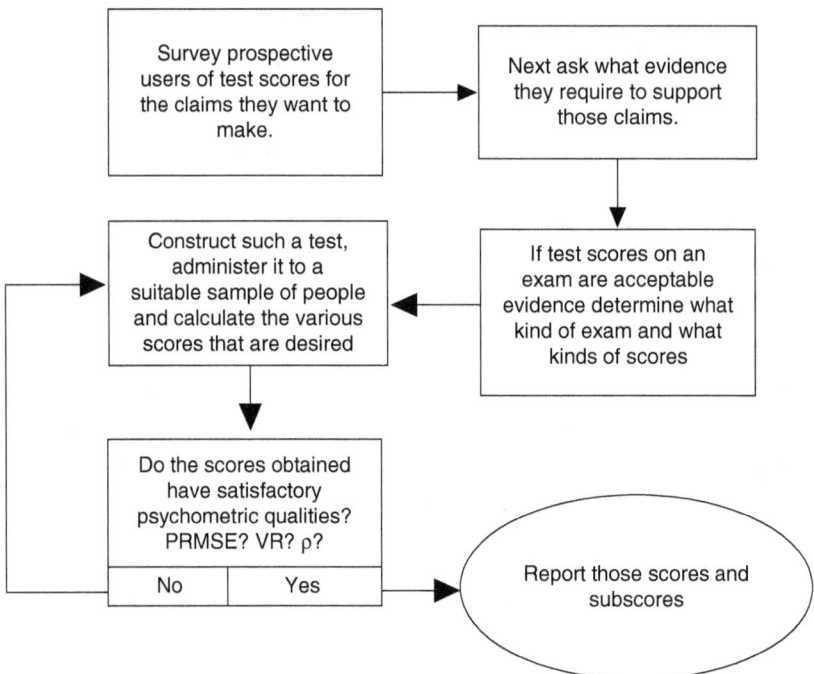

Figure 6.1 Flow chart showing how a test can be built expressly to provide supporting evidence for claims.

those claims. If as result of this survey users require both a measure of overall performance (a total score) and measures of performance on various component parts of the overall score (subscores), the test developers then get to work building a test that has enough items associated with each of the subareas of interest to yield an assessment of them with the required precision. Figures 4.1 to 4.9 and Table 4.2 should be helpful in this process. For example, if the test is used for teacher licensing, then Table 4.2 and Figures 4.4 to 4.6 suggest that the average disattenuated correlation among the subscores of the test would most likely be around 0.80, and consequently, Figure 4.7 suggests that the average subtest length should be 30 to yield subscores that are 50% likely to have added value.

The resulting test is then reviewed for all the characteristics that tests must have (e.g., content completeness, factual accuracy, sensitivity concerns, and many others). Once it passes all these hurdles, the test is administered to a representative sample of examinees, and their response data are gathered.

The resulting data are examined to see if they satisfy all the usual quality control requirements, but, apropos of the topic of this book, we also calculate each subscore's PRMSE (proportional reduction in mean square error) and its VAR (value-added ratio) to confirm that the subscore is both reliable enough and sufficiently independent of other items to provide a measure that adds value over just using the total score. If it passes all these hurdles, report it.

But if it doesn't, what do we do? The *best choice* is to send the flawed subscore back to the test developers for revision – perhaps to add more items or improve its component items or through other redesigns guided now by the data that have been gathered. But what if such reengineering is not possible/practical? We still have options, and these were described in Chapter 5 and depicted in Figure 5.8.

Our actions in this situation depend on exactly why the particular subscore in question is not adding value to the assessment, over and above the total score.

If it is just too unreliable (usually because it contains too few items – see the results in Figures 4.1 and 4.2), you can boost its reliability using one or more of the augmentation schemes described in Chapter 3. The boost of the subscore's reliability through such an augmentation comes at the cost of the subscore's orthogonality from the rest of the test. But this is often a cost worth paying because the resulting augmented subscore will not mislead its users into actions that might only be chasing noise.

Thus, if unreliability is the only issue, you can now report the subscores without concerns that they will mislead score users. Of course, in the worst-case scenario, augmented subscores may not be any different than just reporting the total score repeatedly with different names, but sins engendered by this approach are venial, whereas sins of reporting unreliable subscores, because they can lead to unjustified actions, can be mortal.

If augmentation does not provide enough of a boost in reliability to justify reporting and yet there are contractual stipulations requiring the reporting of subscores whether they have any value or not, we can only advise perhaps reporting them graphically highlighted in some way (maybe in red) with a clear indication that they should not be used for any serious purpose. We realize that negotiation may be needed to ensure that appropriate disclaimers are provided, but professional obligations must be honored.

There are a number of suggestions on how to communicate the uncertainty of empirical measure effectively in Chapter 13 of Wainer (2009) and, more specifically, consider the ideas illustrated in Figures 13.12 and 13.13 of that book.

6.4 Score Reports

Score reports serve many audiences (e.g., examinees, the institution that the examinee comes from, the institution that required the examinee to take the exam) and have many purposes. Each audience/purpose is likely to require reports of a somewhat different character and maybe different content. Our focus here is on reports to audiences that for one reason or another want to see subscores. As we hope we have made abundantly clear, we have found no empirical evidence that justifies reporting subscores that do not add informational value over and above that of the total score. We recognize that sometimes a situation might arise in which one is contractually obligated to report such meaningless subscores. When that occurs, the only ethical way to cut that Gordian knot is to augment the subscores with information contained in the rest of the test so that what is reported is at least reliable, even if it does not provide any unique information. Often this will be equivalent to reporting the total score, rescaled into the metric of the subscores, multiple times.

But once we have reportable scores, what are some good ways to report them? This is not the place for an exhaustive discussion of score reports,[2] but two kinds of representational errors occur that we feel are worth discussing: the organization of the subscores in the report and the representation of error in that report. We shall go into each in turn.

---

[2] One useful place to start might be consulting Roberts and Gierl (2010) for several suggestions they make on the reporting of diagnostic scores and then applying them to the more general task of reporting of subscores.

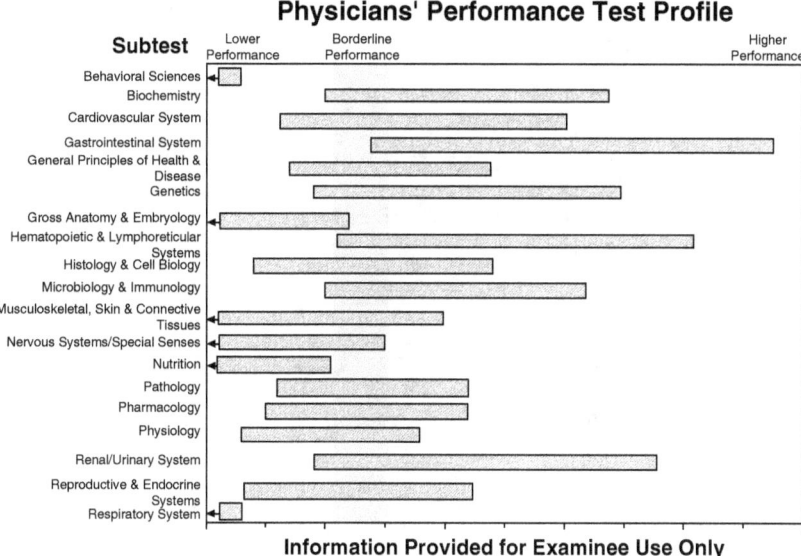

Figure 6.2 A typical performance profile showing the scores for 19 subtests measuring a medical worker's skills. The performance bands reflect the precision of the measurement based on the number of items in the subscore.

In Figure 6.2 is a sample performance profile for an examinee on an imaginary test. This report shares many characteristics of many score reports (see the selection in Chapter 2). Like many other score reports, it displays the scores of this examinee on 19 subtests in alphabetical order from Behavioral Sciences to the Respiratory System. The subscores are represented as bands that are commonly described vaguely but hint at being something like one standard error of the score in each direction (exactly what the bands depict is rarely made explicit). Down the center of the plot is another band that represents what we are often told is the "borderline" performance in that area, ranging from "low pass" to "high pass." Although there is almost never an explicit statement of the value-added of each subscore, we are sometimes warned that there may be interpretative problems because the same item may appear in more than one subscore. The left-pointing arrows are a common convention to indicate that the lower bound of that subscore lies below the range of scores depicted.

6.4.1 Ordering: We're Only Rarely Interested in "Alabama First"

The single display issue we will focus on here is traditionally referred to as the issue of "We're not interested in Alabama First" (Wainer, 1997, p. 35).

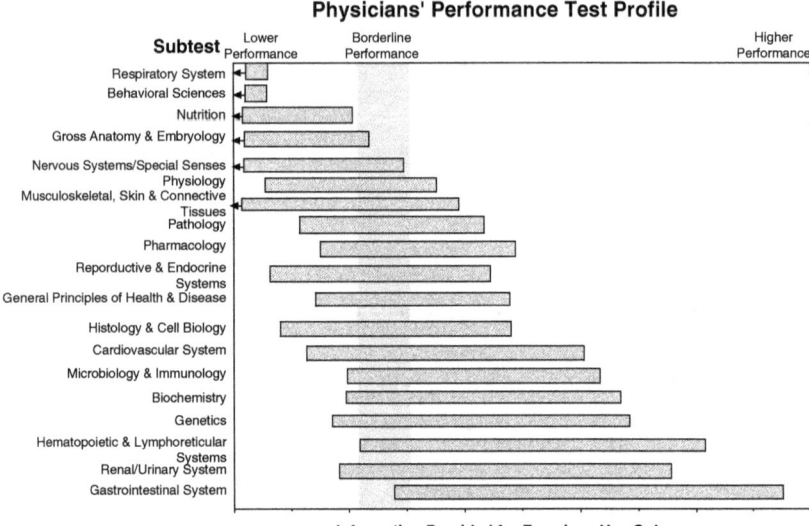

Figure 6.3 One suggested revision in which the subscores shown in Figure 6.2 were sorted by size – low to high.

Specifically, data displays are rarely improved by organizing their contents alphabetically. Instead, it is usually wise to order the display by the data it contains. A reorganized version of the previous display is shown as Figure 6.3.

This organizing principle makes it obvious (if we can believe the data) in which areas the examinee is strongest (e.g., gastrointestinal system and renal/urinary system) and in which areas they are the weakest (e.g., respiratory system). Whether to rank the results from strongest to weakest or vice versa depends on the prospective use of the scores. Ordering the display by the data is an easy redesign that allows the reader to use the powerful visual system to see patterns, not all of them expected, that arise in the data.

6.4.2 Representation of Error

> Anyone can calculate a mean,
> but it takes a statistician
> to calculate a variance.
> *Paul Holland (1982)*

The practical value of a score is diminished considerably if we don't know how accurate it is. If we stand on a bathroom scale and its reading randomly fluctuates by ±100 pounds, we will treat its readings differently than if the fluctuations were only ±2 pounds. A common representation is to show the standard error of a score, which typically is of use because it can be used to compute other error terms of more immediate value. Two obvious sorts of uses for the error term are:

(i) To know the likelihood that an observed score represents examinee ability above (or below) some passing standard
(ii) To know the likelihood that two different observed scores represent different examinee ability, for example, whether the examinee really knows more about pathology than biochemistry

But to make these sorts of comparative judgements, we need the standard error of the difference between the two measures we wish to compare. Such a statistic is easily calculated from the individual standard errors, but it makes the task of the users of the score report easier if the computation is done automatically and directly depicted visually on the score report.

There is yet one more complication that we must consider – we don't know how many such comparisons the reader of the report is going to make. Obviously if 10 or 20 such comparisons are going to be made, the standard error must be expanded (using, e.g., the Bonferroni inequality as one obvious choice) to accommodate the increased likelihood of finding a "significant" difference by chance. In the example shown in Figure 6.3, there are 19 comparisons involving each subscore with the indicated borderline, so the required alpha level needs to be shrunken by that amount. The issue gets more profound when we have to accommodate to the possible (likely?) desire to compare each subscore with every other one. This means that there will not be just 19 comparisons but now there will be 19 choose 2 or 171 *additional* comparisons. The truth of Holland's observation (quoted earlier) about such issues not being amenable to solutions by small children (or those untrained in the art of statistics) is clear. Happily, users of such score reports can safely make such comparisons visually, if those who prepare score reports construct error bars that display the correct error term.

6.5 Hopes, Dreams, Myths, and Urban Legends

I am too familiar with the manner in which actual data are met with the suggestion that other data, if they were collected, might show something else, to believe it to have any value as an argument.

"Statistics on the table, please," can be my sole reply.
In a letter by Karl Pearson to the *London Times* in 1910

Hope springs eternal, but alas, hope is not enough. We have found that when there is no evidence that subscores yield added value overall, they generally also do not yield value in more specific analyses. The following subsections discuss seven unrequited and unsupported hopes.

6.5.1 Maybe It'll Work in Some Unique Subgroups

One popular myth is that when there is no evidence that subscores yield added value overall, there might be some specific subgroup within which there is added value.

Heterogeneity among the examinees might change the story, but although many have claimed the possibility of such an event, we have seen no convincing evidence. On the contrary, we have found the added value to generally be uniform over subgroups (e.g., Sinharay & Haberman, 2014); thus, we have been forced to conclude that if the subscores do not yield added value for the full sample, it is extremely unlikely that added value will be found in some specific subgroup.[3]

"Statistics on the table, please."

6.5.2 An Unusual Subscore Must Mean Something

Another common misconception is that even when there is no evidence that subscores yield added value overall, a sufficiently unusual subscore could indicate a specific strength or weakness.

We have looked at outliers at times. The only real uses we have found for such extreme cases involved unauthorized collaboration and problems with incorrect scoring or incorrect data entry by the test taker. These cases are sometimes of great interest in test quality control and security but have no relation to traditional uses of subscores.

"Statistics on the table, please."

6.5.3 Isn't Weak Information Better than Nothing?

When there is no evidence that subscores yield added value overall, if we are trying to remediate academic weaknesses in a student, it is almost forgivable to be clutching at straws. This persists despite the wisdom of

---

[3] We recognize that a test may be inappropriate for a subgroup and then a different assessment is needed. A test for students in middle school is unlikely to be appropriate for kindergarteners. Our advice here assumes that the tests are appropriate for the test takers.

Josh Billings' previously cited observation, "I honestly believe that it is better to know nothing than to know what ain't so."

There is no credible evidence that we have ever seen suggesting that lousy subscores improve student learning. Indeed, it is very hard to find any literature on formative assessment that indicates they help at all. In repeated examinations of this literature over many years, we have commonly noted the poor quality of such studies. Thus, we were forced to conclude that it would be dishonest to provide information that has the appearance of value when value does not exist. Consequently, we have been convinced that it is much more honest to state clearly that there is no there there. We would welcome randomized controlled trials studying the efficacy of various training approaches utilizing subscores of no apparent value – but continue to believe that one's spare time could be more fruitfully spent in other activities, like gardening. We would be delighted to be proved wrong.

"Statistics on the table, please."

6.5.4 Can Weak Subscores Gain Value When Used in Conjunction with Validity Data?

When there is no evidence that subscores yield added value overall, we have found no boost in their value over that of total score when measured against a validity criterion.

Validity evidence concerning tests varies quite a bit. For tests like the SAT, validity data do indeed exist. You can argue that the incremental validity of the SAT above grades in high school is not as large as desired, but it is not negligible for criteria such as first-year grades, especially once range restriction is considered. Professional licensure tests in general have proven more difficult, but they often do receive serious validity consideration.

The subscore situation is much different. The problem is really whether tailored advice is useful beyond the advice based on the overall score. Saying that your score is barely below the cut versus very low indeed does have value in terms of what resources should be applied and whether there is hope. We can indicate in various ways what a person with a given score can and cannot do with such and such probability. We can also inform test takers of what inferences can rationally be drawn from the available data. We can indicate to test takers what the distribution of results given their scores is if they retake the test. But this is hypothesizing in advance of data.

"Statistics on the table, please."

6.5.5 Can't a Weak Subscore Still Be Used as a Prod to Encourage a Student to Work Harder?

Tests can serve three purposes:

(i) Tests as contests – I got a higher score, so I won (got admitted, got the scholarship).
(ii) Tests as measurements – My score improved 10 points, which was double last year.
(iii) Tests as prods – Why is Johnny studying? He's got a test tomorrow.

Subscores that show no added value are not likely to serve purpose (ii), but it is not far-fetched to believe that an examinee getting a lower score on one subtest or another, regardless of its actual worth, might be motivated to study that aspect (purpose [iii]). Whether the score or the study is of any value can be determined only from a careful data gathering effort. But in advance of data from such efforts, it is unethical to, even implicitly, suggest an action to the examinee that is likely to be wasted effort.

"Statistics on the table, please."

6.5.6 When Is It Legitimate to Insist That an Examinee Must Pass on All Subscores?

When there is no evidence that subscores yield added value overall, is it still legitimate to insist that an examinee must pass on all subscores, rather than just overall, to pass the test?

Suppose we have an *n*-part test (where *n* might be 8 to 10) and, as is common, there is little evidence that the subscores based on each of those *n* parts yield any marginal value over total score.

So far, we are playing on a familiar field.

But the rules of the game are that to pass the test, you need to pass each of the *n* parts individually (which means we are taking the values of the subscores very seriously indeed), and if you don't pass, you can retake just those parts of the exam you had failed previously.

So, where are we? Certainly, it seems to be a violation of our rules of the game to make serious use of subscores that have no added value, yet this doesn't seem to be an unfamiliar approach in licensing exams. Is there any sense in which this might be an acceptable policy?

Perhaps. Note that this test is not necessarily a measurement task but is, at least partially, a contest.

People who passed a section won; those who failed lost – the measurement characteristics matter less, so long as the testing and scoring are fair to all examinees.

The second (and possibly third or fourth) attempts should be viewed as consolation heats. If viewed in this way, this approach is ethically (and maybe even psychometrically) valid.

6.5.7 With Limited Resources, Isn't There Anything We Can Do?

When there is no evidence that subscores yield added value overall, and there are no resources available to reengineer the test, is there anything positive we can do?

Yes, there is! If subscores have no added value over total score, and the reliability of the total score is greater than needed, we can make use of the Spearman–Brown slow diminution of reliability as the test grows shorter. We can still have acceptable reliability with a much shorter test. The tradeoff between test length and reliability was shown for a typical professionally prepared test in Figure 1.1 (repeated here as Figure 6.4), which shows the dramatic declining marginal value of extra items, after about the twentieth. If we use as a rough rule of thumb that a generic multiple-choice item can be answered in about a minute, we see that we lose very little reliability by replacing a 100-item (100-minute) exam with a 40- or even 25-item (-minute) exam. Such a shortening of the exam saves in several ways. A completed (written, edited, and pretested) test item typically costs more than $2,500. Thus, cutting the length of the test in half cuts the costs to the testing organization in half as well. It also cuts the costs for test administration by a similar proportion. Presumably, some proportion of these savings can be passed on to the examinees. In addition, and of perhaps greater importance, the time required of each examinee is also reduced by the same proportion. This is the biggest saving, since it is multiplied by what is often a very large number of examinees.

What's the catch? Actually, there are three. First, there are no subscores to be shared. This is really a positive in the situation we have described, for there were no viable subscores to be shared anyway, and shortening the test reduces the temptation to promulgate nonsense. The second loss is a technical one. With fewer items, there is diminished domain coverage, but if random coverage of domains (the subject matter domains, aggregated over the entire examinee population) is acceptable, this need not be a problem. Of course, such

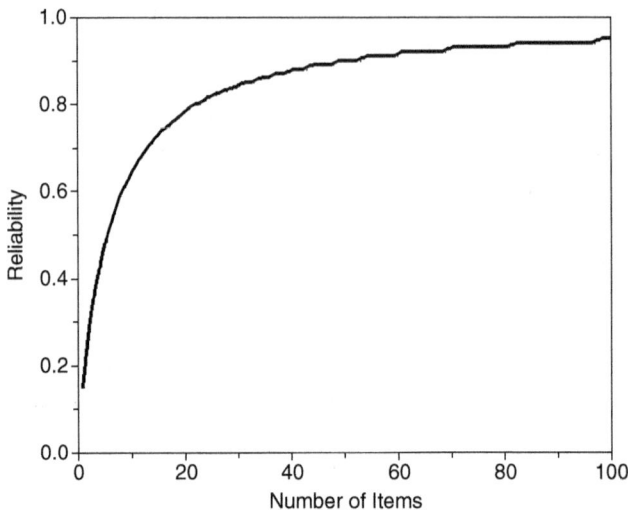

Figure 6.4 Spearman–Brown function showing the reliability of a test as a function of its length if a one-item test has a reliability of 0.15. This is a repeat of Figure 1.1.

random coverage reduces the item development cost advantages but not the test administration savings. We are assured from research dating back at least 40 years (e.g., Bell & Lumsden, 1980) that such shortening has minimal effect on validity.

But, finally, to gain these savings in both time and treasure, the testing organization must admit (at least to itself) that they have no viable subscores.

6.6 One Last Story

There is an ancient Native American adage: "If you tell me a fact, I will learn it. If you tell me a truth, I will believe it. But if you tell me a story, it will live in my heart forever." So let us end with a story that can here serve as an instructive parable and that is credited to W. Edwards Deming (1900–1993), the famous statistician credited with developing modern quality control. It happened that one day there was unusually high absenteeism on an automobile assembly line, but the assembly line's speed was left unchanged. Unsurprisingly, this resulted in an increase in the number of errors. Happily, these errors were caught at the final checking station, and the affected cars were shunted aside and the errors corrected. But correcting errors takes a while because the car needs to be disassembled a bit to fix the problem. A manager, watching the whole process from high above the factory floor, saw the backup at the checking station and, seeking to relieve congestion, ordered some workers off the assembly line to move to the checking station to help out. Of course, this magnified the problem. This story has been used to illustrate many important lessons. It does not take much insight to see that moving tax money from education to law enforcement is an immediate analog. It also illustrates the pitfalls of local optimization. But our point here is directly parallel to that expressed by both Deming and Mussabini: You cannot inspect quality into a product – you must build it in in the first place.

Most of the content of this book has been focused on quality control – describing effective methods for inspecting subscores for their viability, as well as reporting the outcome of such checks on a substantial sample of existing tests. The news was not encouraging. Clearly, the effort needed to build viable subscores into tests has too rarely been expended. If such subscores are important evidence needed to support the claims that users of the test scores want to make, the character of such subscores within the entirety of the test must be established from their very beginnings. The tools we have described here allow us to know how successful we have been, and by showing what kind of subscores work and what kinds don't, may thus provide guidance for future tests. But, remembering back to the lessons learned from census development of small area estimates, effective subscores are not likely to be cheap in either treasure or examinee time.

6.7 And Finally

We firmly believe that the key to answering the sorts of nagging questions posed here is to build tests thoughtfully, with their ultimate use in mind, and then to gather data from which we can construct convincing statistics to put on the table. In this way, the arguments do not have to rely on opinions – not even ours. We realize executing the studies that would generate such data may be expensive, but, in the long run, it is nowhere nearly as expensive as not gathering them.

Appendix
The Data Sets That Are Used in the Survey of Chapter 4

Given an ever-increasing demand for subscores, it is not surprising that many researchers have analyzed data from a wide variety of operational tests in an attempt to determine whether the subscores on those tests had added value over the total score using the proportional reduction in mean square error (PRMSE) and/or the value-added ratio described in Chapter 3 as well as in Haberman (2008a) and Feinberg and Wainer (2014). We were also able to determine whether the subscores have added value for three additional data sets; the reliabilities of and covariances among the subscores for these data sets have been made available by Haladyna and Kramer (2004), Longabach and Peyton (2018), and Wilson (2000). A strength of the PRMSE-based method for determining added value is that it can be applied to existing data sets for which only the reliabilities of and covariances among the subscores are available. Thus, for example, for a test with four subscores, only 14 numbers are required to determine the added value of the subscores on the test.

A.1 Data for Which PRMSEs and/or Value-Added Ratios Are Available

In a comprehensive survey, Sinharay (2010) determined the added value of subscores using data from 25 large-scale operational tests. The 25 data sets considered by Sinharay (2010) originated from a state reading test for 5th grade students (the data analyzed originally by Ackerman & Shu, 2009); the SAT I Verbal, SAT I Math, SAT I, and Praxis Educators' Content Knowledge examinations (Haberman, 2008a); the preliminary ACT English and Mathematics examinations (Harris & Hanson, 1991); the major field test in business (Ling, 2012; the Swedish Scholastic Aptitude Test (Lyren, 2009); eight teacher licensure tests (Puhan, Sinharay, Haberman, & Larkin, 2010); a

Table A.1 *Reliabilities and value-added ratios for the subscores on the National Board of Medical Examiners Part I examination*

Content area	Reliability	Value-added ratio
Behavioral Science	0.76	2.06
Biochemistry	0.87	1.21
Anatomy	0.86	1.16
Pharmacology	0.84	1.10
Pathology	0.83	1.08
Physiology	0.85	1.07
Microbiology	0.82	1.05

test of cognitive and technical skills (Sinharay & Haberman, 2008); two tests of mastery of a language (Sinharay & Haberman, 2008); two tests of achievement of a discipline (Sinharay & Haberman, 2008); two tests of school and individual student progress (Sinharay & Haberman, 2008); and the Delaware Student Testing Program 8th grade mathematics assessment (Stone, Ye, Zhu, & Lane, 2010). Subscores are operationally reported for most of these 25 tests.[1] The PRMSEs indicated that 16 of the 25 tests had no subscores with added value, while each of the remaining nine tests had one, two, or four subscores with added value.

Feinberg and Jurich (2017) analyzed the added value of subscores for a data set from the part examinations administered by the National Board of Medical Examiners (e.g., Swanson, Case, & Nungester, 1991). These examinations, which involved three parts – Parts I, II, and III – have since been replaced by the United States Medical Licensing Examination (USMLE). The National Board of Medical Examiners Part I was a two-day, 950-item multiple-choice examination that was intended to cover seven content areas. Table A.1 shows the seven content areas, the reliabilities for the corresponding subscores, and the value-added ratios for the examination – these values are reproduced from Feinberg and Jurich (2017). The rows are sorted according to the decreasing order of value-added ratio. Noting that a subscore has added value when its value-added ratio is larger than 1, all the subscores for the National Board of Medical Examiners Part I examination have added value.

Meijer, Boeve, Tendeiro, Bosker, and Albers (2017) used PRMSEs to investigate the added value of subscores on two examinations from a degree program in psychology at a Dutch University. Here, we consider the first examination

---

[1] For some of these tests, such as SAT I, we treat the operationally reported section scores (e.g., verbal and mathematics) as the subscores in our analysis.

Table A.2 *Some information regarding subscores on two sections of the TOEFL Primary test*

Section	Number of subscores	Average subtest length	Average reliability
Reading	3	10	0.70
Listening	4	7.5	0.52

(34 items), assessing knowledge on test theory, which involved the following two subscores: factual knowledge (14 items) and conceptual understanding of test construction and test use (20 items). The value-added ratios were 0.82 and 0.74 for the two subscores – so none of the subscores for the test theory examination considered by Meijer et al. had added value.

Papageorgiou and Choi (2018) and Choi and Papageorgiou (2020) employed PRMSEs to investigate the added value of several Reading and Listening subscores of the Test of English as a Foreign Language (TOEFL) Primary® test, which intends to measure the English-language skills of young learners (ages eight and older) of English as a foreign language. Papageorgiou and Choi (2018) also investigated the added value of eight Reading and Listening subscores for the Test of English for International Communication (TOEIC®) Listening and Reading subsections. Here, we include the results for the Reading and Listening sections of the TOEFL Primary test in Choi and Papageorgiou (2020). Table A.2 shows the number of subscores, average subtest length, and average reliability for the two sections.

Lim and Lee (2020) analyzed the added value of the two subscores on a large-scale French language test and six subscores on a large-scale physics test. The subscores on these two tests comprised an average of 32 and 12 multiple-choice items, respectively. Their computed PRMSEs revealed that none of the subscores on the two tests had added value.

Liu, Robin, Yoo, and Manna (2018) computed PRMSEs for six subscores – biological, cognitive, social, developmental, clinical, and other – on three forms of the Graduate Record Examination (GRE®) Psychology test. We include results for the second of the three forms that they considered. The average subscore length and reliability were 34 and 0.80, respectively. Two of the six subscores had added value for the form.

Dai, Svetina, and Wang (2017) analyzed a data set from the eighth-grade mathematics test from the 2011 administration of the Trends in International Mathematics and Science Study (TIMSS) assessment that measures achievement in countries around the world every four years and collects a rich array of information about the educational contexts for learning mathematics and science. The following four subscales were defined for the test: number, algebra, geometry, and data and chance. The test includes 32 dichotomously scored items, with 6 to 9 items belonging to each subscale. The data set that we analyzed contains item scores from 765 students.

A.2 Data for Which PRMSEs or Value-Added Ratios Are Not Available

We were able to compute the PRMSEs and value-added ratios for a data set from Part I of the examination for dentists that was analyzed by Haladyna and Kramer (2004)[2] – the examination includes 100 multiple-choice items on each of the following four subareas: (1) dental anatomy and occlusion, (2) biochemistry and physiology, (3) microbiology and pathology, and (4) anatomic sciences. The value-added ratios for the corresponding subscores were 1.11, 1.02, 1.02, and 0.99, respectively – so three of the four subscores have added value.

Wilson (2000) performed dimensionality assessment using multiple data sets from the 1992 administrations of the TOEIC test. We computed, using the data summaries provided in Wilson (2000), the PRMSEs and value-added ratios for the listening comprehension section of the test – the section includes four subtests – (1) single picture, (2) question response, (3) short conversations, and (4) short talks – comprising 20, 30, 30, and 20 dichotomously scored items, respectively. The value-added ratios were 0.83, 0.84, 0.89, and 0.92 – so none of the four subscores had added value.

Finally, we were able to compute the PRMSEs and value-added ratios using summary statistics available in Longabach and Peyton (2018) for a state English language proficiency assessment.[3] We considered five subscores – Speaking, Writing-Rubric, Reading, Writing, and Listening – and the value-added ratios were 1.47, 1.35, 1.03, 0.95, and 0.89, respectively, so three of the five subscores had added value.

Most of the aforementioned tests included only multiple-choice items. For these tests, the "length" of a subscore refers to the number of items contributing to the subscore. Some tests had constructed response items, and for a subtest involving such items, the "length" refers to the maximum score (e.g., for a subscore with four items, each with three score categories, 0, 1, and 2, the length is 8).

---

[2] Haladyna and Kramer (2004) did not perform any computations on Part II of the examination, which included 500 multiple-choice items distributed among 10 subareas – the chances of establishing subscore validity with that part seemed remote to them.

[3] While Longabach and Peyton (2018) analyzed data from several grade ranges, we consider only the grade range 9 through 12 (results for the other grade ranges are similar).

Glossary

Aggregate-level subscore: An average subscore for a group of test takers.

Augmented subscore: A predicted true subscore s_{sx} based on both the subscore and the total score.

Average proportional reduction of mean square error: The average proportional reduction $\text{APRMSE}_{\text{tott}}$ of mean square error for the true subscores in a test from linear prediction by the true total score.

Best linear predictor: For variables X and Y, the best linear predictor of Y by X is the linear function $L = a + bX$ of X that minimizes the mean square error $E\left([Y-L]^2\right)$. For a positive integer k and variables X_1 to X_k, the best linear predictor of Y by X_1 to X_k is the linear function $L = a + b_1 X_1 + \ldots + b_k X_k$ that minimizes the mean square error $E\left([Y-L]^2\right)$.

Brennan utility index: The proportional reduction $\text{PRMSE}_{\text{tot}}$ of mean square error from use of the total score to predict the true subscore.

Canonical analysis of reliability: The simultaneous decomposition of the standardized true subscores and the standardized subscores into uncorrelated components with mean 0 and variance 1.

Category performance indicator: An indicator of whether the subscores of an examinee are significantly larger or smaller compared to their overall performance on the test.

Correlation coefficient: For two variables X and Y, the expectation $\rho(X,Y) = E(z(X)z(Y))$ of the product of their standardized values.

Cronbach's alpha: A reliability approximation for a score equal to the sum of item scores based on the variance of the score and the sum of the variances of the item scores.

Cut score: A specified value in which a test taker's score must meet or exceed to merit a passing outcome.

Diagnostic classification model: A multidimensional model for item responses that intends to diagnose examinees' mastery status of a set of discretely defined skills or attributes, thereby providing them with detailed information regarding their specific strengths and weaknesses.

Evidence-centered design: A framework for the design and development of assessments that ensures consideration and collection of validity evidence from the onset of the test design.

Expectation: The average $E(X)$ of a variable X.

Generalized partial credit model: A model used in item-response theory in which the conditional log odds of two item values is a linear function of a latent variable with a slope proportional to the difference between the item values.

Half test: A test consisting of half the items in the original test.

Incremental validity: The increase in proportional reduction of mean square error for prediction of a validity variable from use of both a subscore and total score rather than just a total score.

Item mapping: A procedure that involves the use of exemplar items to characterize what examinees at particular score points know and can do.

Item-response model: A model for responses to items in a test in which the item responses are assumed to be conditionally independent given a latent variable or vector.

Kelley estimate: The best linear predictor s_s of a true subscore s_t by a subscore s.

Latent variable: An unobserved variable such that, given the variable, item scores are conditionally independent.

MSE (mean square error): The average of the squared error from prediction of a variable by a predictor.

Measurement error: The difference between a score and its true score.

Multidimensional item-response model: An item-response model in which a latent vector is present.

Objective performance index: An estimate of an examinee's true score on a subarea based on the performance of the examinee on that subarea and the rest of the test. This estimate is similar conceptually to augmented subscores but is computed using an item-response theory model, unlike augmented subscores.

Parallel form: An alternative test that is equivalent to the original test.

Partial correlation: For three variables X, Y, and Z, the correlation $\rho(X,Y \mid Z)$ of the residual error X_{Zr} of the linear prediction of X by Z and the residual error Y_{Zr} from linear prediction of Y by Z.

Partial regression coefficient: For three variables X, Y, and Z, the slope $\beta(X \mid YZ)$ of the linear regression of the residual error X_{Zr} of the linear prediction of X by Z on the residual error Y_{Zr} from linear prediction of Y by Z.

Principal-components analysis: In this book, a decomposition of the standardized values of the true subscores into uncorrelated components with mean 0 and variance 1.

PRMSE (proportional reduction in mean square error): The proportional decrease in mean square error from prediction of a variable by one or more predictors instead of prediction by a constant. Usually in this book, the predicted variable is a true subscore.

PRMSE$_{aug}$ (proportional reduction in mean square error from use of augmented subscore): The proportional reduction in mean square error from prediction of the true subscore s_t by the augmented subscore s_{sx}.

PRMSE$_{irt}$: Proportional reduction in mean square error from use of item-response theory to predict a true transformed subscore.

PRMSE$_{res}$ (proportional reduction in mean square error from best linear prediction of residual true subscore by subscore and total score): The proportional reduction in mean square error from prediction of the true subscore s_t by the subscore s and the total score x.

PRMSE$_{psub}$ (proportional reduction in mean square error from use of Kelley estimate for subscore of a parallel form): The proportional reduction in mean square error from prediction of the subscore s' of a parallel form by the Kelley estimate s_s.

PRMSE$_{punb}$ (proportional reduction in mean square error from use of subscore to predict subscore of a parallel form): The proportional reduction in mean square error from use of the subscore s to provide an unbiased prediction of the subscore s' of a parallel form.

PRMSE$_{sub}$ (proportional reduction in mean square error from use of Kelley estimate for true subscore): The proportional reduction in mean square error from prediction of the true subscore s_t by the Kelley estimate s_s.

PRMSE$_{tot}$ (proportional reduction in mean square error from use of total score): The proportional reduction in mean square error from best linear prediction of the true subscore s_t by the total score x.

PRMSE$_{unb}$ (proportional reduction in mean square error from use of subscore): The proportional reduction in mean square error from use of the subscore s to provide an unbiased prediction of the true subscore s_t.

PRMSE$_{waug}$ (proportional reduction in mean square error from use of Wainer-augmented subscore) The proportional reduction in mean square error from prediction of the true subscore s_t by the Wainer-augmented subscore.

Profile: A collection of subscores.

Profile plot: A graphical plot showing all the subscores, often in standardized form, of a subset of examinees.

Prophecy formula: A formula for prediction of the reliability coefficient of a test similar to a given test but with more or fewer items.

Reliability coefficient: The correlation of scores on a test and on a parallel form. For a subscore s denoted by ρ_s^2. For a total score x denoted by ρ_x^2.

Repeated test: A repeat administration of a test using a parallel form.

Residual subscore: The error s_{rx} from best linear prediction of a subscore s by a total score x.

Residual true score: The error s_{rxt} from best linear prediction of a true subscore s_t by a true total score x_t.

Scale anchoring: A procedure that involves making claims about what examinees at different score points know and can do.

Scaled score: A transformation of a score for reporting purposes.

SNR (signal-to-noise ratio): The ratio of the variance of the true score to the variance of measurement.

Standard deviation: For a variable X, the square root $\sigma(X)$ of its variance $\sigma^2(X)$.

Standardized value: For a variable X, the ratio $z(X) = [X - E(X)] / \sigma(X)$ of the difference between the variable and its expected value compared to its standard deviation.

Stratified alpha: A variation of Cronbach's alpha used for sums of subscores.

Subscore: A score on a portion of the items on a test.

Total score: The sum of all scores of the items on a test.

True score: The average score of a test taker on a randomly selected test form from a collection of parallel forms.

True-score theory: A psychometric theory in which a test score is decomposed into a true score and an error of measurement.

VAR (value-added ratio): The ratio of the proportional reduction of mean square error from prediction of a true subscore by a total score compared to the proportional reduction of mean square error from prediction of a true subscore by a subscore.

Variance: For a variable X, the expectation $\sigma^2(X) = E\left(\left[X - E(X)\right]^2\right)$ of the squared deviation of X from its expectation $E(X)$.

Wainer-augmented subscore: The best linear predictor s_w of a true subscore by use of all subscores in a test.

References

Ackerman, T., & Shu, Z. (2009). *Using confirmatory MIRT modeling to provide diagnostic information in large scale assessment*. Paper presented at the meeting of the National Council on Measurement in Education, San Diego, CA.

ACT. (2022). *ACT technical manual*. Iowa City, IA: ACT.

ACT. (2023). Make sense of your scores. www.act.org/content/dam/act/unsecured/documents/2021-2022-Student-Rpt-with-Write-sample-data.pdf

Adams, R. J., Wilson, M., & Wu, M. (1997). Multilevel item response models: An approach to errors in variables regression. *Journal of Educational and Behavioral Statistics*, 22(1), 47–76. https://doi.org/10.3102/10769986022001047

Albanese, M. A. (2014). The testing column: Differences in subject area subscores on the MBE and other illusions. *The Bar Examiner*, 83(2), 26–31.

Almond, R., Steinberg, L., & Mislevy, R. (2002). Enhancing the design and delivery of assessment systems: A four-process architecture. *The Journal of Technology, Learning and Assessment*, 1(5). https://ejournals.bc.edu/index.php/jtla/article/view/1671

American Board of Internal Medicine Maintenance of Certification (ABIM MOC). (2023). *Enhanced score report*. www.abim.org/Media/f4pp1das/score-report.pdf

American Educational Research Association, American Psychological Association, & National Council on Measurement in Education. (1999). *Standards for educational and psychological testing*. Washington, DC: American Educational Research Association.

American Educational Research Association, American Psychological Association, & National Council on Measurement in Education. (2014). *Standards for educational and psychological testing*. Washington, DC: American Educational Research Association.

Angoff, W. H. (1971). Scales, norms, and equivalent scores. In R. L. Thorndike (Ed.), *Educational measurement* (pp. 508–600). Washington, DC: American Council on Education.

Armed Services Vocational Aptitude Battery (ASVAB). (2023). *Understanding your ASVAB results*. www.asvabprogram.com/media-center-article/28

Beaton, A. E., & Allen, N. L. (1992). Interpreting scales through scale anchoring. *Journal of Educational Statistics*, 17, 191–204. https://doi.org/10.2307/1165169

Bell, R., & Lumsden, J. (1980). Test length and validity. *Applied Psychological Measurement*, 4(2), 165–170. https://doi.org/10.1177/014662168000400203
Bertin, J. (1983). *Semiology of graphics: Diagrams, networks, maps* (Translated into English by Berg, W. J.). Madison: University of Wisconsin Press.
Biancarosa, G., Kennedy, P. C., Carlson, S. E., Yoon, H., Seipel, B., Liu, B., & Davison, M. L. (2019). Constructing subscores that add validity: A case study of identifying students at risk. *Educational and Psychological Measurement*, 79(1), 65–84. https://doi.org/10.1177/0013164418763255
Brennan, R. L. (2012). *Utility indexes for decisions about subscores*. CASMA Research Report 33. Iowa City, IA: Center for Advanced Studies in Measurement and Assessment.
Brinton, W. C. (1939). *Graphic presentations*. New York: Brinton.
Brown, G. T. L., O'Leary, T. M., & Hattie, J. A. C. (2019). Effective reporting for formative assessment: The asTTle case example. In D. Zapata-Rivera (Ed.), *Score reporting research and applications (The NCME Applications of Educational Measurement and Assessment Book Series)* (pp. 107–125). New York: Routledge. https://doi.org/10.4324/9781351136501-11
Brown, W. (1910). Some experimental results in the correlation of mental abilities. *British Journal of Psychology*, 3(3), 296–322. https://doi.org/10.1111/j.2044-8295.1910.tb00207.x
Bulut, O., Davison, M. L., & Rodriguez, M. C. (2017). Estimating between-person and within-person subscore reliability with profile analysis. *Multivariate Behavioral Research*, 52(1), 86–104. https://doi.org/10.1080/00273171.2016.1253452
Casella, G. (1985). An introduction to empirical Bayes data analysis. *The American Statistician*, 39(2), 83–87. https://doi.org/10.2307/2682801
Choi, I., & Papageorgiou, S. (2020). Evaluating subscore uses across multiple levels: A case of reading and listening subscores for young EFL learners. *Language Testing*, 37(2), 254–279. https://doi.org/10.1177/0265532219879654
Comprehensive Clinical Science Examination (CCSE). (2023). *Examinee performance report*. www.nbme.org/sites/default/files/2022-12/CCSE_Examinee_Performance_Report_2022.pdf
Cronbach, L. J. (1951). Coefficient alpha and the internal structure of tests. *Psychometrika*, 16, 297–334. https://doi.org/10.1007/bf02310555
Cronbach, L. J., Schönemann, P., & McKie, D. (1965). Alpha coefficients for stratified-parallel tests. *Educational and Psychological Measurement*, 25, 291–312. https://doi.org/10.1177/001316446502500201
CTB/McGraw-Hill. (2001). *TerraNova, the second edition: Individual profile report*. Monterey, CA: Author.
Dai, S., Svetina, D., & Wang, X. (2017). Reporting subscores using R: A software review. *Journal of Educational and Behavioral Statistics*, 42, 617–638. https://doi.org/10.3102/1076998617716462
Dai, S., Wang, X., & Svetina, D. (2019). Subscore: Sub-score computing functions in classical test theory (R Package Version 3.1) [Computer Software]. http://CRAN.R-project.org/package=subscore
Davison, M. L., Davenport, E. C., Chang, Y.-F., Vue, K., & Su, S. (2015). Criterion-related validity: Assessing the value of subscores. *Journal of Educational Measurement*, 52, 263–279. https://doi.org/10.2307/43940571

DiBello, L. V., Roussos, L., & Stout, W. F. (2006). Review of cognitive diagnostic assessment and a summary of psychometric models. In C. R. Rao, & S. Sinharay (Eds.), *Handbook of statistics*, Volume 26 (pp. 979–1030). Amsterdam: Elsevier Science B.V. https://doi.org/10.1016/s0169-7161(06)26031-0

Dorans, N. J., & Walker, M. E. (2007). Sizing up linkages. In N. J. Dorans, M. Pommerich, & P. W. Holland (Eds.), *Linking and aligning scores and scales* (pp. 179–198). New York: Springer. https://doi.org/10.1007/978-0-387-49771-6_10

Duolingo English Test. (2023). *Sample certificate*. https://englishtest.duolingo.com/sample_certificate

Draper, N. R., & Smith, H. (1998). *Applied regression analysis*. New York: Wiley. https://doi.org/10.1002/9781118625590

DuBois, P. H. (1970). *A history of psychological testing*. Boston: Allyn & Bacon.

Dwyer, A., Boughton, K. A., Yao, L., Steffen, M., & Lewis, D. (2006, April). *A comparison of subscale score augmentation methods using empirical data*. Paper presented at the meeting of the National Council on Measurement in Education, San Francisco, CA.

Ebel, R. L. (1962). Content standard test scores. *Educational and Psychological Measurement*, 22, 15–25. https://doi.org/10.1177/001316446202200103

Educational Testing Service. (2008). *PraxisTM 2008–09 information bulletin*. Princeton, NJ: Educational Testing Service.

Educational Testing Service. (2020). *TOEFL® Research insight series, Volume 3: Reliability and comparability of TOEFL iBT® scores*. Princeton, NJ: Author.

Educational Testing Service. (2021). *The Praxis study companion, elementary education: Content knowledge*. Princeton, NJ: Educational Testing Service.

Edwards, M. C., & Vevea, J. L. (2006). An empirical Bayes approach to subscore augmentation: How much strength can we borrow? *Journal of Educational and Behavioral Statistics*, 31, 241–259. https://doi.org/10.3102/10769986031003241

Everitt, B. (2011). *Cluster analysis*. Chichester, UK: Wiley.

Every Student Succeeds Act, 20 U.S.C. § 6301 (2015). www.congress.gov/bill/114th-congress/senate-bill/1177

Feinberg, R. A., & Clauser, A. L. (2016). Can item keyword feedback help remediate knowledge gaps? *Journal of Graduate Medical Education*, 8(4), 541–545. https://doi.org/10.4300/jgme-d-15-00463.1

Feinberg, R. A., & Jurich, D. P. (2017). Guidelines for interpreting and reporting subscores. *Educational Measurement: Issues and Practice*, 36(1), 5–13. https://doi.org/10.1111/emip.12142

Feinberg, R. A., & von Davier, M. (2020). Conditional subscore reporting using the compound binomial distribution. *Journal of Educational and Behavioral Statistics*, 45(5), 515–533. https://doi.org/10.3102/1076998620911933

Feinberg, R. A., & Wainer, H. (2011). Extracting sunbeams from cucumbers. *Journal of Computational and Graphical Statistics*, 20(4), 793–810. https://doi.org/10.1198/jcgs.2011.204a

Feinberg, R. A., & Wainer, H. (2014). When can we improve subscores by making them shorter? The case against subscores with overlapping items. *Educational Measurement: Issues and Practice*, 33(3), 47–54. https://doi.org/10.1111/emip.12037

Feinberg, R. A., & Wainer, H. (2014). A simple equation to predict a subscore's value. *Educational Measurement: Issues and Practice*, 33(3), 55–56. https://doi.org/10.1111/emip.12035

Flanagan, J. C. (1948). *The aviation psychology program in the Army Air Forces.* Report 1, AAF Aviation Psychology Program Research Reports, US Government Printing Office, pp. xii+316.

Fleiss, J. L. (1975). Measuring agreement between two judges on the presence or absence of a trait. *Biometrics*, 31, 651–659. https://doi.org/10.2307/2529549

Friendly, M., & Wainer, H. (2021). *A history of data visualization and graphic communication.* Cambridge, MA: Harvard University Press. https://doi.org/10.4159/9780674259034

George, A. C., Robitzsch, A., Kiefer, T., Gross, J., & Uenlue, A. (2016). The R package CDM for cognitive diagnosis models. *Journal of Statistical Software*, 74(2), 1–24. https://doi.org/10.18637/jss.v074.i02

Goodman, D. P., & Hambleton, R. K. (2004). Student test score reports and interpretive guides: Review of current practices and suggestions for future research. *Applied Measurement in Education*, 17, 145–220. https://doi.org/10.1207/s15324818ame1702_3

Goodman, L. A., & Kruskal, W. H. (1954). Measures of association for cross classifications. Part I. *Journal of the American Statistical Association*, 49, 732–764. https://doi.org/10.2307/2281536

Haberman, S. J. (2008a). When can subscores have value? *Journal of Educational and Behavioral Statistics*, 33, 204–229. https://doi.org/10.3102/1076998607302636

Haberman, S. J. (2008b). *Subscores and validity.* ETS Research Report Series (ETS Research Report No. RR-08-64). Educational Testing Service. https://doi.org/10.1002/j.2333-8504.2008.tb02150.x

Haberman, S. J. (2008c). *Outliers in assessments.* ETS Research Report Series (ETS Research Report No. RR-08-41). https://doi.org/10.1002/j.2333-8504.2008.tb02150.x

Haberman, S. J. (2013). *A general program for item-response analysis that employs the stabilized Newton-Raphson algorithm.* ETS Research Report Series (ETS Research Report No. RR-13-32). https://doi.org/10.1002/j.2333-8504.2013.tb02339.x

Haberman, S. J., & Sinharay, S. (2010). Reporting of subscores using multidimensional item response theory. *Psychometrika*, 75, 209–227. https://doi.org/10.1007/s11336-010-9158-4

Haberman, S. J., & Sinharay, S. (2013). Does subgroup membership information lead to better estimation of true subscores? *British Journal of Mathematical and Statistical Psychology*, 66, 451–469. https://doi.org/10.1111/j.2044-8317.2012.02061

Haberman, S. J., Sinharay, S., & Puhan, G. (2009). Reporting subscores for institutions. *British Journal of Mathematical and Statistical Psychology*, 62, 79–95. https://doi.org/10.1348/000711007x248875

Haberman, S. J., & von Davier, M. (2007). Some notes on models for cognitively based skills diagnosis. In C. R. Rao & S. Sinharay (Eds.), *Handbook of statistics*, Vol. 26 (pp. 1031–1038). Amsterdam: Elsevier North-Holland. https://doi.org/10.1016/s0169-7161(06)26040-1

Haberman, S., & Yao, L. (2015). Repeater analysis for combining information from different assessments. *Journal of Educational Measurement*, 52, 223–251. https://doi.org/10.1111/jedm.12075

Haberman, S. J, Yao, L, & Sinharay S. (2015). Prediction of true test scores from observed item scores and ancillary data. *British Journal of Mathematical and Statistical Psychology*, 68, 363–85. https://doi.org/10.1111/bmsp.12052

Haladyna T. M., & Kramer, G. A. (2004). The validity of subscores for a credentialing test. *Evaluation and the Health Professions*, 27(4), 349–368. https://doi.org/10.1177/0163278704270010

Hambleton, R. K., & Zenisky, A. L. (2013). Reporting test scores in more meaningful ways: A research-based approach to score report design. In K. F. Geisinger (Ed.), *APA handbook of testing and assessment in psychology: Vol. 3. Testing and assessment in school psychology and education* (pp. 479–494). Washington, DC: American Psychological Association. https://doi.org/10.1037/14049-023

Harris, D. J., & Hanson, B. A. (1991, April). *Methods of examining the usefulness of subscores*. Paper presented at the meeting of the National Council on Measurement in Education, Chicago, IL.

Hegarty, M. (2019). Advances in cognitive science and information visualization. In D. Zapata-Rivera (Ed.), *Score reporting research and applications (The NCME Applications of Educational Measurement and Assessment Book Series)* (pp. 19–34). New York: Routledge. https://doi.org/10.4324/9781351136501-4

Huff, K., & Goodman, D. P. (2007). The demand for cognitive diagnostic assessment. In J. Leighton, & M. Gierl (Eds.), *Cognitive diagnostic assessment for education: Theory and applications* (pp. 19–60). Cambridge: Cambridge University Press. https://doi.org/10.1017/cbo9780511611186.002

Junker, B. W., & Sijtsma, K. (2001). Cognitive assessment models with few assumptions, and connections with nonparametric item response theory. *Applied Psychological Measurement*, 25, 258–272. https://doi.org/10.1177/01466210122032064

Kelley, T. L. (1923). *Statistical method*. New York: Macmillan.

Kibby, M. W. (1981). Test review: The degrees of reading power. *Journal of Reading*, 24(5), 416–427. www.jstor.org/stable/40032381

Kolstad, A., Cohen, J., Baldi, S., Chan, T., DeFur, E., & Angeles, J. (1998). *The response probability convention used in reporting data from IRT assessment scales: Should NCES adopt a standard?* Washington, DC: American Institutes for Research.

LaFlair, G. T. (2020). *Duolingo English test: Subscores* (Duolingo Research Report No. DRR-20-03). Duolingo.

Lane, S., Raymond, M. R., Haladyna, T. M., & Downing, S. M. (2015). Test development process. In S. Lane, M. R. Raymond, & T. M. Haladyna (Eds.), *Handbook of test development* (2nd ed., pp. 3–18). New York, NY: Routledge.

Lazer, S., Mazzeo, J., & Weiss, A. with Campbell, J., Casalaina, L., Horkay, N., Kaplan, B., & Rogers, A. (2001). *Final report on enhanced achievement level reporting and scale anchoring activities*. Unpublished report prepared on behalf of the National Assessment Governing Board.

Leighton, J. P., & Gierl, M. J. (2007). *Cognitive diagnostic assessment for education: Theory and applications*. New York: Cambridge University Press. https://doi.org/10.1017/cbo9780511611186

Leighton, J. P., Gierl, M. J., & Hunka, S. M. (2004). The attribute hierarchy model for cognitive assessment: A variation on Tatsuoka's rule-space approach. *Journal of Educational Measurement*, 41, 205–237. https://doi.org/10.1111/j.1745-3984.2004.tb01163.x

Lim, E., & Lee, W. (2020). Subscore equating and profile reporting. *Applied Measurement in Education*, 33, 95–112. https://doi.org/10.1080/08957347.2020.1732381

Ling, G. (2012). Why the major field test in business does not report subscores – Reliability and construct validity evidence (ETS Research Report No. RR-08-64). Educational Testing Service. https://doi.org/10.1002/j.2333-8504.2012.tb02293.x.

Liu, Y., Robin, F., Yoo, H., & Manna, V. (2018). *Statistical properties of the GRE® psychology test subscores*. ETS Research Report Series. https://doi.org/10.1002/ets2.12206

Longabach, T., & Peyton, V. A. (2018). Comparison of reliability and precision of subscore reporting methods for a state English language proficiency assessment. *Language Testing*, 35, 297–317. https://doi.org/10.1177/0265532217689949

Longford, N. T. (1990). Multivariate variance component analysis: An application in test development. *Journal of Educational Statistics*, 15, 91–112. https://doi.org/10.2307/1164764

Lord, F. M., & Novick, M. R. (1968). *Statistical theories of mental test scores*. Reading, MA: Addison-Wesley.

Lord, F. M., & Wingersky, M. (1984). Comparison of IRT true-score and equipercentile observed-score equatings. *Applied Psychological Measurement*, 8, 453–461. https://doi.org/10.1177/014662168400800409

Lovett, B. J., & Harrison, A. G. (2021). De-implementing inappropriate accommodations practices. *Canadian Journal of School Psychology*, 36(2), 115–126. https://doi.org/10.1177/0829573520972556

Luecht, R. (2007). Using information from multiple-choice distractors to enhance cognitive-diagnostic score reporting. In J. Leighton & M. Gierl (Eds.), *Cognitive diagnostic assessment for education: Theory and applications* (pp. 319–340). Cambridge: Cambridge University Press. https://doi.org/10.1017/cbo9780511611186.011

Luecht, R. (2013). Assessment engineering task model maps: Task models and templates as a new way to develop and implement test specifications. *Journal of Applied Testing Technology*, 14, 1–38.

Luecht, R. M., Gierl, M. J., Tan, X., & Huff, K. (2006, April). *Scalability and the development of useful diagnostic scales*. Paper presented at the annual Meeting of the National Council on Measurement in Education, San Francisco, CA.

Lyren, P. (2009). Reporting subscores from college admission tests. *Practical Assessment, Research, and Evaluation*, 14, 1–10.

Margolis, M. J., Clauser, B. E., Winward, M., & Dillon, G. F. (2010). Validity evidence for USMLE examination cut scores: Results of a large-scale survey. *Academic Medicine*, 85(10), 93–97. https://doi.org/10.1097/acm.0b013e3181ed4028

McDermott, P. A., Glutting, J. J., Jones, J. N., Watkins, M. W., & Kush, J. (1989). Core profile types in the WISC-R national sample: Structure, membership, and applications. *Psychological Assessment: A Journal of Consulting and Clinical Psychology*, 1, 292–299. https://doi.org/10.1037/1040-3590.1.4.292

McFadden, D. (1974). Conditional logit analysis of qualitative choice behavior. In P. Zarembka (Ed.), *Frontiers in econometrics* (pp. 105–142). New York: Academic Press.

Meijer, R. R., Boevé, A. J., Tendeiro, J. N., Bosker, R. J., & Albers, C. J. (2017). The use of subscores in higher education: When is this useful? *Frontiers in Psychology*, 8, 1–6. https://doi.org/10.3389/fpsyg.2017.00305

Menard, S. (2000). Coefficients of determination for multiple logistic regression analysis. *The American Statistician*, 54(1), 17–24. https://doi.org/10.2307/2685605

Mertler, C. A. (2018). Norm-referenced interpretation. In B. Frey (Ed.), *The SAGE encyclopedia of educational research, measurement, and evaluation* (pp. 1161–1163). Thousand Oaks, CA: SAGE. https://doi.org/10.4135/9781506326139.n478

Mislevy, R. J., Steinberg, L. S., & Almond, R. G. (2003). On the structure of educational assessments. *Measurement: Interdisciplinary Research and Perspectives*, 1, 3–67. https://doi.org/10.1207/S15366359MEA0101_02

Morey, L. C. (2004). The Personality Assessment Inventory (PAI). In M. E. Maruish (Ed.), *The use of psychological testing for treatment planning and outcomes assessment: Instruments for adults* (pp. 509–551). Mahwah, NJ: Lawrence Erlbaum Associates Publishers. https://doi.org/10.4324/9781410610614

Muraki, E. (1992). A generalized partial credit model: Application of an EM algorithm. *Applied Psychological Measurement*, 16, 159–176. https://doi.org/10.1177%2F014662169201600206

National Assessment of Educational Progress (NAEP). (2023). *Student groups.* https://nces.ed.gov/nationsreportcard/guides/groups.aspx

New York State Testing Program (NYSTP). (2023). *NYS grades 3-8 2021 technical report.* www.nysed.gov/common/nysed/files/programs/state-assessment/3-8-technical-report-2021w.pdf

Paolino, J. (2020). Teaching linear correlation using contour plots. *Teaching Statistics*, 43(1), 13–20. https://doi.org/10.1111/test.12239

Papageorgiou, S., & Choi, I. (2018). Adding value to second-language listening and reading subscores: Using a score augmentation approach. *International Journal of Testing*, 18, 207–230. https://doi.org/10.1080/15305058.2017.1407766

Pashler, H., Cepeda, N. J., Wixted, J. T., & Rohrer, D. (2005). When does feedback facilitate learning of words? *Journal of Experimental Psychology: Learning, Memory, and Cognition*, 31(1), 3–8. https://doi.org/10.1037/0278-7393.31.1.3

Pearson Longman. (2010). *The official guide to PTE: Pearson test of English academic.* Hong Kong SAR: Pearson Longman Asia ELT.

Perie, M., Marion, S., & Gong, B. (2009). Moving toward a comprehensive assessment system: A framework for considering interim assessments. *Educational Measurement: Issues and Practice*, 28(3), 5–13. https://doi.org/10.1080/01619561003685304

Personality Assessment Inventory (PAI). (2023). *The PAI police and public safety selection report.* https://post.ca.gov/portals/0/post_docs/publications/psychological-screening-manual/PAI_PolicePubSftyRpt.pdf

Pieper Bar Review. (2017). *Bar examiners to provide (slightly) more information to candidates who fail the bar exam.* http://news.pieperbar.com/bar-examiners-to-provide-slightly-more-information-to-candidates-who-fail-the-bar-exam

Praxis. (2023). *Interpreting Your Praxis® Test Taker Score Report.* www.ets.org/s/praxis/pdf/sample_score_report.pdf

Puhan, G., & Liang, L. (2011). Equating subscores under the non equivalent anchor test (NEAT) design. *Educational Measurement: Issues and Practice*, 30(1), 23–35. https://doi.org/10.1111/j.1745-3992.2010.00197.x

Puhan, G., Sinharay, S., Haberman, S. J., & Larkin, K. (2010). The utility of augmented subscores in a licensure exam: An evaluation of methods using empirical data. *Applied Measurement in Education*, 23, 266–285. https://doi.org/10.1080/08957347.2010.486287

R Core Team. (2022). *R: A language and environment for statistical computing.* Vienna, Austria: R Foundation for Statistical Computing. www.R-project.org/

Ramsay, J. O. (1973). The effect of number of categories in rating scales on precision of estimation of scale values. *Psychometrika*, 38(4, Pt. 1), 513–532. https://doi.org/10.1007/bf02291492

Rasch, G. (1966). An individualistic approach to item analysis. In P. F. Lazarsfeld, & N. W. Henry (Eds.), *Readings in mathematical social science* (pp. 89–107). Cambridge, MA: MIT Press.

Raymond, M. R. (2001). Job analysis and the specification of content for licensure and certification examinations. *Applied Measurement in Education*, 14, 369–415. https://doi.org/10.1207/s15324818ame1404_4

Reckase, M. D. (2009). *Multidimensional item response theory*. New York: Springer. https://doi.org/10.1007/978-0-387-89976-3

Reckase, M. D., & Xu, J. R. (2014). The evidence for a subscore structure in a test of English language competency for English language learners. *Educational and Psychological Measurement*, 75, 805–825. https://doi.org/10.1177/0013164414554416

Roberts, M. R., & Gierl, M. J. (2010). Developing score reports for cognitive diagnostic assessments. *Educational Measurement: Issues and Practice*, 29(3), 25–38. https://doi.org/10.1111/j.1745-3992.2010.00181.x

Roussos, L. A., DiBello, L. V., Stout, W. F., Hartz, S. M., Henson, R. A., & Templin, J. H. (2007). The fusion model skills diagnostic system. In J. Leighton, & M. Gierl (Eds.), *Cognitive diagnostic assessment for education: Theory and applications* (pp. 275–318). New York: Cambridge University Press. https://doi.org/10.1017/cbo9780511611186.010

Rupp, A. A., & Templin, J. L. (2009). The (un)usual suspects? A measurement community in search of its identity. *Measurement*, 7(2), 115–121. https://doi.org/10.1080/15366360903187700

Rupp, A. A., Templin, J., & Henson, R. A. (2010). *Diagnostic measurement: Theory, methods, and applications*. New York: Guilford Press.

Sands, W. A., Waters, B. K., & McBride, J. R. (1997). *Computerized adaptive testing: From inquiry to operation*. Washington, DC: American Psychological Association. https://doi.org/10.1037%2F10244-000

SAT. (2023). *Understanding your score report*. https://satsuite.collegeboard.org/media/pdf/sample-sat-score-report.pdf

Sawaki, Y., & Sinharay, S. (2018). Do the TOEFL iBT® section scores provide value-added information to stakeholders? *Language Testing*, 35, 529–556. https://doi.org/10.1177/0265532217716731

Sinharay, S. (2010). How often do subscores have added value? Results from operational and simulated data. *Journal of Educational Measurement*, 47, 150–174. https://doi.org/10.1111/j.1745-3984.2010.00106.x

Sinharay, S. (2013). A note on assessing the added value of subscores. *Educational Measurement: Issues and Practice*, 32, 38–42. https://doi.org/10.1111/emip.12021

Sinharay, S. (2014). Analysis of added value of subscores with respect to classification. *Journal of Educational Measurement*, 51, 212–222. https://doi.org/10.1111/jedm.12043

Sinharay, S., & Haberman, S. J. (2008). How much can we reliably know about what students know? *Measurement: Interdisciplinary Research and Perspectives*, 6, 46–49. https://doi.org/10.1080/15366360802715486

Sinharay, S., & Haberman, S. J. (2011). Equating of augmented subscores. *Journal of Educational Measurement*, 48, 122–145. https://doi.org/10.1111/j.1745-3984.2011.00137.x

Sinharay, S., & Haberman, S. J. (2014). An empirical investigation of population invariance in the value of subscores. *International Journal of Testing*, 14, 22–48. https://doi.org/10.1080/15305058.2013.822712

Sinharay, S., Haberman, S. J., & Lee, Y. -H. (2011). When does scale anchoring work? A case study. *Journal of Educational Measurement*, 48(1), 61–80. https://doi.org/10.1111/j.1745-3984.2011.00131.x

Sinharay, S., Haberman, S. J., & Puhan, G. (2007). Subscores based on classical test theory: To report or not to report. *Educational Measurement: Issues and Practice*, 26(4), 21–28. https://doi.org/10.1111/j.1745-3992.2007.00105.x

Sinharay, S., Haberman, S. J., & Wainer, H. (2011). Do adjusted subscores lack validity? Don't blame the messenger. *Educational and Psychological Measurement*, 71, 789–797. https://doi.org/10.1177/0013164410391782

Sinharay, S., Puhan, G., & Haberman, S. J. (2010). Reporting diagnostic subscores in educational testing: Temptations, pitfalls, and some solutions. *Multivariate Behavioral Research*, 45, 553–573. https://doi.org/10.1080/00273171.2010.483382

Sinharay, S., Puhan, G., & Haberman, S. J. (2011). An NCME instructional module on subscores. *Educational Measurement: Issues and Practice*, 30(3), 29–40. https://doi.org/10.1111/j.1745-3992.2011.00208.x

Sinharay, S., Puhan, G., Haberman, S. J., & Hambleton, R. K. (2019). Subscores: When to communicate them, what are their alternatives, and some recommendations. In D. Zapata-Rivera (Ed.), *Score reporting research and applications (The NCME Applications of Educational Measurement and Assessment Book Series)* (pp. 35–49). New York: Routledge. https://doi.org/10.4324/9781351136501-5

Skorupski, W. P., & Carvajal, J. (2010). A comparison of approaches for improving the reliability of objective level scores. *Educational and Psychological Measurement*, 70, 357–375. https://doi.org/10.1177/0013164409355694

Slater, S., Livingston, S. L., & Silver, M. (2019). Score reports for large-scale testing programs. In D. Zapata-Rivera (Ed.), *Score reporting research and applications (The NCME Applications of Educational Measurement and Assessment Book Series)* (pp. 91–106). New York, NY: Routledge. https://doi.org/10.4324/9781351136501-10

South Carolina College- and Career-Ready Assessments (SCREADY). (2023). *Individual student report*. https://ed.sc.gov/tests/tests-files/sc-ready-files/spring-2022-sample-individual-student-report-english/

Spearman, C. (1904). The proof and measurement of association between two things. *American Journal of Psychology*, 15, 72–101. https://doi.org/10.2307/1412159

Spearman, C. (1910). Correlation calculated from faulty data. *British Journal of Psychology*, 3, 271–295. https://doi.org/10.1111/j.2044-8295.1910.tb00206.x

Spencer, B. D. (Ed.). (1997). *Statistics and public policy*. Oxford: Clarendon Press.

Stanton, H. C., & Reynolds, C. R. (2000). Configural frequency analysis as a method of determining Wechsler profile types. *School Psychology Quarterly*, 15(4), 434–448. https://doi.org/10.1037/h0088799

Stone, C. A., Ye, F., Zhu, X., & Lane, S. (2010). Providing subscale scores for diagnostic information: A case study when the test is essentially unidimensional. *Applied Measurement in Education*, 23, 63–86. https://doi.org/10.1080/08957340903423651

Swanson, D. B., Case, S. M., & Nungester, R. J. (1991). Validity of NBME Part I and Part II scores in prediction of Part III performance. *Academic Medicine*, 66, S7–S9. https://doi.org/10.1097/00001888-199109001-00004

Tanaka, V. (2023). *A framework for reporting technically-sound and useful subscores on state assessments*. www.nciea.org/blog/promoting-effective-practices-for-subscore-reporting-and-use/

Tatsuoka, K. K. (1983). Rule space: An approach for dealing with misconceptions based on item response theory. *Journal of Educational Measurement*, 20, 345–354. https://doi.org/10.1111/j.1745-3984.1983.tb00212.x

Theil, H. (1970). On the estimation of relationships involving qualitative variables. *American Journal of Sociology*, 76, 103–154. https://doi.org/10.1086/224909

Thissen D. (2013). Using the testlet response model as a shortcut to multidimensional item response theory subscore computation. In R. Millsap, L. van der Ark, D. Bolt, & C. Woods (Eds.), *New developments in quantitative psychology: Presentations from the 77th Annual Psychometric Society Meeting* (pp. 29–40). New York: Springer. https://doi.org/10.1007/978-1-4614-9348-8_3

Tufte, E. R. (2001). *The visual display of quantitative information* (2nd ed.). Cheshire, CT: Graphics Press.

United States Medical Licensing Examination (USMLE). (2023). *Updated sample Step 2 CK annual school report*. www.nbme.org/sites/default/files/2022-08/2022_Enhanced_USMLE_Step_2_CK_School_Report_Sample.pdf

Von Davier, M. (2008). A general diagnostic model applied to language testing data. *British Journal of Mathematical and Statistical Psychology*, 61, 287–307. https://doi.org/10.1348/000711007x193957

Wainer, H. (1984). How to display data badly. *The American Statistician*, 38(2), 137–147. https://doi.org/10.2307/2683253

Wainer, H. (1997). *Visual revelations*. New York: Copernicus Press. https://doi.org/10.4324/9780203774793

Wainer, H. (2009). *Picturing the uncertain world*. Princeton, NJ: Princeton University Press. https://doi.org/10.1515/9781400832897

Wainer, H. (2015). On the crucial role of empathy in the design of communications: Genetic testing as an example. In *Truth or truthiness: Distinguishing fact from fiction by learning to think like a data scientist* (pp. 82–90). Cambridge: Cambridge University Press. https://doi:10.1017/CBO9781316424315.012

Wainer, H., Dorans, D. J., Eignor, D., Flaugher, R., Green, B. F., Mislevy, R. J., Steinberg, L., & Thissen, D. (2000). *Computerized adaptive testing: A primer* (2nd ed.). Hillsdale, NJ: Lawrence Erlbaum Associates. https://doi.org/10.4324/9781410605931

Wainer, H., & Feinberg, R. A. (2017). For want of a nail: Why unnecessarily long tests may be impeding the progress of Western civilization. In M. Pitici (Ed.), *The best writing on mathematics* 2016 (pp. 321–330). Princeton, NJ: Princeton University Press. https://doi.org/10.1515/9781400885602-030

Wainer, H., Gessaroli, M., & Verdi, M. (2006). Finding what is not there through the unfortunate binning of results: The Mendel Effect. *Chance*, 19(1), 49–52. https://doi.org/10.1080/09332480.2006.10722771

Wainer, H., & Robinson, D. (2023). Why testing? Why should it cost you? *Chance*, 36(1), 48–52. https://doi.org/10.1080/09332480.2023.2179281

Wainer, H., Sheehan, K. M., & Wang, X. (2000). Some paths toward making Praxis scores more useful. *Journal of Educational Measurement*, 37, 113–140. https://doi.org/10.1111/j.1745-3984.2000.tb01079.x

Wainer, H., Vevea, J. L., Camacho, F., Reeve, B. B., Rosa, K., Nelson, L., et al. (2001). Augmented scores: "Borrowing strength" to compute scores based on small numbers of items. In D. Thissen & H. Wainer (Eds.), *Test scoring* (pp. 343–387). Mahwah, NJ: Erlbaum Associates. https://doi.org/10.4324/9781410604729-16

Wang, X., Svetina, D., & Dai, S. (2019). Exploration of factors affecting the added value of test subscores. *Journal of Experimental Education*, 87, 179–192. https://doi.org/10.1080/00220973.2017.1409182

Wilson, K. M. (2000). An exploratory dimensionality assessment of the TOEIC test. ETS Research Report Series (ETS Research Report No. RR-00-14). https://doi.org/10.1002/j.2333-8504.2000.tb01837.x

Yao, L., Sinharay, S., & Haberman, S. J. (2014). *Documentation for the software package SQE* (ETS Research Memorandum No. RM-14-02). Educational Testing Service.

Yen, W. M. (1987). *A Bayesian/IRT index of objective performance*. Paper presented at the meeting of the Psychometric Society, Montreal, Canada.

Zapata-Rivera, D., VanWinkle, W., & Zwick, R. (2012). *Applying score design principles in the design of score reports for CBAL™ Teachers*. (ETS Research Memorandum RM-12-20). Princeton, NJ: Educational Testing Service.

Zenisky, A. L., & Hambleton, R. K. (2012). Developing test score reports that work: The process and best practices for effective communication. *Educational Measurement: Issues and Practice*, 31(2), 21–26. https://doi.org/10.1111/j.1745-3992.2012.00231.x

Zenisky, A. L., & Hambleton, R. K. (2015). A model and good practices for score reporting. In S. Lane, M. R. Raymond, & T. M. Haladyna (Eds.), *Handbook of test development* (2nd ed., pp. 585–602). New York: Routledge.

Zieky, M. J., Perie, M., & Livingston, S. A. (2008). *Cutscores: A manual for setting standards of performance on educational and occupational tests*. Princeton, NJ: Educational Testing Service.

Zwick, R., Senturk, D., Wang, J., & Loomis, S. C. (2001). An investigation of alternative methods for item mapping on the national assessment of educational progress. *Educational Measurement: Issues and Practice*, 20(2), 15–25. https://doi.org/10.1111/j.1745-3992.2001.tb00059.x

Name Index

Abrahams, H., 136
Ackerman, T., 150
Adams, R. J., 74
Albanese, M. A., 124
Albers, C. J., 151
Allen, N. L., 125
Almond, R. G., 130, 136
Angoff, W. H., 21

Barksdale, J., 138
Beaton, A. E., 125
Bell, R., 148
Bertin, J., 104
Biancarosa, G., 135
Billings, J., 87
Bingham, W. V., 10
Boeve, A. J., 151
Bosker, R. J., 151
Boughton, K. A., 122
Brennan, R. L., 43, 55, 59, 106
Brown, G. T. L., 39
Brown, W., 48, 79
Bulut, O., 64, 66

Carvajal, J., 120, 121
Case, S. M., 151
Casella, G., 114
Cepeda, N. J., 124
Chang, Y.-F., 109
Choi, I., 130, 152
Clauser, A. L., 124
Clauser, B. E., 106
Cronbach, L. J., 48, 70–73, 76, 79, 113

Dai, S., 71, 120–122, 152
Davenport, E. C., 109

Davison, M. L., 82, 109
Deming, W. E., 88, 148, 149
DiBello, L. V., 131
Dillon, G. F., 106
Dorans, N. J., 55, 57
Draper, N. R., 126, 128
DuBois, P., 6, 8
Dwyer, A., 122

Edwards, M. C., 120
Everitt, B., 131

Feinberg, R. A., xi, 21, 33, 41, 59, 106, 107,
   124, 127, 128, 150, 151
Flanagan, J., 11, 12
Fleiss, J. L., 77
Friendly, M., 41

George, A. C., 133
Gessaroli, M., 21
Gierl, M. J., 131, 132, 140
Glutting, J. J., 117
Gong, B., 22, 23
Goodman, D. P., 19, 110, 122
Goodman, L. A., 130
Gross, J., 133
Gulliksen, H., 12

Haberman, S. J., x, xi, 45, 52, 57, 59–62, 65,
   67, 71–74, 82, 83, 85, 109, 111, 113–115,
   120, 121, 126–128, 133, 144, 150, 151
Haladyna, T. M., 45, 81, 99, 102, 106–109,
   150, 153
Hambleton, R. K., 19, 40, 122
Hanson, B. A., 99, 150
Harris, D. J., 99, 150

Harrison, A. G., 19
Hattie, J. C. A., 39
Hegarty, M., 41
Henson, R. A., 131
Holland, P. W., 110, 142
Hubbard, H. D., 3
Huff, K., 110
Hunka, S. M., 132

Jenckes, T., 7
Johnson, P., 17
Jones, J. N., 117
Junker, B. W., 132, 133
Jurich, D. P., 59, 106, 151

Kelley, T. L., 45, 46, 53–56, 58, 59, 62, 85, 114, 116
Kibby, M. W., 125
Kiefer, T., 133
Kolstad, A., 126
Kramer, G. A., 45, 81, 99, 102, 106–109, 150, 153
Kruskal, W. H., 130
Kush, J., 117

LaFlair, G. T., 32
Lane, S., 40, 151
Larkin, K., 150
Lee, W., 152
Leighton, J. P., 131, 132
Lewis, D., 122
Liang, L., 44
Lim, E, 152
Ling, G., 150
Link, H., 9
Liu, Y., 120, 152
Livingston, S. A., 40, 126
Longabach, T., 150, 153
Longford, N. T., x, 83, 128
Loomis, S. C., 125
Lord, F. M., 99, 127
Lovett, B. J., 19
Luecht, R., 130, 135
Lumsden, J., 148
Lyren, P., 150

Manna, V., 120, 152
Margolis, M. J., 106
Marion, S., 22, 23
McDermott, P. A., 117
McFadden, D., 104

Meijer, R. R., 151, 152
Menard, S., 104
Mertler, C. A., 22
Mislevy, R. J., 130, 136
Morey, L. C., 37
Morrison, T., xii
Muraki, E., 74
Mussabini, S., 136, 149

Novick, M. R., 99
Nungester, R. J., 151

O'Leary, T. M., 39

Paolino, J., 104
Papageorgiou, S., 130, 152
Pashler, H., 124
Pearson, K., 143
Pendleton, G. H., 7
Perie, M., 22, 23, 126
Peyton, V. A., 150, 153
Puhan, G., 44, 113, 120, 150

Ramsay, J. O., 21
Rasch, G., 127, 130
Raymond, M. R., 106
Reckase, M. D., 131
Ree, M., 13
Reynolds, C. R., 117
Roberts, M. R., 140
Robin, F., 120, 152
Robinson, D. H., 81
Robitzsch, A., 133
Rohrer, D., 124
Roussos, L. A., 131, 132
Rupp, A. A., 131, 133

Sands, W. A., 14
Sawaki, Y., 108
Senturk, D., 125
Sheehan, K., ix, x
Shu, Z., 150
Sijtsma, K., 132, 133
Silver, M., 40
Sinharay, S., x, xi, 24, 43, 53, 59, 61, 66, 71, 73, 108, 113, 120, 121, 133, 135, 144, 150, 151
Skorupski, W. P., 120, 121
Slater, S., 40
Smith, H., 126, 128
Spearman, C., 45, 48, 63, 79

Spencer, B. D., 81
Stanton, H. C., 117
Steffen, M., 122
Steinberg, L. S., 130
Stone, C. A., 121, 151
Stout, W. F., 131
Su, S., 109
Sumner, C., 7
Svetina, D., 120–122, 152
Swanson, D. B., 106, 107, 151

Tanaka, V., 134
Tatsuoka, K. K., 132
Templin, J., 131, 133
Tendeiro, J. N., 151
Theil, H., 104
Thissen, D., x, 120
Thorndike, E. L., 9
Thurstone, L. L., 10
Tufte, E. R., 18, 41
Twain, M., 145

Uenlue, A., 133

VanWinkle, W., 40
Verdi, M., 21
Vevea, J. L., 120

von Davier, M. J., 21, 107, 127, 128, 132, 133
Vue, K., 109

Wainer, H., ix, x, xi, 21, 33, 41–43, 48, 59, 68,
    81, 107, 114, 120, 121, 140, 141, 150
Walker, M. E., 55, 57
Wang, J., 125
Wang, X., x, 120–122, 152
Watkins, M. W., 117
Wilson, K. M., 107, 150, 153
Wingersky, M., 127
Winward, M., 106
Wixted, J. T., 124

Xu, J. R., 131

Yao, L., 71, 72, 122
Ye, F., 151
Yen, W. M., 121
Yerkes, R. M., 8, 9
Yoo, H., 120, 152

Zapata-Rivera, D., 40
Zenisky, A. L., 40
Zhu, X., 151
Zieky, M. J., 126
Zwick, R., 40, 125

Subject Index

X^2-type statistic, 121, 122
36 data set survey, 88–91

ACT report, 27
actual subscores, 117, 120–122
added value subscores. *See* value-added subscores
adequate yearly progress (AYP), 14–15
AFQT. *See* Armed Forces Qualification Test (AFQT)
AGCT. *See* Army General Classification Test (AGCT)
aggregate-level subscores, 49, 83–85
Alpha test, 10
American Board of Internal Medicine Maintenance of Certification Examination (ABIM MOC), 27–30
American Community Survey, 4
Armed Forces Qualification Test (AFQT), 10
  score, 10–11
Armed Services Vocational Aptitude Battery (ASVAB), 9, 10, 30
  compared with Census, 13–14
  performance of, 11–12
  reliability of, 12
  and scores, 10–11
  subtests of, 10–11
Army Alpha test, 9–10
Army Beta test, 9
Army General Classification Test (AGCT), 10, *See also Army Alpha* test
assessment
  critical thinking, 36–37
  engineering, 130
  formative, 22–23
  large-scale, 126

  subscores on educational, ix
  summative, 23, 43
  TIMSS, 152
  types, 22–23
Assessment Tools for Teaching and Learning (asTTle), 39–40
asTTle. *See* Assessment Tools for Teaching and Learning (asTTle)
ASVAB. *See* Armed Services Vocational Aptitude Battery (ASVAB)
augmented subscores, x, 46, 60, 61, 111
  correlations of, 63
  examinees, 123
  scores, 114
  language test and, 61–62
  PRMSEs of, 112
  rational argument in, 62
  reporting, 111–112, 114–121
  subscores vs. total scores, correlations, 62–63
  use of, 111
  validity of, 121
  VAR of, 61
  vs. objective performance index, 122–123
average proportional reduction of mean square error, 64
AYP. *See* adequate yearly progress (AYP)

best linear predictor, 47, 62
between-items multidimensional item-response models, 74
Brennan utility index, 59

canonical analysis, 47–48
  reliability coefficient, 68, 69
  true subscores

correlations of, 68–69
prediction of, 67–69
card-sorting test, 9
category performance indicators, 128–130
CCSE. *See* Comprehensive Clinical Science Examination (CCSE)
ceteris paribus, 1
cognitive diagnostic model, 131–133
Comprehensive Clinical Science Examination (CCSE), 33–34
conditional subscores, 126–130
construct definition, 81, 106
contour lines, 103, 104
correlation coefficient, 61, 62
critical thinking assessment, 36–37
Cronbach's alpha, 48, 70
    approximation to reliability coefficient, 70–71
    estimation, 70–71
    standard errors, reliability coefficients, 71
cut scores, 77–79

diagnostic classification model, 131–133
difference score, 51–52
disattenuated correlation, 98–99, 105, 107, 108
displaying data, principles, 41
Duolingo English Test, 30–32

Educational Testing Service (ETS), ix
efficacy, test scores, 11
eigenvalue, 66
eigenvector, 66
Elementary Education: Content Knowledge test, 113–116, 121, 122
ETS. *See* Educational Testing Service (ETS)
Every Student Succeeds Act, 110
evidence-centered design, 130, 136
Examination a, 9, *See also Army Alpha* test
extrapolations, 3–4

fitted quadratic function, 2–3
formative assessments, 22–23
    asTTle report, 39–40
    focus of, 23
    SC Ready, 32–33
    types of, 22–23

generalized partial credit model, 74–75
group subscore mean, 84–85
group test, intelligence, 8

half test, 72–73
heterogeneity, 144

incremental validity, 47–49, 81–83
intelligence, group test, 8
isarithms, 104
item mapping, 125–126
item-level feedback, 124–125
item-response theory, 73–74, 86
    cut scores, 77–79
    latent variable and true subscore by, 75
    multidimensional models, 74–76, 86
    scaled subscores, 76–77
    true transformed subscore by, 76

job analysis, 106

Kelley estimation, 53–55
    application of, 53
    improvement from, 54
    of total score, 55, 56
    of writing score, 55, 56

language test
    augmented subscores and, 61–63
    correlations
        subscores vs. total scores, 62–63
        true subscores vs. total scores, 63–64
    data, 49–50
    eigenvalue in, 66
    estimation, 70
    half-tests in, 72
    PRMSE
        canonical score results, 68–69
        and partial regression coefficients, 62
        and VAR, 59
    $PRMSE_{res}$ in, 65
    reliability of cut scores, 78
    standard errors, reliability coefficients, 71
    structure of, 50
large-scale assessments, 126
latent variables prediction, 74–76
linear predictor, 68
linear regression, 126
logical evidence, 106
logistic regression model, 103–105

maximum-likelihood estimation, 75
mean square error (MSE), 46, 47
meaningful subscores, 5
measurement error (S_e), 51–52, 72, 73
mirt program, 73, 75, 77

MSE. *See* mean square error (MSE)
multidimensional item-response models, 74–76, 86, 133–134

NAEP. *See* National Assessment of Educational Progress (NAEP)
National Adult Literacy Survey, 126
National Assessment of Educational Progress (NAEP), 23, 126
National Board of Medical Examiners (NBME), x, 151
National Council on Measurement in Education (NCME), xi
NBME. *See* National Board of Medical Examiners (NBME)
NCME. *See* National Council on Measurement in Education (NCME)
New York State Testing Program (NYSTP), 41
No Child Left Behind Act, ix, 14
non-overlapping subscores, 108
normal approximation case, 76, 77
norming group, 22
NYSTP. *See* New York State Testing Program (NYSTP)

objective performance index, 121–124
orthogonality, 6

PAI. *See* Personality Assessment Inventory (PAI)
parallel-form subscore, 50, 51
  PRMSE estimation of, 58
parallel-form total score, 50, 51
partial correlation coefficient, 61
partial regression coefficient, 61–62
Pearson Test of English Academic, 131
Personality Assessment Inventory (PAI), 37–38
practice analysis, 106
practitioners recommendations, 138–140
Praxis test, 24–25
principal-components analysis, 47, 65–67
  true subscores with, 67
PRMSE. *See* proportional reduction in mean square error (PRMSE)
$PRMSE_{aug}$, 47, 61, 62
$PRMSE_{irt}$, 75–77
$PRMSE_{psub}$, 54, 57
$PRMSE_{punb}$, 54
$PRMSE_{res}$, 65
$PRMSE_{sub}$, 46–47, 79–80
$PRMSE_{tot}$, 46–47, 59, 64, 113

$PRMSE_{unb}$, 54
$PRMSE_{waug}$, 48, 68
procedural evidence, 106
profile, 47–48
profile analysis, ix, 117
profile bands, 20, 21
prophecy formula, 79
proportional reduction in mean square error (PRMSE), 46–47, 108, 139
  of augmented subscores, 112
  available data for, 150–153
  language test
    and partial regression coefficients, 62
    and VAR, 59
  for parallel-form scores estimation, 58
  strength of, 150
  from true subscores, 53
    conditionally unbiased property/estimation, 54–55
  unavailable data for, 153
psychometric quality, 19, 24, 40
psychometric-based approach, 131

reading tests, value-added subscores, 107
receptive subscore, 52
reliability, 1, 6
  ASVAB scores, 12
  coefficients, 45–46, 50–53, 79
    canonical analysis, 68, 69
    Cronbach's approximation to, 70–71
    half-sample estimation, 73
    incremental validity in, 48–49
    for numbers of items, 79–81
    of residual subscores, 83
    satisfactory, 46
    standard errors estimation, 71
    variances and, 52
  and correlation requirements, 99–103
  cut scores in language test, 78
  estimation of, 48
  on National Board of Medical Examiners, 151
  of residual subscores, 82
  subscore, 12–13, 86
    report, 45–46
  test scores, 12
repeated test, 72–73
residual subscores, 47, 63–65
  reliability, 82
residual true score, 64
residual-based indicators, 128–129
response percent/probability (RP), 125

Subject Index

rhythm test, 10
rudimentary proficiency testing, 6

SAT report, 25–27
scale anchoring process, 125
scaled subscores, 76–77
scatter analysis, ix
score report, 140–141, *See also* subscores
   ABIM MOC, 27–30
   ACT, 27
   assessment types, 22–23
   asTTle report, 39–40
   ASVAB, 30
   categorical performance indicators, 20, 21
   CCSE, 33–34
   complexity of, 18–20
   comprehensive framework in, 40
   critical thinking assessment, 36–37
   Duolingo English Test, 30–32
   empathy in communication of results, 41–42
   error representation, 142–143
   ordering, 141–142
   PAI Law Enforcement, Corrections, and Public Safety report, 37–38
   percent correct, 20–21
   percentile score, 20, 21
   practices on, 40–42
   Praxis test, 24–25
   profile bands, 20, 21
   raw score, 20, 44
   SAT, 25–27
   SC Ready, 32–33
   user types, 23–24
   USMLE, 34–36
scores, history of, 6–8
signal-to-noise (SNR), 55
SNR. *See* signal-to-noise (SNR)
South Carolina College-and Career-Ready Assessments (SC Ready), 32–33
Spearman–Brown function, 2, 147, 148
   prophecy formula, 79
specific subgroups, 144
specificity, 6, 13–14
standard deviations (SD), 115
Stanford–Binet intelligence test, 8
standardized value, 58
step-by-step process, 138
stratified alpha, 48, *See also* Cronbach's alpha
subscores
   aggregate-level, 49, 83–85
   augmented, x, 46, 60, 61

   average reliability, 95–98
   cases of, 5–6
   chance of adding value, 103–105
   characteristics, 6
   conditional, 126–130
   on educational assessments, ix
   examinees, 123
      score, 115–116
   gain value, 145–146
   history of, 6–8
   incremental validity in, 48–49
   information. *See* score report
   insisting examinee pass on, 146–147
   involvement with, ix–xi
   limited resources, 147–148
   meaningful, 5
   non-overlapping, 108
   open-source software packages, 71
   orthogonality, 6
   outliers, reporting, 126–130
   parallel-form, 50, 51
   psychometric-based approach, 131
   receptive, 52
   reliability, 6, 12–13, 86
   report complexity, 18–20
   report on practices, 40–42
   residual, 47, 63–65
   scaled, 76–77
   specificity, 6, 13–14
   testing programs by, 14–15
   unreporting, 124
   unusual, 144
   used as prod, 146
   values, 20–22
   variance of, 51
   vs. total score prediction, 60–63
   Wainer-augmented, 68
   weak information, 144–145
subtests
   of ASVAB, 10–11
   history of, 6–8
   length of, 92–95
   mean score and reliability, 113
summative assessments, 23, 43
   ACT, 27
   ASVAB report, 30
   Duolingo English Test, 30–32
   SAT, 25–27
Swedish Scholastic Aptitude Test, 105

TerraNova test, 122
test developer, 106–107

test development process, 106
test length, 81
  effect on subscore, 79–81
  modification, 48
Test of English for International Communication (TOEIC) test, 153
test publishers, 23, 24, 44, 111
test scores, 1, See also reliability, coefficients
  efficacy, 11
  reliability, 12
test specifications, 40
test takers, 72, 83–84, 86
testing organizations, ix, 48, 49, 83, 85–86
testing programs. See also specific test programs
  subscores by, 14–15
tests, history of, 6–8
TIMSS assessment. See Trends in International Mathematics and Science Study (TIMSS) assessment
TOEFL, 83, 108
TOEFL Primary® test, 130, 152
TOEIC test. See Test of English for International Communication (TOEIC) test
total scores
  alternatives approach, 65
  canonical analysis, 67–69
  principal-components analysis, 65–67
  vs. subscore prediction, 60–63
Trends in International Mathematics and Science Study (TIMSS) assessment, 152
true score, 45–46, 48, 52, 63, 69, 72, See also true subscores
  predictors of, 74, 86
  principal-components with, 67
  profiles, 64
  residual, 64
  variances of, 73
true subscores
  canonical analysis prediction, 67–69
  conditionally unbiased property/ estimation, 54
    PRMSE for, 54–55
  by item-response theory, 75
  Kelley estimation, 53–55
  prediction, 53–58
    options for, 46–47
  residual, 47
  total score vs. subscore, 60–63
  predictors of, 74
  PRMSE from, 53
  scree plot of, 67
  vs. total scores, 47–48
    correlations of, 64
    prediction, 58–60
true-score theory, 48
two-category transformation case, 76

US, mental testing in, 8–10
unidimensional item response model, 121–122
United States Medical Licensing Examination (USMLE), 34–36, 151
unreliable subscore, 86, See also reliability, subscore
unusual subscores, 144
US census
  decennial census, 2–5
  extrapolations, 3–4
  lessons, 4
  population, factors of, 4
user types, subscore, 23–24

validity
  augmented subscores, 121
  evidence, 106, 109
  external criterion, 82
  incremental, 81–83
value-added ratio (VAR), 46, 59, 60, 108, 139
  augmented subscores of, 61
  available data for, 150–153
  on National Board of Medical Examiners, 151
value-added subscores
  in practice, 91–92
  reading tests, 107
  uniqueness of, 105–107
VAR. See value-added ratio (VAR)
variances
  half-sample estimation, 73
  of measurement, 73
  and reliability coefficients, 52
  of subscores, 51

Wainer-augmented subscore, 68
weighting, 21

For EU product safety concerns, contact us at Calle de José Abascal, 56–1°,
28003 Madrid, Spain or eugpsr@cambridge.org.

www.ingramcontent.com/pod-product-compliance
Lightning Source LLC
LaVergne TN
LVHW021714060526
838200LV00050B/2664